UNDERSTANDING STATEBUILDING

To Scott

Understanding Statebuilding
Traditional Governance and the Modern State in Somaliland

REBECCA RICHARDS
University of Lancaster, UK

LONDON AND NEW YORK

First published 2014 by Ashgate Publishing

2 Park Square, Milton Park, Abingdon, Oxon OX14 4RN
711 Third Avenue, New York, NY 10017, USA

Routledge is an imprint of the Taylor & Francis Group, an informa business

First issued in paperback 2016

Copyright © Rebecca Richards 2014

Rebecca Richards has asserted her right under the Copyright, Designs and Patents Act, 1988, to be identified as the author of this work.

All rights reserved. No part of this book may be reprinted or reproduced or utilised in any form or by any electronic, mechanical, or other means, now known or hereafter invented, including photocopying and recording, or in any information storage or retrieval system, without permission in writing from the publishers.

Notice:
Product or corporate names may be trademarks or registered trademarks, and are used only for identification and explanation without intent to infringe.

British Library Cataloguing in Publication Data
A catalogue record for this book is available from the British Library

The Library of Congress has cataloged the printed edition as follows:
Richards, Rebecca.
　　Understanding statebuilding : traditional governance and the modern state in Somaliland / by Rebecca Richards.
　　　　pages cm
　　Includes bibliographical references and index.
　　ISBN 978-1-4724-2589-8 (hardback)
1. Nation-building--Somaliland (Secessionist government, 1991–)
2. Newly independent states--Somaliland (Secessionist government, 1991–)
3. Somaliland (Secessionist government, 1991–)--Politics and government. 4. Somaliland (Secessionist government, 1991–)--Ethnic relations. I. Title.
　　JZ5584.S58R53 2014
　　320.96773--dc23
　　　　　　　　　　　　　　　　　　　　　　　　　　　　　　　　　2014003398

ISBN 978-1-4724-2589-8 (hbk)
ISBN 978-1-138-26726-8 (pbk)

Contents

Acknowledgements   *vii*

1	Introduction	1
2	Norms, Ideals and Modern Statebuilding	19
3	Legitimacy and the 'Built' State	39
4	The Clan, Governance and the Build-up to Breakdown	63
5	The Emergence of the New State	95
6	The Institutionalisation of the Traditional	123
7	Somaliland at the Crossroads?	153
8	Conclusions	177

Bibliography   *195*
Index   *213*

Acknowledgements

My thanks go to the numerous people who have helped and guided me throughout the process of writing this, from the proposal stage to completion. It is impossible to mention everyone by name, but I would like to acknowledge the support provided by family, friends, academics, organisations and many many individuals.

Firstly, I would like to thank Professor Mark Duffield, who has consistently provided invaluable advice, comments, critiques and seemingly endless support. Thanks also to Vanessa Pupavac and Martin Gainsborough for comments on earlier drafts; to Adam Morton for his continued support; to Berit Bliesemann de Guevarra, Nina Caspersen, Ian Spears and Stuart Gordon for pushing me to think further, and to Will Reno, I.M. Lewis and especially Mark Bradbury for all of their assistance and guidance.

In Somaliland I would like to give thanks to everyone at the Academy for Peace and Development, especially Mohammed Gees, Bobe Yusuf Duale Nassir Osman Sheikh Hassan and Abdi Aw Rabaax. A special thank you goes to Mohammed Hassan Gani for all of his guidance, insight and special ambushing skills. Their support and assistance were very much unexpected but overwhelmingly accepted. Thanks also need to go to all the men of the Somaliland *Guurti*. They called me the 'walking contradiction' at first but accepted me as one of their own at the end. Special thanks at the *Guurti* must go to Abdullahi Habane and his staff for all of their assistance and document retrievals. I would also like to thank Ulf Terlinden and Genti Miho for everything.

Finally, unquantifiable thanks must go to my family and friends for their patience, understanding and support. And to Robert – I could not have done this without you.

Chapter 1
Introduction

Anyone who has watched enough documentaries on dangerous or 'no-go' places in the world is sure to hear about Somaliland at some point. Somaliland is a 'place that does not exist'. Officially on most government no-go lists because it is technically a part of Somalia, the idea of traveling to Somaliland has an air of intrigue, mystery and daring to it. Anyone actually planning a trip to Somaliland, though, will encounter a different experience. Visitors can obtain visas from small offices hosting Somaliland consulates prior to their arrival (these are unofficial offices, of course. In London it can be found in a standard terrace on a back street in Whitechapel). Regular flights from Addis Ababa, Nairobi and Dubai on major carriers make Somaliland easy to reach. As mysterious travel goes, it is all fairly mundane. Upon arrival, you disembark in a relatively developed airport, pass through immigration and customs, and are met outside by taxi drivers in cars with Somaliland license plates clamouring to get your custom. The roads in the cities are paved and maintained, the Somaliland flag flies above most buildings and adorns almost anything imaginable in a show of nationalistic pride. It is against the law to use certain plastic bags in the market as the thin blue variety have a tendency to escape and collect in the bushes and trees, turning them an odd shade of blue in an otherwise dusty and brown environment. The democratic government is stable, political debate is commonly heard in most tea houses and cafes, and the opposition is very vocal. The capital, Hargeisa, is growing, it is vibrant and it is booming. Most notable, though, is the remarkably peaceful and orderly nature of Somaliland. The conflict that plagues the south is conspicuously absent, and sometimes you have to remind yourself that you are indeed technically in Somalia. Ask any Somalilander why Somaliland is different and they are certain to reply with 'we are not like Somalia. We are civilized and peaceful'. Somaliland may be on the list of places that do not exist, but being in Somaliland tells a completely different story. Somaliland is a state without being a state, and for more than 20 years it has been undergoing, and undertaking, a remarkable self-led statebuilding process. Guided by both external expectations and internal necessities, it has created the apparent antithesis to its parent-state, Somalia. The question is, however, how did it do it?

The 1991 failure and collapse of the state in Somalia ushered in what was to become a long-term and largely unsuccessful effort aimed at internationally driven post-conflict state reconstruction and statebuilding. Since 1992 Somalia has been the subject of numerous peace conferences and a succession of attempts at re-establishing the state apparatus and a government. The current government in Somalia continues to be plagued with difficulties, not only from within the government itself but also from various factions within society, including an increasingly outward looking and al Qaeda aligned militant movement: al-Shabaab. The 2006 return of Somalia's government from more than a decade in exile in Kenya was not met with jubilation in the streets, but rather the continuation of violence so intense in the capital city of Mogadishu that the returning government opted to base itself in Baidoa, nearly 160 miles away. Today's unstable and unpredictable situation in Somalia leads one to question the sustainability of not only the current incarnation of the government but also, more broadly, of an externally created government within the archetypal failed state. Despite the persistent failures at re-building the state, the international community and Somalia's neighbours continue their endeavours aimed at building a stable and accountable Somalia. Where the international community and its statebuilding activity is largely absent, however, pockets of locally created governance have emerged. In many areas outside the major cities, clan governance continues to provide social and physical stability and security to the people. In the northeast province of Puntland, a long-standing regional government offers basic services and security to the population. And in the northwest territory of Somaliland, the most organised and developed of these pockets of governance, a new 'state' that exhibits the central democratic government that has so far eluded the south is emerging. It is here that an extraordinary project of domestically-led statebuilding is taking place within the larger failure of Somalia.

Throughout the literature on failed states and that of statebuilding, the ongoing project in Somalia is a frequent point of reference. Within these studies the self-declared independent territory of Somaliland is often referred to as a region of Somalia or as a breakaway territory that refuses to engage with the wider project of reconciliation and rebuilding of the state. Whilst it is true that there is minimal contact between Somalia and Somaliland on the nature of Somaliland's status, the continuation of viewing Somaliland as region or territory of Somalia creates a situation in which the causes for Somaliland's secession and the successes in creating a state are not acknowledged. Instead, the existence of an independent Somaliland is problematic for the long-standing goal of re-establishing a government able to exercise its power throughout the entirety of Somalia. The insistence on the territorial integrity of Somalia coming from the West as well as strongly from the African Union ensures that very little official attention is paid to the statebuilding process in Somaliland. It therefore remains conspicuously absent from much of the statebuilding policy, practice and literature.

The insistence on an externally-led project of creating a central democratic state in Somalia reflects the current development trend of promulgating a universally applied style of state. Indeed, statebuilding in Somalia, as the first post-Cold War statebuilding project informed by the idealistic New World Order, marked the start of the promotion of an idealised modern democratic state through statebuilding and development projects. With a flux of new Eastern European states creating increased competition for investment and development assistance from the West, the message portrayed to states seeking support regarding what was needed to obtain support became clear. As Dowden, in reference to African states, recollects:

> Europe and America gave African governments three conditions for their continued, if diminishing support: pursue free market policies, as laid down in the Washington consensus, respect human rights, and hold democratic elections – by which they meant multi-party democracy.[1]

These demands reflect wider expectations of what the state should be. However, whilst broader academic examinations of the state and the changing understanding of it are nothing new, within literature and indeed policy on statebuilding, what the state 'is' is often assumed rather than analysed. And whilst expectations of what the state should be are commonly found within development literature and policy, these too reflect assumptions surrounding the state. The literature on theory and philosophy of the state is vast, and the intention here is not to provide an overarching theoretical picture of the state. What is of primary interest, however, is how the state is portrayed and treated in practice and the assumptions and expectations encompassing and underpinning that. It is this treatment that informs not only external policies, but also in some instances internal action.

The 'State'

The 1648 Peace of Westphalia is widely accepted as the landmark agreement that laid the foundation for the creation of independent demarcated sovereign states as well as the beginnings of the interstate system. Control of territory and a monopolisation of force necessary to extract rents and taxes was considered vital to the growth and sustainability of the state.[2] Indeed, the early emphasis on control of a clearly demarcated territory as the primary characteristic of the state is still reflected in Max Weber's widely accepted definition of the state.[3] The Westphalian state and the development of the concept of sovereignty, with the emphasis on the sovereign's ability to control a territory and accumulate the capital necessary to ensure and maintain the territorial integrity and security of the state, left little room or concern for what took place within the boundaries

---

1   R. Dowden, 'An Alien Inheritance', *Prospect* (September 2008), pp. 42–45: p. 43.

2   See J. Herbst, *States and Power in Africa: Comparative Lessons in Authority and Control* (Princeton: Princeton University Press, 2000); A. Morton, 'The Age of Absolutism: Capitalism, the Modern State System and International Relations', *Review of International Studies* 31.3 (2005), pp. 495–517.

3   See M. Weber, *The Theory of Social and Economic Organisation (1947)*, ed. Talcott Parsons (New York: Free Press, 1964); M. Weber, 'Politics as Vocation (1948)', in H.H. Gerth and C. Wright Mills (eds), *From Max Weber: Essays in Sociology* (London: Routledge, 1967), pp. 77–128.

of the state. Even within Weber's augmentation of the rudimentary Westphalian conception of the state, where there is an acknowledgment of the empirical actions of the state, the concern with the empirical maintains the focus on state actions in maintaining juridical security and control within the state rather than the more human focused state actions that have become associated with more contemporary assessments of the state. Consistently for Weber, if the monopoly of force by the national government is absent, the territory exists in a realm of statelessness. Whilst social, humanitarian, economic and political responsibilities may be interpretively derived from this definition through an examination of the elements of control or organisation, whether charismatic leadership, traditional leadership, or bureaucratic control,[4] engrained in this definition is the persistent emphasis placed on the monopolisation or legitimisation of force necessary to first achieve and then maintain statehood. This force-centric understanding of the state continues to underpin contemporary conceptions of the state, yet they do not occupy the entirety of the space in understandings and expectations of what the state is and should be.

Whilst control and a monopoly of force remain essential components of modern statehood, the evolution of what it means to be a state has resulted in increased importance being placed on the actions of the central government outside the realm of physical or territorial security. Drawing on the criteria of statehood codified in the 1933 Montevideo Convention on the Rights and Duties of States, Ian Brownlie describes the state as a legal entity – recognised by international law – with four main elements: a defined territory; a permanent population; an *effective government*; and independence, or the right to enter into relations with other states.[5] Although the Montevideo Convention simply states 'government' as one of its criteria for statehood, Brownlie added emphasis on the internal occurrences and practices of the sovereign with his identification of 'effective government'. In a similar theme, Robert Jackson articulates that modern states must exhibit not only juridical – or legal territorial – statehood, but also empirical statehood – or fulfilling domestic sovereign responsibilities through institutional authority and organisational capacity – in order to be 'complete' states.[6] Development and statebuilding policy and discourse extend the empirical much further than Jackson's authority-based conception and into the realm of good governance. Indeed, the mere existence of the term 'failed state' indicates

---

4 M. Weber, 'Politics as Vocation', op. cit.; M. Weber, *The Theory of Social and Economic Organisation*, op. cit., pp. 154–6.

5 I. Brownlie, *Principles of Public International Law*, 5th edition (Oxford: Clarendon Press, 1998): pp. 70–72, Emphasis added; International Conference of American States, 'Convention on Rights and Duties of States', Seventh International Conference of American States, Montevideo, Uruguay (26 December 1933), available at http://avalon.law.yale.edu/20th_century/intam03.asp.

6 R. Jackson, *Quasi-States: Sovereignty, International Relations and the Third World* (Cambridge: Cambridge University Press, 1990), p. 21.

the dominant expectation that even though the state may juridically and therefore legally exist, merely maintaining sovereign borders is not enough to fully meet modern expectations of statehood.

As Jessop notes, the notion of what it means to be a state is a perpetually incomplete and constantly evolving understanding.[7] Although Jessop discusses the changing nature of the state as a result of changing economic practice, the observation can also be applied to changes resulting from normative values determining what it means to be a state. In other words, what has changed is not the state, per se, but rather the *conception* or understanding of the state. This is clear in evolving understandings not only since its inception at Westphalia but also since the time of Weber's now dominant conception of the state was written.[8] Concerns over the empirical attributes of statehood have gone beyond a sovereign or government able to exert institutional control and authority through a monopolisation of force. Following rapid decolonisation, juridical statehood trumped the existence of an empirical state, and as such, according to Jackson,

> many [ex-colonial states] have not yet been authorized and empowered domestically and consequently lack the institutional features of sovereign states ... They disclose limited empirical statehood: their populations do not enjoy many of the advantages traditionally associated with independent statehood. Their governments are often deficient in the political will, institutional authority, and organized power to protect human rights or provide socioeconomic welfare.[9]

Caught in the geopolitical struggle of the Cold War, however, the concern regarding many of these new states, as well as many 'old' states, was predominantly

---

7 See B. Jessop, *State Theory: Putting the Capitalist State in its Place* (Oxford: Polity, 1990).

8 For the evolution of the conception of the state, see, for example, I.W. Zartman (ed.), *Collapsed States: the disintegration and restoration of legitimate authority* (Boulder: Lynne Rienner, 1995); R. Jackson, *Quasi-states: Sovereignty*, op. cit.; R. Jackson, 'Quasi-States, Dual Regimes, and Neoclassical Theory', *International Organisation* 41.4 (1987), pp. 519–49; R. Jackson, 'Surrogate Sovereignty? Great Power Responsibility and "Failed States"', University of British Columbia Institute of International Relations Working Paper 25 (1998); M. Weber, 'Politics as Vocation', op. cit.; M. Weber, *The Theory Social and Economic Organisation*, op. cit.; D. Carment, 'Assessing State Failure: Implications for Theory and Policy', *Third World Quarterly* 24.3 (2003), pp. 407–27; J. Milliken (ed.), *State Failure, Collapse and Reconstruction* (Oxford: Blackwell, 2003); R. Rotberg, 'Failed States, Collapsed States, Weak States', in R. Rotberg (ed.), *State Failure and State Weakness in a Time of Terror* (Washington DC: Brookings Institution Press, 2003), pp. 1–28; R. Rotberg, *When States Fail: Causes and Consequences* (Princeton: Princeton University Press, 2004); B. Jessop, *State Theory*, op. cit.; A. Morton, op. cit.; State Failure Task Force, 'State Failure Task Force Reports: Phases II-III Findings', College Park, MD: Centre for International Development and Conflict Management (31 July 1998; 4 August 2003).

9 R. Jackson, *Quasi-States: Sovereignty*, op. cit., p. 21.

ideological; again the empirical concerns stopped at whether the state was 'for us or against us'. It was not until the end of the Cold War that focus increasingly and rapidly shifted towards the relationship between the state, governance and the population: a focus dominated by issues now associated with not only good, but also legitimate governance and the exercising of empirical sovereignty within those states that Jackson implies were 'behind' or 'problematic' from the start. Vital to this shift is the expectation of international political and financial cooperation, perceived to best be achieved through the establishment of liberal democracies. Indeed, the push for familiar and proven liberal democracies as a 'sure bet' form of statehood reflects the prioritisation of external expectations of the state; expectations that are perceived to be necessary not only for the legitimacy and security of the state in question, but also for the political, physical and economic security of the system. It must be clear, though, that the legitimacy referred to here is not solely domestic acceptance of a government; it also refers to an international acceptance of the actions and functions of the state.

In the 1990s, humanitarian considerations and good governance replaced ideological leanings and the militarisation of the state as points of attention. As evidenced in President George H.W. Bush's short-lived New World Order, and later prevalent in the output and actions of the United Nations, as well as the advent of humanitarian intervention, the empirical actions of state leadership in regards to the treatment and conditions of the populace challenged the state's juridical sovereign right to non-intervention.[10] Whilst provision of public goods and empirical statehood are not new concepts in relation to the state, the conception of expected state action, both externally and domestically, shifted from a focus on force or control to a focus on provision, both to the international community and the domestic population of the state in question. It is within this realm where the legal state separates from the normative state. Whereas there continues to be an emphasis on the legalistic monopolisation of force, contemporary conceptions of effective statehood have come to include the state's ability to provide for its citizens in the realm of territorial security as well as in terms of political, social, economic, and human security. Whilst the legal definition of sovereignty and statehood has changed little since the formation of the early European states, the normative conception of statehood has evolved. Further, following the end of the Cold War the notion of a link between the liberal state and systemic security became dominant, firmly entrenching the empirical occurrences in an individual

---

10 B. Boutros-Ghali, *An Agenda for Peace: Preventive Diplomacy, Peacemaking and Peacekeeping* (New York: United Nations, 1992); G.H.W. Bush, 'Address Before a Joint Session of the Congress on the Persian Gulf Crisis and the Federal Budget Deficit', Washington DC, 11 September 1990; G.H.W. Bush, 'Address Before a Joint Session of Congress on the Cessation of the Persian Gulf Conflict', Washington DC, 6 March 1991. See also International Commission for Intervention and State Sovereignty (ICISS), *The Responsibility to Protect* (Ottawa: International Development Research Centre, 2001), Appendix A, 'Elements of the Debate', p. 10.

state in the security of others, particularly the liberal democratic states of the West. With this link made, threats emanating from states became much more than just military or territorial ones and not only the style of state but also domestic actions of the government became a concern of more than just the population inhabiting a sovereign territory.

In his oft-cited work, Rotberg expounds upon the increasing emphasis on state expectation and provisions in maintaining that modern states are responsible for mediating the 'constraints and challenges of the international arena' with the 'dynamism of their own internal economic, political, and social realities'. Noting the importance of security in the conception, and indeed in Rotberg's work on assessment of the state, he also notes that it is not the sole purpose for the existence of a state:

> [n]ation-states exist to provide a decentralized method of delivering political (public) goods to persons living within designated parameters (borders) ... modern states focus and answer the concerns and demands of citizenries ... [political goods] encompass indigenous expectations, conceivably obligations, inform the local political culture, and together give content to the social contract between ruler and ruled that is at the core of regime/government and citizenry interactions.[11]

Rotberg accurately and succinctly captures the picture of state expectation that is widely found within policy and practice. He stresses that the provision of political goods is vital to the domestic legitimacy of the state, and as such in assessing the performance, or even worthiness, of a state key political goods are hierarchically identified as valid tools of judgment and evaluation. States that do not fulfil these criteria are 'failing' or 'failed', in this assessment, making those that do 'successful'. Within this, territorial security is the top priority for successful states, and Rotberg makes clear the importance placed on the existence of an acceptable or successful liberal state for global security. However, other more social-political goods are also ranked as being fundamental to a state's legitimacy and success, such as enforceable rule of law, free and fair participation in the political process, the provision of social goods such as health care and education, physical and economic infrastructure, communications infrastructure, environmental protection, sound and logical fiscal policy and even the promotion of civil society.[12] Under these assessments, states are not functioning or legitimate if they are lacking in the empirical provision of public goods that are perceived as essential to effective rule. States that fail this assessment are targets for attention or some form of intervention, be it through a direct presence or some form of conditional aid. Successful states perform in a

---

11 R. Rotberg, 'The Failure and Collapse of Nation-States: Breakdown, Prevention and Repair', in R. Rotberg (ed.), *When States Fail: Causes and Consequences* (Princeton: Princeton University Press, 2004), pp. 2–3.

12 R. Rotberg, 'Failed States, Collapsed States, Weak States', op. cit., p. 3.

way that legitimises governmental rule both domestically and internationally by protecting the interests and security of not only the sovereign and the territory, but the population as well. Failed or failing states must be 'fixed' for the benefit of all.[13] Although the sovereign boundaries of recognised states stand, absolute sovereignty is no longer a guarantee. Whilst physical intervention in various forms is a common feature in development and security policies, what is less obvious is ideational intervention; a form of intervention that can be both externally enacted and domestically adopted.

This emphasis on conforming to the dominant international norms informs projects aimed at responding to or remedying state failure, including statebuilding projects.[14] The response to what are seen as financial, political social and security concerns or problems is a prescribed 'one size fits all' approach[15] to modern idealised statehood in order to create stability in not only the state in question, but also the international system of states. This 'ideal' state conforms to liberal notions of acceptable statehood, exhibiting not only a democratic government and a secure territory, but also exercising good governance, providing public and political goods to the population, engaging in the international economy through liberal policies and eager for political interactions with other states and international institutions. In other words, the 'ideal' state is one which is 'governed' within the liberal rubric: it is one in which political, economic and security threats are eliminated and the practices, policies and structures of the state are familiar and easily accessible to the international community. The ideal state, therefore, is an extension of liberal intervention and as such is subject to the control or subjugation of powerful states and international institutions. It does not reflect an already existing state structure, but rather comprises a wish list of sorts; it is a composition of factors that together would make the perfect acceptable or successful state not only for security, but also for political and economic relationships with powerful actors in the international community. The promulgation of the ideal state is more a liberal tool than an achievable reality.

---

13 See A. Ghani and C. Lockhart, 'Closing the Sovereignty Gap: An Approach to State-Building', Overseas Development Institute Working Paper 253 (London: ODI, 2005); A. Ghani and C. Lockhart, *Fixing Failed States: A Framework for Rebuilding a Fractured World* (Oxford: Oxford University Press, 2008).

14 Whilst the United Nations entered Somalia under the guise of a peacekeeping mission in 1992 (UNOSOM I), the statebuilding project began in March 1993 with the start of the highly ambitious UNOSOM II mission. United Nations, 'Resolution 814 (26 March 1993)', Security Council Resolution.

15 See S. Chesterman, M. Ignatieff and R. Thakur, 'Introduction: Making States Work', in S. Chesterman, M. Ignatieff and R. Thakur (eds), *Making States Work: State Failure and the Crisis of Governance* (Washington DC: Brookings Institute Press, 2005), pp. 1–10: p. 4.

The Ideal Modern State and Indigenous Governance Structures

Within literature and policy on state failure, statebuilding and state development the successful or acceptable – the ideal – state is portrayed as one that complies with the normative framework of the modern state. As Berger notes, the growing body of literature concerned with failed and failing states 'attempts to facilitate the formulation of policies that will reverse this trend and create a world order of stable, economically dynamic and secure nation-states'.[16] This is also reflected by the technocratic Ghani and Lockhart in the subtitle of their book, *Fixing Failed States: A Framework for Rebuilding a Fractured World*.[17] Failed, fragile, weak or collapsed states are seen as states in crisis and as such are threatening to the cohesiveness and stability of the international system of states. Because of this there is a perceived incompatibility of failed or fragile states and the international system of states, thereby forcing the system to seek a way to strengthen its weaker chains. As Weiner indicates, weak, failed or fragile states create the threat of a bad neighbourhood, with the problems of one state quickly spreading to impact upon the others in its proximity.[18] In line with this, failed, weak, fragile or collapsed states can be seen as crudely akin to a crack house in a residential neighbourhood: the malignant force of a failed state threatens the stability of a surrounding area and therefore must be addressed. Since removal of the entity is unfathomable under current rules of the international system, the response is a prescriptive remedy similar to an urban regeneration scheme that would be established to address a problematic neighbourhood. Berger associates this increased prescriptive attention with an emerging crisis of the nation-state system, with states failing to meet the rigorous demands of modern statehood threatening the stability of a system built on and dependent upon the functioning or legitimate sovereign states. However, the current means of addressing these problems itself are problematic in that the impending crisis is not one which can be addressed by 'technocratic prescriptions for the creation or stabilisation of particular collapsing or failing nation-states or the rehabilitation of the nation-state', but rather the international community must reconsider the dictate of what is acceptable in the modern state.[19]

As models of development have largely been dictated by the dominant discourses of the period, policies such as the push for political reform based on democracy's third wave, the economic sector oriented Washington Consensus and increased awareness of and concern for social and human security within sovereign states have significantly informed today's development policy and therefore

---

16 M. Berger, 'States of Nature and the Nature of States: the fate of nations, the collapse of states and the future of the world', *Third World Quarterly* 28.6 (2007), pp. 1203–14: p. 1203.

17 A. Ghani and C. Lockhart, *Fixing Failed States*, op. cit.

18 M. Weiner, 'Bad Neighbors, Bad Neighborhoods: An Inquiry into the Causes of Refugee Flows', *International Security* 21.1 (1996), pp. 5–42.

19 M. Berger, op. cit., pp. 1203–4.

the normative framework for acceptable statehood.[20] Modernisation of state institutions and practices is integral to this framework; 'backwards' traditional, indigenous or non-democratic structures and procedures are not efficient or effective in meeting the ideals being presented. Thus, modernisation of political and economic structures through democratisation, good governance practices and liberal economics becomes a vital component of the state. Even though a definitive statement of ideal statehood does not exist, policies such as Structural Adjustment Programmes and aid conditionality, together with the promotion of good governance and the modernisation of institutions and government through development policies and, in extreme cases, interventionist statebuilding, support the perception of an ideal, preferred, or acceptable state. As previously discussed, there exists a notion of the type of state that is preferred by the international community; a type of state that is viewed as secure and stable and is preferable to engage with on the social, economic and political levels. In addition to a liberal economy and democracy, the ideal state exhibited within this discourse is one that provides what Jackson terms empirical statehood and what Rotberg identifies as public and political goods.[21] Whilst there are no specifically stated parameters for this state, the popular characteristics defined by developed states and presented in literature and policy create a picture of the ideal that developing states should strive to become and what the international community should build through development projects and statebuilding interventions.

For those entities aspiring to legally recognised statehood, however, creating the ideal state can become more than just conforming to a normative model of statehood; it can become the perceived path to recognition and therefore to the political, social and economic interactions and benefits that accompany legal statehood. In reference to the enlargement of the European Union, Ghani and Lockhart paint a picture of a structured path for aspiring member states, with the accession to the EU being the end reward for following the pre-determined rules and regulations for membership.[22] In a similar manner, the benefits of recognised

---

20   J. Williamson, 'In Search of a Manual for Technopols', in J. Williamson (ed.), *The Political Economy of Policy Reform* (Washington DC: Institute for International Economics, 1994), pp. 9–28; A. Yannis, 'State Collapse and its Implications for Peace-Building and Reconstruction', in J. Milliken (ed.), *State Failure, Collapse and Reconstruction* (Oxford: Blackwell, 2003), pp. 63–82; T. Carothers, *Critical Mission: Essays on Democracy Promotion* (Washington DC: Carnegie Endowment for International Peace, 2004). See also, United Nations, 'Report of the International Conference on Financing for Development (Monterrey Convention)', Monterrey, Mexico, 18–22 March 2002.

21   R. Jackson, *Quasi-States*, op. cit.; R. Jackson, 'Surrogate Sovereignty?', op. cit.; R. Jackson, 'Quasi-States, Dual Regimes', op. cit.; R. Rotberg, 'Failed States, Collapsed States, Weak States', op. cit.; R. Rotberg, 'The Failure and Collapse of Nation-States', op. cit.; R. Rotberg, 'Strengthening Governance: Ranking Countries Would Help', *The Washington Quarterly* 28.1 (2004–2005), pp. 71–81; R. Rotberg, 'The New Nature of Nation-State Failure', *The Washington Quarterly* 25.3 (2002), pp. 85–96.

22   A. Ghani and C. Lockhart, *Fixing Failed States*, op. cit., pp. 30–31.

statehood are the carrot being dangled in front of those territories wanting to be states. In the context of what Jean-François Bayart identifies as a strategy of extraversion,[23] or actively seeking external sources of financial or political benefit, creating the ideal state with the aim of gaining recognition of statehood can become a means through which a territorial entity can benefit from interaction with the international community; the state becomes a strategic tool. Through the medium of legally recognised statehood, unrecognised states endeavour to gain access to those areas largely reserved for states, such as legal financial frameworks, developmental assistance through international organisations and increased access to trade and other political activities taking place in the international realm of states. The process of creating an ideal modern state, therefore, can be a means to a financially, politically and socially beneficial end.

The concern here, however, is the uniform approach to creating stable or successful states using the blueprinted framework of the ideal state, particularly within non-Western states or those with a reliance upon or strong tradition of non-Western governance structures. How are local structures and dynamics accommodated in the creation or formation of a state, particularly within territories or entities with little or no experience of the modern or democratic state? Further, the model of modern acceptable or successful statehood discounts the centralisation of indigenous or traditional governance structures, particularly in Africa, as they are believed to be backwards, corrupt, unpredictable or unstable. Although indigenous structures are viewed as useful when engaging locally in governance or development projects, as Duffield notes, reminiscent to systems of indirect rule, their role in externally-led projects is accepted only if in a devolved manner.[24] Their exclusion from the central state creates a situation in which the expectation is the creation of a modern and acceptable state in varied social or political contexts. As a result, modes of social and political organisation that are specifically tailored to the territory and society, yet do not follow the Western model of statehood, are often the target of reform or co-option by external donors and institutions rather than inclusion in the central mechanisms of government as those unfamiliar alternatives do not conform to the ideal and trusted picture of the successful state.

The Ideal 'State', Statebuilding and Somaliland

Although the ideal state is a reflection of desires rather than a recreation of an existing state structure, this rubric of statehood is exhibited in policy as the desired

---

23 See J-F. Bayart, 'Africa in the World: A History of Extraversion', *African Affairs* 99.395 (2000), pp. 217–67; J-F. Bayart, *The State in Africa: Politics of the Belly* (London: Longman, 1993).

24 M. Duffield, *Development, Security and Unending War* (Cambridge: Polity, 2007), pp. 172–9.

outcome of interventionist actions. It extends far beyond active development or statebuilding policy, however. The dominance of this style of state in the normative liberal framework guiding international relations also creates an environment in which alternatives to or deviations from this blueprint of statehood and the path through which to reach it are not trusted, regardless of any success that may be exhibited. As such, international norms of what it means to be a state also direct domestic policy within developing states and, in particular, unrecognised states. For the latter, conforming to these acceptable standards of statehood is considered vital to achieving international recognition. By exploring conceptions of the acceptable or ideal state it is possible to understand, and also critique, the expectations for modern statebuilding. An ideal case study for this is Somaliland. A separate entity from its southern neighbour, Somaliland is often referred to as a model in Africa: on empirical grounds it 'fulfils the principle criteria for statehood' and ticks the boxes of what a stable, modern state should be.[25] By all pretences it is a state, albeit one that lacks international recognition of sovereignty. A 2005 report commissioned by the World Bank, however, unveils a perceived problem with the state in Somaliland: a deviation from the liberal blueprint in the inclusion of traditional authority in the unrecognised state's central government structure.[26]

The stated goal of creating a modern state is the same in both Somalia and Somaliland, but Somaliland has taken a drastically different path to achieving this and has set about creating a state on its own. Its exclusion from international involvement in the statebuilding process, offered under the guise of reconstructing Somalia as a unitary state, however, has meant that the territory has been subjected to little direct interference from the international community. This relative isolation has allowed for Somaliland to define its own conditions for the introduction of demands for modern statehood, including democracy, in the governing structure and practices of the territory. The formation of the state in Somaliland reflects not only the normative dominance of the idealised acceptable or successful modern statehood, but also adapts these demands to Somaliland society. What is being created is a hybrid state that is inclusive of both familiar traditional governance structures as well as the newly introduced modern democratic government.[27]

Outwardly, the outcome of the statebuilding process in Somaliland appears to be a modern democratic state – albeit an unrecognised one – and the modern practices of the state are widely referred to in Somaliland's quest for international

---

25 M. Bryden, 'The Banana Test: Is Somaliland Ready for Recognition?' *Annales d'Éthiopie* 19 (2003), pp. 341–64.

26 A. Hashi, 'The Implication of Traditional Leadership, "Guurti" and Other Non-State Actors in Local Governance in Somaliland', Study Report for the Community Empowerment and Social Inclusion Program of the World Bank Institute (June 2005).

27 It must be noted here that using the terms 'traditional' and 'customary' is done without connotation, normative judgments or any comment on the often contentious use of the terms. The terms were chosen for purposes of distinction and analysis, and should not be read as more than that.

recognition of sovereignty. The imposition of modern democracy within the complexities of Somaliland's political and social environment was not as simple as just creating a democratic government and modern state practices, however, and was viewed as potentially destabilising by the founders of Somaliland. Because of this, a compromise was reached between clan governance and modern democracy, resulting in a deviation from the model of the modern state with the formation of a hybrid government in Somaliland. The government is thus a product of reconciliation between 'old' traditional structures and the 'new' democratic structures and practices, what can also be viewed as domestic needs and external demands, creating a central government inclusive of and dependent upon both. This book examines the creation of such a state, asking why a modern democratic state was created, why the traditional was included in this state, and how the complex relationship between the old and the new functions in the formation, legitimisation, growth and future of the state. This book also considers what the implications of the success this hybrid government are for not only for Somaliland, but for the broader picture in the context of the discourses on state formation and statebuilding.

Somaliland proves an interesting case in that what is occurring in the territory is statebuilding, and within that state formation, that is informed and guided by international norms and standards of statehood, but is also proceeding as an indigenous process with minimal direct external intervention.[28] In contrast to the fraught filled long-term international statebuilding project taking place in Somalia, Somaliland is an oasis of calm in the chaos of the archetypal failed state. Although Somaliland appears to conform to the standards and requirements of acceptable statehood, despite its declaration of independence in 1991 it is not recognised as a sovereign entity separate from Somalia. Because of its inability to access international structures and institutions that are reserved for sovereign states, achieving recognition of statehood has become a primary goal of the government in the territory, with the creation of a democratic state at the centre of Somaliland's strategy. Whilst on the surface the state does exhibit the characteristics of a successful modern state and the government engages in an aggressive international public relations campaign advertising and espousing its successes, it does deviate from the ideal statehood mould in that it has incorporated traditional Somali forms

---

28 Although there is an international presence within Somaliland, much of this is under the guise of the wider Somalia projects. Most international involvement or intervention also targets humanitarian rather than political concerns. The primary external actor in Somaliland – the Diaspora – is in interesting one as it is both an internal and an external actor. So as not to reduce the role of the Diaspora in the statebuilding process in Somaliland, here it is treated separately from considerations of non-Somaliland international involvement; the Diaspora is considered an external domestic actor, but not an international actor. Wherever possible, involvement by the international community is referred to as 'external' intervention or 'international' intervention. As the Diaspora arguably is not an interventionist actor, and to distinguish its unique role, it is referred to as 'the Diaspora'.

of governance in the central state structure in the form of a house of parliament. Whilst the traditional nature of this body is not hidden, its promotion as a primarily legislative body downplays those functions of the institution that are associated with the indigenous clan governance structure.[29] With the objective of obtaining recognition of sovereignty in order to be capable of fully participating in the international system of states, and with the structure and function of the state apparatus appearing to conform to the acceptable state framework, the question must be raised of why a traditional institution was included, and retained, in the government of this aspiring state? Indeed, without the inclusion of this traditional element from the beginning of the process, the territory would not exhibit the level of peace and stability that exists today; and without peace and stability the introduction of a modern, yet foreign, democratic governing structure would have encountered significant difficulties. Whilst the inclusion of the traditional was essential to the initial stages of statebuilding, however, its continuance in the growing and evolving central government has begun to be questioned by elements within the Somaliland government and society. In order to maintain the uniquely Somaliland structure that has ensured stability, re-negotiating the relationship between the old Somali governance system and the new democratic structures and practices in the hybrid government is the focus of the next phase of statebuilding in the territory. Seen as a process rather than a project, this tailoring and continual re-negotiation of the state and statebuilding in Somaliland, as well as the flexibility afforded by that, proves invaluable from an analytical standpoint.

Whilst to an extent Somaliland follows the normative frameworks for acceptable or successful statehood, the inclusion of indigenous or traditional rule in the government sets Somaliland apart from the dominant 'blueprint approach'. This inclusion still puts Somaliland on the path towards the ideal of liberal democracy, but it does so in a way not defined by the international community but rather by Somaliland itself. The state being created in the territory is one that makes democracy, and the state, work by tailoring the ideal to fit and therefore be possible, and legitimate, in Somaliland. In balancing a desire for recognition of sovereign statehood with the need to create a stable governing structure in Somaliland, the shapers of this government have created an interesting case of statebuilding for study. The case of Somaliland raises interesting questions concerning not only dominant statebuilding and state formation discourse, policy and practice, but also questions the 'cookie cutter' approach commonly found in both literature and policy.

The hybrid government in Somaliland was integral to establishing peace and stability, and the statebuilding process taking place in the territory, as a carefully tailored and flexible process, provides empirical grounds for analysis and understanding of statebuilding and what it could be. With that said, it should

---

29 Interviews with author, August-September 2006, Hargeisa. It is very common to be told that the traditional inclusion in Somaliland's government, the Upper House of Parliament, is comparable to the United States Senate.

be noted that whilst the approach to statebuilding taken by Somaliland has been successful, it is not the intention here to suggest that the territory is perfect, or that the territory's distinctive experience should be carbon copied by other territories or states. What has worked for Somaliland is a tailored fit, and it is one that has been altered and has evolved as obstacles are encountered or as need demands. Its importance is not that it has created a blueprint for non-Western statebuilding – Somaliland itself is not and should not be a model – but that what has taken place in Somaliland and what has been created provides analytical commentary not only on the conception of the ideal state, but also on how to achieve it: statebuilding. The territory provides an excellent platform for the study of contemporary statebuilding, particularly how this is shaped or reactive to normative values of statehood. The territory also proves interesting in examining the interaction between Western ideals and traditional practices and structures in contemporary statebuilding. Somaliland is an example of how the model of acceptable statehood fails to acknowledge the importance of local social and political dynamics in contributing to the stability, legitimacy and success of a developing, re-building or forming state, and its process is useful in exploring what statebuilding could, and should, be. It is because of this that the examination of the government in Somaliland here focuses on the deviation that has proved to be the foundation for stability in and legitimacy of the forming state: the inclusion of the indigenous traditional governance structures into the Somaliland government. It must also be noted that it is not the purpose of this book to assess Somaliland through the discourse of right to self-determination. The legal and political complexity surrounding the international community's response to and policy regarding Somaliland's declaration of independence is a vast and separate project itself. However, it would be misleading to present the assumption that the inclusion of traditional authority in Somaliland's government is a reason for lack of recognition. Whilst the power of the clan authority in the institutions and functions of government has been noted as a concern, issues regarding Somaliland's placement within Somalia and expressed policy protecting territorial integrity in the region are considerable obstacles to recognition. Until Somalia is stabilised, Somaliland is unlikely to be recognised. The isolation due to this, however, has been beneficial to Somaliland as the territory has been granted the time and space to 'go it alone'.[30]

Challenging the Ideal

The desire to shape states to meet the needs of other more powerful neighbours is not new. Encouraging or forcing conformity for the purposes of cooperation and international stability is a practice that can be traced back to the days of empire. The end of empire and a new order based on the concept of independent sovereign states halted the direct paternalism being used to foster cooperation and

---

30   G. Prunier, 'Somaliland Goes it Alone', *Current History* 97.619 (1998), pp. 225–8.

relationships based on common values, but it did not end the push for conformity or efforts to encourage, or in some cases impose, it. When the new order appeared challenged due to state failure and fragility, state collapse and state weakness, the need for stability within and amongst sovereign states increased as a priority amongst policymakers and political thinkers, particularly those within the West. Conformity, in the form of liberal democracy and an exhibition of good governance, became a security concern, and the need to maintain international stability amongst independent states has resulted in many projects that have sought to rebuild those that threatened due to failure or collapse. Whilst there are many examples, Somalia exists as both a historic and contemporary model of this impulse. Somaliland, on the other hand, challenges how we understand it.

This book seeks to fill a gap in the literature on statebuilding and Somaliland. Statebuilding literature is rife with criticisms and examples of what has gone wrong, but there is very little on what has gone right. In the literature on Somaliland, there is emphasis on the technical components of the statebuilding process on the one hand,[31] and the role of the clan in Somali society on the other.[32] The literature on Somaliland is also dominated by discussions on and justifications for sovereign recognition. However, there is a distinct lack of literature that brings these areas together. By placing Somaliland in the context of statebuilding and by asking the question 'what went right', this book seeks to contribute to bridging that gap. The purpose here is to examine the often mentioned but underexplored aspect of creating the state in Somaliland – the role of the clan – in the context of statebuilding. The focus here is examining the relationship between internal and external demands in the self-led statebuilding process in Somaliland, specifically focusing on the utilisation of the clan as a mechanism of that relationship and that process. As a point of 'deviance' in Somaliland as the utilisation of traditional authority brings with it connotations of unpredictability and backwardness in an otherwise seemingly 'modern' democratic state, the inclusion of the clan is particularly interesting, raising the question of why was it included in the process of creating what aspires to be a state that conforms to external expectations. Much of this book is a historical story. By looking at and telling the story of the process through history, it is not only possible to extract the importance of the clan and how it relates to or facilitates internal and external expectations, but also its evolving role in a growing and strengthening 'state'. This opens the door for placing that very Somaliland necessity – the clan in the state – in the context of statebuilding and in balancing the internal and the external. The constant evolution and renegotiation of the hybrid Somaliland state, processes which have maintained stability thus far, pose significant challenges for discourse and policy that outline specific guidelines and offer blueprints for the development of effective governance and political reform necessary to meet the requirements of the modern

---

31 See, for example, M. Bradbury, *Becoming Somaliland* (Oxford: James Currey, 2008).

32 See, for example, the works of I.M. Lewis.

acceptable state. In looking at conclusions pertaining to local capabilities and local ownership, negotiation versus imposition, and statebuilding as a process rather than a project, failings of technocratic statebuilding are identified and highlighted.

The book provides a general introduction to conceptions of acceptable statehood found within literature and policy, as well as an explanation and a critical examination of externally-led statebuilding – a form of intervention aimed at creating acceptable or ideal statehood in states perceived to be fragile, failed, failing, threatening or concerning. Within this, problems with externally-led statebuilding are identified, particularly in establishing local ownership and legitimacy within an externally-built state. In contrast to this, domestically-led statebuilding in unrecognised states is introduced, leading to an examination of this process in Somaliland. Before attention is turned to Somaliland, a brief history of the Somali people and the Somalia state, including the role of the clan, is given. Following this, an examination of the statebuilding process in Somaliland, focusing on the role of the clan as a legitimising actor and the process of locally owning the state, is given. Starting with a critical historical explanation of Somaliland both pre- and post- 1991, the latter half of the book focuses on the utilisation of the clan as a mechanism of governance and legitimacy within the statebuilding process in Somaliland and as a means through which the gap between internal and external was bridged. This book then examines problems with the juxtaposing of the 'old' and the 'new' in a modernising government, posing questions pertaining to what the future Somaliland state will look like as the statebuilding process progresses. Finally, the book concludes with a critical re-examination of not only the hybrid government in Somaliland, but also returning to this in the context of statebuilding and lessons to be drawn from that. This book examines statebuilding as a process rather than a project, and as such it is acknowledged throughout that what is taking place in Somaliland is ongoing. It is also acknowledged throughout that whilst the clan has played a key role in the Somaliland statebuilding process, it is not the only actor involved. Although the focus here is on the clan, other important actors are acknowledged.

The purpose here is not to romanticise the clan and traditional authority in Somaliland, or to see the statebuilding process in Somaliland through rose coloured spectacles. To do so would offer a misleading picture of the statebuilding process in Somaliland. After all, the placement of the clan in the central government is Somaliland has not been resulted in a utopian tale or ending. It is fully acknowledged here that the ongoing process in Somaliland has not been problem free and that some of the obstacles facing Somaliland as it continues in its statebuilding process centre on the clan inclusion. However, fear of romanticising an aspect of the process or concerns about accusations of romanticism only result in an incomplete view and therefore understanding of the process, just as disregarding aspects like history excludes contextual information necessary to provide analysis, particularly in regards to political occurrences or structures. With that in mind, these reservations should be considered by the reader, and the examination of the inclusion of the clan should be read as a component, albeit an important component, of the overall ongoing process.

Chapter 2
Norms, Ideals and Modern Statebuilding

The rise and fall of states is nothing new. Further, as Clapham notes, 'states have historically derived from various specific and by no means universally realised conditions, and the global political system has until recent times comprised areas under the control of states, areas regulated by other forms of governance, and areas with no stable government at all'.[1] From the time of Westphalia and European absolutism, states have come and gone in the historical processes of state formation, failure and collapse.[2] The modern Western state has taken centuries to reach what is exhibited today, with a Darwinistic survival of the fittest approach contributing to the evolution of the membership of the international community of states: the modern Western state is the product of a lengthy process rather than a unitary declaration or act. However, following decolonisation the bestowing of sovereignty and therefore statehood upon the former colonial territories, the majority of which are located in Africa, thrust these new non-Western states into the international system as fully sovereign states on par with those states that have existed for centuries. Herbst notes the obvious in recognising that state formation and consolidation in post-Westphalian Europe differs greatly from that in independent Africa,[3] as within the latter the creation of independent states was superseded by decolonisation and the granting of blanket sovereignty. As a result, what took place within the majority of former colonial territories was state 'bestowing' that took for granted the existence of state structures and practices. All of this together makes obvious one of the most fundamental yet most erroneous normative assumptions of policy and research surrounding state formation and failure: that all states will reflect or even follow the 'European path'. The blanket sovereignty granted by the international community – through the UN – following decolonisation bestowed juridical sovereignty upon the new states regardless of the existence, or lack thereof, of what are widely identified as 'functioning' or 'acceptable' state structures and practices. As Jackson states, '[t]o be a sovereign state today one needs only to have been a formal colony yesterday. All other

---

1 C. Clapham, 'The Global-Local Politics of State Decay', in R. Rotberg (ed.), *When States Fail: Causes and Consequences* (Princeton: Princeton University Press, 2004), pp. 77–93: p. 77.

2 R. Rotberg, 'The Failure and Collapse of Nation-States: Breakdown, Prevention, and Repair', in R. Rotberg (ed.), *When States Fail: Causes and Consequences* (Princeton: Princeton University Press, 2004), pp. 1–50: p. 1.

3 See J. Herbst, *States and Power in Africa: Comparative Lessons in Authority and Control* (Princeton: Princeton University Press, 2000).

considerations are irrelevant'.[4] However, this is not taken into account when these states are judged.

Whilst empirical statehood was not an explicit concern in the granting of statehood following decolonisation, the opposite is apparent today. Current development policy centres on good governance, or what it means to be a legitimate, competent and accountable state, as vital to development and growth. Value-laden terminology often used in discussions on good governance, such as 'sound', 'unaccountable', 'acceptable', 'legitimate' and 'competent' denote not only an act of assessment, but also a sense of superiority and judgment – in this case in reference to the developed world towards the developing. These assessments and judgements are apparent nowhere more strongly than in literature and policy regarding what have been termed 'failed' states and how to 'fix' them. Assessing of the effectiveness of states, specifically those within the 'developing world', and the degree of 'goodness' in the governance of those states evidences the dominance of what Jackson distinguishes as empirical statehood in modern conceptions of what it means to be a state.[5] This is not only a sharp departure from the Westphalian statehood applied to the early European states, but also from what was required for statehood in the immediate post-colonial era.

Much of the current development focus of the international community, particularly those areas concerned with states perceived to be fragile or on the brink of failure, is closing the gap between juridical and empirical statehood by focusing on the functions and the provisions of the state apparatus and institutions. The empirical basis on which these assessments are made are rooted in the liberal state, informed primarily by Western-derived normative conceptions of statehood, government structure and government action. It is this basis of assessment that informs not only what a state is, but what a state should be, and it is this that underpins and guides much of current development and security policies and practices, including that of statebuilding.

Failed States, Successful States

The assessment of state performance reached a pinnacle with the attention on failed states. With the post-Cold War focus shifting to the humanitarian or governance state, the criteria through which to assess state performance also altered. Whilst control of territory and therefore physical security remain of high importance in the assessment of state performance, these new governance-centric benchmarks for statehood are clearly evidenced in literature concerning failed states.

Semantically, the term 'failed state' is relatively new, although the concept of state failure is not. As Bøås and Jennings ascertain:

---

4 R. Jackson, *Quasi-States: Sovereignty, International Relations and the Third World* (Cambridge: Cambridge University Press, 1990), p. 17.

5 Ibid.

[a]lthough the rhetorical and policy adoption of 'failed states' is quite recent, intellectually speaking the concept has been around for a long time. Indeed, 'failing' or 'failed' are simply the most recent in a long list of modifiers that have been used to describe or attempt to explain why states residing outside of the geographical core of Western Europe and North America do not function as 'we' think they are supposed to.[6]

They continue in identifying previously used terms within scholarship, including 'neopatrimonial', 'lame', 'weak', 'quasi', and 'premodern'.[7] Morton and Bilgin share this view, arguing that the failed state is nothing more than the latest representation of the problematic 'post-colonial' state.[8] Whereas the term 'failed state' was made popular by Madeleine Albright during her tenure as United States Ambassador to the United Nations,[9] after 11 September 2001 it became the dominant term associated with states in which there has been an 'implosion of government'[10] and where the absence of central authority creates a vacuum of sovereignty. Indeed, a commonly used definition identifies failed states as those in which 'the central government ceased to function and [is] unable to provide for the well-being of its population or protect it from internal or external threats'.[11] A failed state is unsuccessful at maintaining the most basic Weberian norms of statehood as well as in the areas of social provision and human security.[12] The Fund for Peace in its Failed States Index also considers economic conditions in its consideration of state failure, and the State Failure Task Force adds to these factors such as environmental protection and 'democracy level' as variables in its statistical determination of a failed state.[13]

---

6 M. Bøås and K. Jennings, 'Insecurity and Development: The Rhetoric of the "Failed State"', *The European Journal of Development Research* 17.3 (2005), pp. 385–95: p. 387.

7 Ibid.

8 A. Morton and P. Bilgin, 'Historicising Representations of "Failed States:" Beyond the Cold War Annexation of the Social Sciences?' *Third World Quarterly* 23.1 (2002), pp. 55–80.

9 J. Gros, 'Towards a Taxonomy of Failed States in the New World Order: decaying Somalia,
Liberia, Rwanda and Haiti', *Third World Quarterly* 17.3 (1996), pp. 448–61: p. 455.

10 A. Yannis, 'State Collapse and its Implications for Peace-Building and Reconstruction', in J. Milliken (ed.), *State Failure, Collapse and Reconstruction* (Oxford: Blackwell, 2003), pp. 63–80: p. 64, footnote 1.

11 D. Carment, 'Assessing State Failure: Implications for Theory and Policy', *Third World Quarterly* 24.3 (2003), pp. 407–27: p. 409.

12 In particular, this is evident in works by Robert Rotberg and the Harvard Failed States Project. See also Bøås and Jennings, op. cit., for more discussion on the relationship between the state and human security in the context of the failed state.

13 State Failure Task Force, 'State Failure Task Force Findings I (30 November 1995), II (31 July 1998), III (20 September 2000), IV (18 November 2003), V (3 September 2005)',

Although 'failed state' is a popularly used term within academia and policy, definitional ambiguity exists surrounding what the phenomena actually is. Definitions range from simply *etat sans gouvernement*, or 'state without government', to a state that is 'tense, deeply conflicted, dangerous, and contested bitterly by warring factions', characterised by criminal violence, poverty, corruption, flawed institutions and deteriorating or destroyed infrastructures.[14] Some usages of the term even include those states that are 'aggressive, arbitrary, tyrannical or totalitarian' in governing or those that are undergoing revolutionary wars, ethnic wars, mass killings and adverse or disruptive regime change.[15] Within these offerings a wide definitional expanse becomes clear, with everything from complete lack of government to poor governance to violent state actions falling into the broad conception of state failure. Exactly what constitutes state failure, how to assess failure, who assesses failure and whether or not there is an identified threshold that if crossed indicates failure remains uncertain. The exact meaning of the failure of a state is left open to interpretation and assessment, with the control against which a state is assessed being unspecified beyond vague criteria such as citizens' needs and desires and legitimate government. What is clear, though, is that within the wide definitional scope there is one commonality: states that dramatically fail to meet the expectations of modern acceptable statehood. Brinkerhoff exemplifies this in saying that state failure is a,

> breakdown of law and order where state institutions lose their monopoly on the legitimate use of force and are unable to protect their citizens, or those institutions are used to oppress and terrorise citizens; (b) weak or disintegrated capacity to respond to citizens' needs and desires, provide basic public services, assure citizens' welfare or support normal economic activity; (c) at the international level, lack of a credible entity that represents the state beyond its borders.[16]

It is within the work surrounding what state failure is perceived to be that the criteria of state success, and therefore acceptableness, can be drawn out.

What is consistent throughout the literature, however, is the prevalence of assessment and judgement based on conceptions of Western democratic statehood and the model or ideal state portrayed through normative assumptions. These value

---

College Park, MD: Centre for International Development and Conflict Management; Fund for Peace, '2013 Failed States Index Scores', available at http://www.fundforpeace.org/.

14 D. Thürer, 'The "failed state" and international law', *International Review of the Red Cross* No. 836 (December 1999), pp. 731–61: p. 731; R. Rotberg, op. cit., pp. 5–7.

15 D. Thürer, op. cit., p. 731; State Failure Task Force, 'Phase I Findings', op. cit., p. vii.

16 D. Brinkerhoff, 'Rebuilding Governance in Failed States and Post-Conflict Societies: Core Concepts and Cross-Cutting Themes', *Public Administration and Development* 25.1 (2005), pp. 3–14: p. 4. A similar definition is given by the Fund for Peace in the explanation of their annual Failed States Index.

laden comparisons of success and dysfunction, particularly those that compose state performance taxonomies,[17] paint a picture of superior versus inferior state forms, organisations and actions. The term – the classification, even – brings with it the semantically valued implication that '[a] failed state[s] is a polity that is no longer able or willing to perform the *fundamental tasks* of a nation-state in the modern world',[18] 'a ghostly presence on the world map' that is 'utterly incapable of sustaining itself as a member of the international community': they are the 'threat of ungoverned space'.[19] These states which are, according to Rotberg, 'black holes' where a 'dark energy' exists and where 'the forces of entropy have overwhelmed the radiance that hitherto provided some semblance of order', are antithetic to secure liberal democratic states.[20] Whereas this language may appear to be overdramatic, the sense of pessimism and even despair portrayed is typical of the posture found throughout literature on failed states. Yannis less colourfully states that there are 'minimum standards of governance that reflect a universal consensus about the minimum requirements of *effective* and *responsible* government',[21] and that failed states are those that do not meet them. Although Yannis does not specify what these minimum requirements are, it is clear throughout the rest of his work, and indeed throughout most of the work on state failure, that they are based on liberal expectations of good governance.

The emphasis on the ideals of successful statehood highlights an important distinction that is prevalent throughout current state failure literature: that of societal responsibility. Yannis, amongst others, makes clear there is an idealised point or standard of statehood at which to aspire that goes beyond the existence of a central government; a standard which incorporates Rotberg's political or public goods. It is here that the normative assumptions of what a state is expected to be become clearer: a central democratic government is expected to protect the territory

---

17 In addition to the Failed States Index and the State Failure Task Force, op. cit., see for example USAID, 'US Foreign Aid: Meeting the Challenges of the Twenty-first Century', US Agency for International Development (2004); USAID, 'Proposed Typology in Order to Classify Countries Based on Performance and State Capacity', US Agency for International Development (2003); Prime Minister's Strategy Unit, 'Countries at Risk of Instability Reports' (February 2005); J. Gros, op. cit.
18 R. Rotberg, 'The Failure and Collapse of Nation-States', op. cit., p. 6. Emphasis added.
19 D. Thürer, op. cit., p. 731; State Failure Task Force, 'Phase I Findings', op. cit., p. 1; M. Duffield, *Development, Security and Unending War* (Cambridge: Polity, 2007), p. 170.
20 R. Rotberg, 'Failed States, Collapsed States, Weak States: Causes and Indicators', in R. Rotberg (ed.), *State Failure and State Weakness in a Time of Terror* (Washington DC: Brookings Institute Press, 2003), pp. 1–28: p. 9. See also, S. Chesterman, M. Ignatieff and R. Thakur, 'Introduction: Making States Work', in S. Chesterman, et al. (eds), *Making States Work: State Failure and the Crisis of Governance* (New York: United Nations University Press, 2005), pp. 1–10.
21 A. Yannis, op. cit., p. 64, footnote 1. Emphasis added.

and the people as well as provide certain goods and services, including '[w]hat are considered in the West to be norms of civilised state behaviour – including those pertaining to human rights of individuals and groups'.[22] States that do not achieve this, therefore, have failed the standards of statehood, a departure from the more innocuous and literal *etat sans gouvernement* conception of the failed state. These standards of governance are echoed by Jackson, who claims failed states are those states that 'cannot or will not safeguard minimal civil conditions for their populations: domestic peace, law and order, and good governance'.[23] The implication of failure to society as an aspect of state failure not only displays the value placed on societal responsibilities of states to their populations, but also links the existence of an effective central government to societal stability.

As Gourevitch critically observes, by viewing state failure as domestic anarchy, analysts and policymakers 'do not have to understand the local dynamics driving the crisis ... Instead they can simply treat it as chaos'.[24] Implicit in this analysis is that by identifying state failure in Western terms – that is, applying the assessment of failure, chaos or anarchy to situations that do not comply with norms of statehood – the self-image of the ideal Western state is reinforced and intervention to 'fix' or 'remake' the chaotic state is justified. Forms of political organisation that do not mimic or comply with the familiar Western state or the picture of an ideal modern state are often present in states identified as failed. As a result, non-Western forms of political organisation and practice are often overlooked as legitimate forms of state organisation and are therefore excluded from acceptable solutions and conceptions of success. Within this is the underlying assumption that the key to a successful state, and the key to preventing state failure, is to create a modern democratic state that is familiar and understandable to the West.

One of the key criticisms of the ideal state is that there is no uniform model in practice. The Western liberal state is hailed as the solution to weak or problematic states, yet there is a significant degree of disparity between the political organisations of Western states, particularly those within Europe. Reviewing statebuilding projects a decade on from Haiti and Bosnia, a report from *The International Peace Academy* concludes that there was still a tendency towards a 'one size fits all' approach to political reform that missed the variety in models of democracy. The report noted that whilst 'mature and advanced democracies' possessed a shared commitment to the values of liberal democracy and market economics, 'there is no uniformity of pattern in the structures, institutions and processes'.[25] This, as well as lack of

---

22 M. Ayoob, 'State Making, State Breaking, and State Failure', in C. Crocker, et al. (eds), *Turbulent Peace: The Challenges of Managing International Conflict* (Washington DC: United States Institute for Peace, 2001), pp. 127–42: p. 133.

23 R. Jackson, *Global Covenant: Human Conduct in a World of States* (Oxford: Oxford University Press, 2000), pp. 295–6.

24 A. Gourevitch, 'The Unfailing of the State', *Journal of International Affairs* 58.1 (2004), pp. 255–60: p. 257.

25 S. Chesterman, M. Ignatieff and R. Thakur, op. cit., p. 4.

recognition of variance in proposed solutions, is a significant gap. Despite the lack of a singular practical model of this ideal state, there is also an inability amongst its proponents to see benefits outside this framework. As a result, non-Western or non-liberal forms of political or state organisation that may challenge the uniform applicability of the ideal state are often overlooked or rejected. This is not to say that in all instances the idea of the state is dead or being abandoned,[26] but rather that not all states and societies exhibit, or benefit, from the uniformity espoused by the ideal state. This does not mean that those states need to be fixed. In some cases, such as Somalia or Iraq, applying a standardised prescription for success through uniformity has been unduly negative and has resulted in chaos. The lack of a central government or the presence of a non-Western or weak government does not automatically mean there is an absence of control or provision, and a weak or absent government does not doom the state to the Hobbesian anarchy as parallel, shadow or social institutions may fill the empirical gaps. Success in a non-Western form of state or political organisation does not mean an abandonment of the state design altogether, but rather an alternative to the political and state organisation enshrined by the ideal state.

Much of the current literature and practice, however, fixates on the supposed anarchy created by the absence of the familiar liberal democratic state, and as such, success or failure is judged primarily on what Western components are missing in non-Western states. As a result, non-Western or non-liberal forms of political or state organisation or even 'deviant' institutions and practices that may challenge the uniform applicability of the idealised liberal democratic state are often overlooked or rejected. This does not mean that states exhibiting these mechanisms of governance need to be fixed. Rather, it indicates that not all states and societies exhibit, or indeed may benefit from, the liberal democratic model of statehood. In some cases, such as Somalia, applying a standardised prescription for success through uniformity has been unduly negative and has resulted in chaos. In others, the firmly held liberal perspective failed to account for or accommodate the socio-political realities on the ground; for example, the role of an individual like Grand Ayatollah Ali al-Sistani in shaping political debate in Iraq does not fit within the liberal understanding or framework of the state. Whilst there is much focus on the value assessment of state success based on the comparison of these states to Western democracies, what is not recognised is the value of alternative forms of political organisation or control and thus alternative sources of public goods, state control and security. The exclusion of 'non-Western' sources of political power

---

26 The argument can be made that provision made by the Zapatistas in Mexico or Hamas in Palestine and Lebanon and their challenge to the central state indicates an abandonment of the state. The same can be said of some militant groups in Somalia, particularly al-Shabaab, an extremist militarised faction of the Union of Islamic Courts. The question of abandoning the state is also raised by Berger in his discussion of state building. M. Berger, 'States of Nature and the Nature of States: the fate of nations, the collapse of states and the future of the world', *Third World Quarterly* 28.6 (2007), pp. 1203–14.

poses significant questions for statebuilding. As will be discussed in the context of Somaliland, the placement or role of an 'unfamiliar' political actor can be a vital component for legitimising the state and stabilising the statebuilding process.

Taught and Learned Statehood

In this focus on the familiar, the liberal democratic state becomes as the path to state success, creating a system of promulgation of this style of state through policy and practice. Robinson, in his book *The Theory of Global Capitalism*, argues that an emerging transnational capitalist class is establishing the framework for a 'transnationalist state', or a state that conforms to values of statehood dependent on economic capability and production which in turn will favour capitalist production. He states that the transnational capitalist class,

> in part by virtue of its position as an 'organized minority' and the resources and networks at its disposal for coordination, works through identifiable institutions and is fairly coherent as a collective actor ... [this ensures] the reproduction of global capitalist relations of production, as well as the creation of and reproduction of political and cultural institutions favourable to its rule.[27]

Robinson's argument is very obviously premised and dependent on the understanding of inter-state relations in the context of capitalist reproduction. However, the recognition of a self-reproducing system ensuring conditions favourable to its continuation raises interesting questions and similarities in regard to the role of the Western-dominated international system in the shaping or restructuring of states. If the Marxist undertones from Robinson's thesis are removed, what is left is a powerful group of states – albeit a minority – creating and working, sometimes through international institutions, to reproduce normative values of statehood that favour those dominant states, as well as acceptable and familiar structures of governance and government. In other words, and taking the application of Robinson further out of the Marxist context, there is a dominant group of states that, through the international system and international institutions, creates a normative framework of acceptable statehood through which values reflecting the desires, interests and demands of those powerful actors are disseminated, enacted and reproduced. As such, this system is promoting the creation of states that reflect the acceptable normative standards of statehood, accomplished through the reproduction of known governance structures. With the dominance of the liberal state, its Western origins and the association this has with security in mind, it can be argued that the self-reproducing system aims to create a style and function of state that is not only seen to be proven, but importantly

---

27 W. Robinson, *The Theory of Global Capitalism: Production, Class and State in a Transnational World* (Baltimore: Johns Hopkins University Press, 2007), pp. 86–7.

one that is user-friendly to the dominant Western states.[28] In this regard, familiar and known structures and functions are deemed not only safe and secure, but also controllable.

Robinson is not alone in identifying the existence and dominance of these global institutions and structures. Although not underpinned by the same Marxist assumptions, Finnemore similarly asserts that international institutions and normative values 'may make uniform behavioural claims upon dissimilar actors. They may shape and define the preferences of actors in ways not related to internal conditions, characteristics, or functional need'.[29] The uniform outcome of the impact of these normative values – the 'one size fits all' approach – ensures the reproduction of those values. What is important to note within Finnemore's work, however, are the relationships between these international institutions, normative values and the state. Whilst Finnemore places emphasis on the role of norms and institutions, she does not divorce them from the state. Rather, states are symbiotically enmeshed in this web of relationships:

> [s]tates are embedded in dense networks of transnational and international social relations that shape their perceptions of the world and their role in that world. States are socialized to want certain things by the international society in which they and the people in them live.[30]

Whilst all states may be embedded in these networks, their role in the establishment of them varies. Within the works of both Finnemore and Robinson, as well as other scholars writing on norms and institutions, one cannot completely overlook the role of dominant states in the international system as the powerful actors in determining the shape and outlook of the institutional and normative frameworks. Those states with the economic, cultural, political and military power will be the decisive factor in the composition of the normative system and the actions of the institutions. As a result of this, it is difficult to separate international institutions, including non-tangible institutions, and the norms surrounding them from those dominant states that govern them. Whereas these institutions may be the agents of change through policies and practices, the role of dominant Western states in the formation and function of these institutions cannot be completely discounted. And although Finnemore highlights the socialisation of individual states through these networks and structures, the impact of this system of socialisation on individual political actors within a state must also be recognised. As will be seen, the socialisation of individuals as a method of embedding developing states in

---

28 For more discussion on this, see M. Duffield, *Development, Security and Unending War* (Cambridge: Polity, 2007), Chapter 7.

29 M. Finnemore, *National Interests in International Society* (London: Cornell University Press, 1996), p. 22.

30 Ibid., p. 2. Emphasis in original.

these dense networks and normative systems is an important component of certain development and statebuilding policies, both externally and internally driven.

Whilst Finnemore stops short of exactly specifying the role of the state in the creation of the normative frameworks guiding policy, what is interesting about her assessment is the differentiation between 'teaching' and 'learning'. It is within this that the implied role of the state becomes clearer. Finnemore argues that the predominant way of interpreting normative values of statehood and the policies that go with them is to understand that functioning as a state reflective of those values is something that can either be taught or learned. There is a *systemic* impetus for the proliferation and reproduction of normative values, and international institutions are the primary teachers of statehood within this system.[31] Roughly analogous with the structure of learning and homework assignments a student receives in school, an example of this would be structural adjustment programmes (SAPs), where the normative values relating to economic liberalisation are taught to recipient states through conditionality agreements. Learning, on the other hand, has its origin *within* the state and is therefore domestically driven.[32] In other words, a state can be self-taught in that it can learn from, and then conform to, systematic normative preferences by voluntarily adapting actions, interests and policies to bring them in line with perceived systemic preferences. The difficult area Finnemore does not venture into, however, is a combination of the two: states which are concurrently instructed and learning the normative model of acceptable or ideal statehood. This is perhaps because a combination of the two is difficult to conceptualise in the context of a domineering and systemic normative framework. It also begs the question of whether learning is indicative of complicity, of manipulation or of both. A combination of being taught *and* independently learning would point to the rare existence of an enthusiastic state overeager to comply with the demands of the international system; returning to the student analogy of the state it is one that does its homework plus asks for extra reading. Just as it is difficult for many teachers to imagine many of their students eager to seek out extra work, in dominant understandings of the international system and of states it is difficult to envision a state willing to relinquish, at least to some extent, autonomy and identity necessary to drastically alter itself in such a way. Indeed, even within understandings of SAPs and conditional aid it is widely accepted that these changes are coercive rather than fully voluntary; states are left with little choice but to comply or suffer. However, this combination of the two is not as rare an occurrence as it may appear. Certainly there are states that have beneficially complied with reform projects and others who have sought them out. More obvious, though, is the combination of teaching and learning taking place within those territories undergoing domestically-led statebuilding projects; a category of political entities that will be returned to further in this chapter.

---

31 Ibid., pp. 11–13.
32 Ibid.

The existence of a normative value system surrounding statehood, as well as both the notions of teaching these values and voluntarily learning and adopting them, stresses the existence of an ideal type of state and preferred state functions and actions. Although not expressly stated or referred to as an 'ideal', a clear conception of a model state preferred by powerful states and international institutions, based on ideas of democracy and security, can be extricated from literature and policy surrounding weak, fragile, failing or failed states. The important question arising from the teaching-learning nexus, though, is how is this model of statehood proliferated?

Building Ideal States?

The teacher-student association highlighted by Finnemore is evident in contemporary literature and theory concerning failed states as well as that aimed at fixing these failures; the successful states guiding the unsuccessful, or the model state serving as an example. While there has long been an impulse of trusteeship within development policy,[33] this push for teaching statehood is different: in most cases there is less intense direct involvement and action is better understood as socialising rather than occupying. Duffield identifies the dominant liberal framework and action as 'a radical development agenda of social transformation' with the aim to 'transform the dysfunctional and war-affected societies it encounters on its borders into cooperative, representative and, especially, stable entities'.[34] However, the same connotations of distrust of the unfamiliar and superiority over other forms of governance that are associated with trusteeship continue, and the socialisation can be intrusive or coercive. Whether through direct action or normative 'teaching', the aim is creating a form of government that covers all the bases or attempts to eliminate risks; to create a government that is functional and a state that is successful. However, the approach taken is creating a government that is from the outset concerned with everything needed to support society rather than going through the slow process of evolving into the successful acceptable state. The element of trusteeship or teacher-student relationship, therefore, is an expedited way to skip ahead to what a state should provide. In more extreme cases, this involves a much more intensive approach that has come to be known as statebuilding.

Since their inception, international institutions have assisted with development programmes, aimed at bringing those states seen to be lagging behind into the fold of being a successful member of the international community. Even before international institutions, individual actors acted in this way; much of the early colonialism was not only financially motivated, but was also aimed at civilising those who were seen as backwards or inferior to the European way of living and

---

33 See M.P. Cowen and R.W. Shenton, *Doctrines of Development* (London: Routledge, 1996), p. 11.
34 M. Duffield, *Global Governance and the New Wars* (London: Zed, 2001), p. 11.

governing. With the advent of international institutions, much of the development focus was economic, as reforming and modernising economic systems through the empowering of complicit technocratic elites within the state was seen as the optimal way to spark and maintain developmental success whilst simultaneously allowing for an outwardly apolitical stance by the institutions. In the 1990s, however, policy prerogatives shifted to include an emphasis on the more political governance reform and the promotion of good governance within conditional assistance agreements. In the 1990s, the concept of good governance became associated with development. As already highlighted, this also became associated with security.

The perceived relationship between good governance and security and the role of the international community in maintaining this relationship was clearly articulated in Boutros Boutros-Ghali's 1992 *An Agenda for Peace* and the immediate policy-made-practice in Somalia. As early as 1973 the World Bank was already including mention of governance in its reports on projects within countries, but it was not until 1992 that the institution gave a clear indication of expectations for establishing mechanisms for good governance as a condition of continued assistance.[35] Still, within this more economy-oriented aspect of development, good governance continued to exist primarily within the realm of economic development. Within Boutros-Ghali's work, however, a link was made between governance and socio-political development, with the expectation that good governance would lead to stability and therefore security of the state and, by extension, the system. In both areas, good governance is viewed as exercising of power in a manner conducive to maximising development and advancement opportunities: governance reflective of that found in the model of the modern state. As Harrison notes, for the World Bank expectations of good governance continued the theme of economic restructuring in that governance reform was the 'promotion of a more efficient public administration, the promotion of accountability, the establishment of the rule of law and a capable judiciary, and transparency'.[36] For Boutros-Ghali and the changing post-Cold War involvement of the UN, however, reform was also aimed at establishing governance that would ensure territorial and human security, and that meant extending beyond the realm of economics and finance.

With the establishment of UNOSOM II in Somalia, Boutros-Ghali's ideas were quickly put to the test. Attempts to establish good governance in Somalia,

---

35 See G. Harrison, *The World Bank and Africa: The Construction of Governance States* (London: Routledge, 2004); G. Harrison, 'The World Bank, Governance and Theories of Political Action in Africa', *British Journal of Politics and International Relations* 7.2 (2005), pp. 240–60; The World Bank, *Governance: The World Bank's Experience* (Washington DC: The World Bank, 1994). For an examination of inclusion of social policy and indicators as a component of assessing governance, see G. Davis, 'A History of the Social Development Network in The World Bank, 1973 – 2002', World Bank Social Development Papers Number 56 (2004).

36 The World Bank, op. cit.; G. Harrison, 'The World Bank, Governance and Theories of Public Action', op. cit., p. 240.

though, required further action than simply reform as the formal political system had collapsed and the power vacuum it created was fuelling further conflict. UN Security Council Resolution 814 (1993) clearly stated the need for not only the maintenance of law and order to resolve the humanitarian crisis in Somalia, but also the 're-establishment of local and regional administrative institutions as essential to the restoration of domestic tranquillity' and the need to set up a transitional government 'leading to the establishment of representative democratic institutions'.[37] Resolution 814 continues in establishing the mandate for the UN to assist in political reconciliation and the re-establishment of institutions and administration. Resolution 814 is not only a clear link between humanitarian concerns, political concerns and security concerns, but it is also the explicit establishment of the practice of statebuilding. Resolution 814 brought the ideas of post-conflict peacebuilding through the re-establishment of institutions of acceptable government from the realm of ideas into the reality of practice.[38]

Statebuilding is often discussed under the guise of peacebuilding. When viewed in the context of post-conflict environments, statebuilding is about delivering 'authoritative, legitimate and capable' governance through the establishment of liberal institutions and practices that 'can provide for security and the necessary rule-of-law conditions for economic and social development' and a means through which further conflict can be prevented.[39] The assumption here, of course, is that poor or abusive governance is a driver of conflict, and that by providing a means through which the voice of the citizens can be heard and political and social goods provided in an effective manner is a way to 'manag[e] social conflicts away from the battlefield and streets and into regularized processes of non-violent resolution'.[40] In states where institutions of authority have been destroyed or disrupted, such as post-conflict states emerging from a period of civil war, re-establishing institutions and ensuring good governance is a way to create a mediating outlet and process for further discontent. The development and security nexus heavily underpins this approach to peacebuilding: while negotiating peace agreements and reconciling at the societal level is important, 'ultimately the extent of peace consolidation is based on the building of a state that is socially accepted as a legitimate, accountable arbiter of social differences and a provider of critical public goods'.[41] Longer term strengthening of institutions and practice through continued support serves to strengthen the state, creating security and stability not only for the population but also for the international system. In post-conflict countries, 'statebuilding is the *telos* (or end goal) of consolidating peace'.[42]

---

37 United Nations, 'Resolution 814 (26 March 1993)', Security Council Resolution.
38 B. Boutros-Ghali, *An Agenda for Peace* (New York: United Nations, 1992), 1.15.
39 T. Sisk, *Statebuilding* (Cambridge: Polity, 2013), p. 1.
40 Ibid.
41 Ibid.
42 Ibid. p. x.

Statebuilding as a security mechanism is not limited to the post-conflict realm, though. With identified risk emanating from weak, failing, fragile or failed states, statebuilding is also seen as a prevention mechanism to keep war from breaking out or to curb the dangers of failure, such as terrorism, humanitarian crises, refugee flows or cross-border conflict, through the strengthening of institutions and liberal democratic practices. Ghani and Lockhart maintain that forty to sixty fragile states contain the roots of many global crises, with 'prolonged conflict or misrule, networks of criminality, violence and terror … providing an ever expanding platform that threatens the entire globe'. They offer a technocratic guide to rebuilding failed states, identifying this policy action as a form of risk management.[43] Rotberg, in his focus on the dangers of state failure, argues that policies towards fragile and failed states must address institutional weaknesses, economic underdevelopment and democratisation through the fostering of elections. Both the UK and US government, amongst other Western states, place 'fragile' and 'conflict prone' states into the same category within security policy, identifying development within these states as a priority in the area of conflict prevention.[44] Tellingly, the UK government strategies and policy documents are produced not only by the Ministry of Defence, but also by the Department for International Development.[45] The now infamous 2002 United States National Security Strategy firmly established state failure and state weakness as a security concern, and subsequent organisational and institutional policies identify key tasks necessary for the establishment of good governance for the purposes of strengthening and stabilisation, tasks undertaken by the US State Department, the US International Development Agency (USAID) and the Department of Defence. USAID, in its self-description, maintains that 'countries that have ineffective government institutions, rampant corruption and weak rule of law have a 30-to-45 per cent higher risk of civil war' than other developing countries, so USAID is working to change that narrative through 'integrating democracy programming'

---

43   A. Ghani and C. Lockhart, 'Closing the Sovereignty Gap: An Approach to State-Building'. London, Overseas Development Institute Report (2005); A. Ghani and C. Lockhart, *Fixing Failed States; A Framework for Rebuilding a Fractured World* (Oxford: Oxford University Press, 2008), p. 23.

44   See UK Government, 'A Strong Britain in an Age of Uncertainty: The National Security Strategy', (London: HM Government, 2010); UK Government, 'Building Security Overseas Strategy', (London: DfID, MOD and FCO, 2011); US Government, 'The National Security Strategy of the United States', (Washington DC: The White House, 2002); S. Woodward, 'State-Building and Peace-Building: What Theory and Whose Role?' in R. Kozul-Wright and P. Fortunato (eds), *Securing Peace: State-Building and Economic Development in Post-Conflict Countries* (London: Bloomsbury Academic, 2011), pp. 87–112: p. 93.

45   See also, UK Prime Minister's Strategy Unit Papers (2005), op. cit.; DfID, 'Country Engagement Plan for Somalia', (London, 2005); DfID, 'Making Government Work for Poor People: Building State Capability', (London: 2001); DfID, 'Why We Need to Work More Effectively in Fragile States', (London, 2005).

throughout their core development work in order to 'prevent conflict, spur economic growth and advance human dignity'.[46] Following the expensive, drawn-out and unpopular statebuilding interventions in Iraq and Afghanistan, though, leading Western states have adopted a more facilitative and supportive rather than interventionist stance. Still, consistent goal of 'democracy building' is maintained, again linking expectations of good governance to security and stability.[47] The United Nations, itself underpinned by ideas of peace-through-democratisation, also identifies a link between state fragility and security within its operational structure, with much of this work undertaken by the relatively new UN Department of Peacebuilding Operations, as well as the UN Department of Political Affairs and the UN Development Programme. As Chandler notes, statebuilding is a key policy practice that has 'increasingly become internationally accepted as [a] central mechanism through which the problems of weak or failing states can be addressed'.[48] Rather than being something concrete or accurately measurable, therefore, the 'fragile' or 'failed' state is best considered as a relation of international governance, particularly liberal global governance.[49]

Within these policies and practices, the problems of global insecurity, poverty, development and conflict are directly linked to the widespread existence of states perceived to be dysfunctional.[50] The ideas behind statebuilding here are fairly simple: the problem with weak, fragile or failing states is poor governance and a failure or inability to provide public and political goods. By addressing those weaknesses and failure through strengthening democratic governance, increasing institutional capacity, eliminating corruption and improving participation, development goals can be reached and the risk of conflict reduces, thereby improving security for the state in question and the system as a whole. The 'solution to these [socio-political-economic] problems' associated with the development-security paradigm is 'therefore that of enabling states and societies to make better choices and decisions and at the same time ensuring that decision-making is more constrained by international frameworks' outlining expectations for good governance.[51] 'Changing the rules of the game' by changing bad governance into good governance serves to overcoming 'institutional blockages' that prevent 'state-society relations from creating a stable social order and which prevent the state from benefiting from the stable social and economic order of institutional society'.[52] Through statebuilding, primarily through institutional

---

46 USAID, *What We Do: Democracy, Human Rights and Governance.* [Online] Available at www.usaid.gov.
47 T. Sisk, op. cit. 163.
48 D. Chandler, *International Statebuilding: The Rise of Post-Liberal Governance* (London: Routledge, 2010), p. 1.
49 M. Duffield, *Development, Security and Unending War*, op. cit., p. 159.
50 D. Chandler, op. cit., p. 5.
51 D. Chandler, Ibid.
52 D. Chandler, Ibid., p. 6.

design and capacity, it is maintained, fragility can be prevented from sliding into failure, thereby protecting not only the population of the state in question but also global security as a whole.

There is no uniform step-by-step guide for statebuilding. Indeed, as Woodward notes, many of the practices found within statebuilding were developed for other purposes and circumstances in the development and peacebuilding realm but have 'evolved in the past two decades as they adjusted to these different conditions'.[53] One of the biggest criticisms of statebuilding is the ad hoc manner of the implementation of these practices and the lack of coordination between agencies. Even within the big interventionist projects such as those seen in Iraq, Afghanistan, Bosnia, East Timor and Kosovo, different agencies and actors were responsible for different elements of the project, creating a situation where lack of continuity or failures in communication and standardisation added to the complexity of attempts at statebuilding. In projects that are smaller-scale and do not have the substantial military support or significant international attention focused on them, the decentralised efforts of the statebuilders is also apparent and often problematic. Despite there not being a guide or a uniform approach, though, there is a clear framework for statebuilding, and within that, there is a clear ideological blueprint. Statebuilding is not characterised by socio-political change or building the state and all of its tangible and intangible components, but rather is concerned primarily with institution building. This blueprint puts emphasis on the creating of democratic and accountable institutions and strengthening institutional capacity in order to fulfil the liberal demands of the state, particularly those pertaining to protection and provision of public goods. Within this, the long-term goals of consolidating peace and creating a sustainable political solution within a state, as Sisk maintains, requires a 'laser-like focus on the institutions of the state'.[54] This emphasis on the institutions and the practices surrounding them as the lynchpin for peace and stability echoes the liberal focus on peace through democratisation and good governance. With the liberal dominance in the international system, though, this is not surprising. The goal of statebuilding is to build the ideal state.

In the dominant discourses of the international community the institutional components of the state and their scope of activity have been largely static in the last two decades. In line with liberal understandings, these components comply with expectations of Weberian bureaucratic administrations and modern acceptable statehood, and through this there is a framework for emerging states to match and a check list for statebuilding projects. Liberal economic institutions and democracy are part of the 'political gold standard' good governance model.[55] Despite the high-profile of the discourse surrounding democracy promotion there

---

53 S. Woodward, op. cit., p. 88.

54 T. Sisk, op. cit., p. 168.

55 M. Cox, 'Wilsonian Resurgent? The Clinton Administration and the Promotion of Democracy', in M. Cox, G.J. Ikenberry, T. Inoguchi (eds) *American Democracy Promotion: Impulses, Strategies and Impacts* (Oxford: Oxford University Press, 200, p. 226.

is very little said about the nature of the democracy being promoted. In the rush of countries making the shift to democracy in the late twentieth century there was only limited space for development of alternate structures or styles of state, and the Western based model of elections, legislature and independent judiciary became a template to be copied as best practice and as a path towards stability and acceptance.

In addition to liberal economics and a democratic government, the final pillar of this institutional state is the advancement of individual rights. As with economic reform and political change, these values are firmly entrenched in ideas of good governance. Exhibited by Boutros-Ghali, alongside the new emphasis on peacebuilding and institutional reform and reconstruction, the 'increasingly common moral perception that spans the world's nations and peoples' of individual human rights and institutional protection for them became a component of expected empirical statehood.[56] Linked with democratic practice and the inclusion of the population in political choice, respect for individual rights is also seen as a legitimising feature of the state, both externally and, importantly, internally. Demands for democracy and respect for human rights, once described by some as a western project, has been adopted beyond the western liberal world as rights have been demanded by communities across the globe. Linking into ideas of good governance, and with the model of liberal democracy being the means through which to ensure these protections, institutional expectations for the state being built become clear.[57]

Institutionalisation and the institutional state is more than simply establishing the tangible bodies of government that are the means through which legitimate power is exercised. Institutionalisation is:

> the process by which a cluster of activities acquires a persistent set of rules that constrain activity, shape expectations, and prescribe roles for actors. Institutionalisation means that sustainability does not depend on any single individual but on a shared commitment to the principles, procedures, and goals of the institution.[58]

Because it involves the embedding of the rules of governance within political practice itself to the point where those rules become a popular expectation for political action, statebuilding thus must not only establish these rules, but also much account for the repetition or enforcement of practice needed to embed these norms, expectations and behaviours not only within the political class, but also within society. In other words, the establishment of institutions and the practices

---

56 B. Boutros-Ghali, op. cit., pp. 8–9.
57 R. Richards and R.G. Smith, 'Imagining the State: Legitimising Kurdistan and Somaliland', EWIS Workshops, Tartu, 2013.
58 C. Call, 'Ending Wars, Building States', in C. Call and V. Wyeth (eds), *Building States to Build Peace* (London: Lynne Rienner, 2008), pp. 1–22: p. 8.

surrounding them must outlive a charismatic leader empowered to lead the process – a common characteristic of international statebuilding – and must exist after the statebuilders leave.

The establishment of this form of institutional state is approached through a combination of external direction and internal adoption. Within this the empirical emphasis is on the tangible institutions, with the expectation that establishing those and increasing institutional capacity will lead to meeting the demands of governance found within the framework and the repetition of such practice will complete the cycle of institutionalisation. Because of the expectation of conformity to systemically maintained structures, norms and values, the primacy here is on external legitimacy – both external expectations for how to achieve domestic legitimacy and external demands for the style of state. It has long been the accepted mantra and practice in the international community that if institutions are built, legitimacy will follow. It is assumed that institutions shaped in the mould of Western liberal democracies will lead to good practice, which in turn will lead to the good governance that is the foundation for stability and legitimacy. This is not to say that domestic acceptance of these institutions and the practices that are expected to follow is not a possibility, but instead it is an assumption rather than a consideration. In many ways, statebuilding has the standing attitude of 'if you build them, it will come' approach to constructing and legitimising the state.[59]

Conclusions

The model of statehood portrayed within development and statebuilding policy and discourse is one of success in terms of compliance and of governance. In addition to Weber's basic definition of statehood, what is now being encouraged, or even imposed, either directly or implicitly, is a legitimate, accountable and non-corrupt 'good' government, preferably chosen through a democratic process and eager to engage with the international community and its demands, dictates and desires.[60] This model of success has become the benchmark of statehood necessary for creating economic and political state-to-state and state-to-institution relationships. Weak, fragile, failing or failed states – those unable or unwilling to engage with the international economy and those exhibiting poor or no governance – are seen as a threat to international stability for a number of reasons, whilst successful states are perceived as being viable and beneficial members of the international community of states.

The expectation of the acceptable successful state and the assumption that it is the path to security, provision and stability is a long standing assumption that has dominated development policy since the end of the Cold War and has

---

59 *Field of Dreams*. [Film] Directed by P.A. Robinson (United States: Gordon Company, 1989).
60 See The World Bank, op. cit., p. xiv.

proliferated the peace and security realm as well. Statebuilding is the epitome of this. Given its rooting in liberal understandings of peace and security, expressed very clearly in Boutros-Ghali's ideas of the maintenance of these, peacebuilding is not a surprising place for statebuilding to fit. However, statebuilding itself goes far beyond areas such as negotiation and reconciliation that are typically associated with peacebuilding. Indeed, statebuilding is a highly intrusive and intensive project that involves establishing both tangible and practical institutions of government with the aim of creating stability through creating good governance and acceptable government. Bliesmemann de Guevara comically notes that the international community guides and intervenes in areas of fragility or collapse with a positive Bob the Builder mentality of 'we can fix it!'[61] With the normative model of the ideal or acceptable liberal state guiding action and intervention in failed, failing, fragile, weak or post-conflict states, the approach taken is one of imbuing, or imposing, what is deemed to work: the institutionalisation of liberal democratic practices and the instilling of good governance in order to create a safe and secure state, both for the population and for the system. Indeed, the 'recovery of state capacities through international assistance has emerged as a leitmotif of international responses' to conflict and fragility.[62] Despite its seemingly good intentions, though, statebuilding has not shown much success in practice, particularly in the intensively interventionist projects.

As Sisk concisely states, 'statebuilding is a complex and problematic process'.[63] It has long been criticised that the dominant liberal approach to statebuilding is narrow and exclusionary; it is one which assumes political and cultural homogeneity and one which ignores not only existing power structures, but also sovereign complexities resulting from the imposition of institutions in target states. There is a tendency to 'assume[e] that the political process is a product of state policies rather than constitutive of them'.[64] Meaningful progress in restoring or stabilising states through statebuilding does not have a good track record, and as the OECD noted is 'frequently bedevilled by liberal "orthodoxies" transplanted from consolidated, democratic countries'.[65] While intentions in statebuilding are good and the logic behind it makes sense, the approach taken have proven to be problematic and unsuccessful. At the heart of this are the assumptions surrounding the type of state to be built. The model of the successful state and the prevailing understanding that this can be achieved through institutionalisation alone runs contrary to the process of both political and social change that is necessary for successfully redesigning or recomposing a state. Charles Call notes that it is erroneous to say that there

---

61 B. Bliesemann de Guevara, 'Statebuilding and State Formation', in B. Bliesemann de Guevara (ed.) *Statebuilding and State-Formation: The political sociology of intervention* (London: Routledge, 2012), pp. 1–20: p. 2.
62 T. Sisk, op. cit., p. 64.
63 Ibid., p. 9.
64 D. Chandler, op. cit., p. 71.
65 T. Sisk, op. cit., p. 76.

is a 'one-size-fits-all' model of statebuilding, and that there is no such thing as a 'state-in-a-box'.[66] In many ways he is correct: there is no set in stone blueprint or checklist outlining and dictating each step to be undertaken. However, he is also wrong in that there is a normative 'one-size-fits-all' expectation for state success, one that demands liberal democratic 'good' governance. Although a normative expectation, its proliferation of the realms of development and security means that it has become a practical expectation, or even, a demand.

Within the proliferation of the liberal democratic state through development policies, including statebuilding, familiar structures and practices familiar are reproduced, leaving very little room for alternative forms of state design or practice. Whilst paying lip service to the importance of local considerations, underlying social structures that shape and determine the relationship between the people and the state are often disregarded in the political process. The institutionalisation of the ideal incorporates known, familiar and predictable institutions of governance into the statebuilding paradigm. This obsession with the known, predictable and controllable is symbolic of what Chandler notes is a hypocritical fear of autonomy.[67] In the quest to achieve the end goal of liberal democracy, a political system dependent upon autonomy of individuals and society, the autonomy of choice in states perceived to be failed or dysfunctional is a frightening prospect: What happens if the choices made to not comply with external expectations of how the state should be? Sisk claims that statebuilding constantly strives to balance a number of the exogenous and the endogenous, between external and internal expectations.[68] The challenge for external actors thus becomes balancing between external goals and agendas and internal expectations and socio-political structures and practices, a balance that too often places the external before, if not above, the internal. Building institutions and encouraging practices of good governance may have the best of intentions, but effective statebuilding must strategise around several key linkages, one of them being those between international interests and agendas versus national interests and legitimacy.[69] If statebuilding takes place without conscious strategies of how to balance the external and the internal, successful consolidation of the peace-bringing liberal state is questionable. Examining this balance is the focus of the next chapter.

---

66 C. Call, op. cit., p. 13.
67 D. Chandler, op. cit.
68 T. Sisk, op. cit., p. 10.
69 See C. Call, op. cit. p. 3.

Chapter 3
Legitimacy and the 'Built' State

The desire to shape states to meet the demands of external actors or a dominant normative consensus is not a new aspect of global politics. In today's world, this often takes the form of development or reform projects. In more extreme cases, statebuilding is employed, often in the name of security. The frameworks of good governance are seen as 'a "silver bullet" capable of assisting states in coping with the problems of our complex globalised world: facilitating sustainable development, social peace and the development of democracy and the rule of law'.[1] Statebuilding is an ideological exercise: with the 'goal of developing and exporting [these] frameworks of good governance',[2] it is characterised by an interventionist project that goes into a state with a list of goals of what to achieve and how to achieve them. It is a highly political externally driven project that may include some deference to local considerations, but the project itself best reflects external demands, agendas and requirements – a check list of sorts. It is what Bendana identifies as top down, externally guided, supply-driven, elitist and interventionist.[3] However, statebuilding projects to date have shown little success, with security situations degrading and shaky political solutions often crumbling once statebuilders leave and sovereign control of the state is handed over to local actors. This is not to say that statebuilding is a bad idea. Indeed, in theory it makes sense – it is potentially a shortcut to political and physical stability for not only the target state and its population, but also for the liberal international order. But in practice it does not work. Statebuilding is a complex process of socio-political change taking place within contentious and often divided societies. To assume that simply creating the institutions will lead to good practice and popular acceptance is a hubristic understatement of the complexities of politics and the state. It is almost clinical in its naivety.

Many question the effectiveness or appropriateness of the narrow liberal framework and the laser-like focus on institutionalisation as the chosen mechanism through which to build the ideal successful state.[4] Ottaway notes that

---

1 D. Chandler, *International Statebuilding: The Rise of Post-Liberal Governance* (London: Routledge, 2010), p. 1.

2 Ibid.

3 A. Bendana, 'What Kind of Peace is Being Built? Critical Assessments from the South', International Development Research Centre Discussion Paper (Ottawa, 2003).

4 See, for example, M. Ottaway, 'Rebuilding State Institutions in Collapsed States', in J. Milliken (ed.) *State Failure, Collapse and Reconstruction* (Oxford: Blackwell, 2003), pp. 254–66; M. Ottaway, 'Promoting Democracy After Conflict: The Difficult Choices',

whereas externally-led reconstruction enforces the creation or re-creation of the empirical-juridical state, internally-led reconstruction follows a more circuitous route similar to the state formation process undergone by the majority of modern states that did not obtain their statehood through decolonisation: control or raw power is first established within the territory, then institutions, either democratic or not, are slowly developed.[5] The short-cut of the externally-led process does not guarantee a stable democratic state exhibiting efficient and accountable institutions. Bypassing the lengthy formation process through the international community's route harbours the hope of quickly achieving the desired goal of a stable democratic state. Without rooting the state and the institutions in society, however, and incorporating internally-led reconstruction efforts what is deemed success is often only temporary. The fast-tracked state reconstruction process has not proved successful in creating the desired stable modern states, leaving the open question of how these states can be established.

Indeed, Ottaway's concerns echo those often found within statebuilding literature. Throughout local ownership has been identified as an aspect vital to state 'success' that is difficult to achieve, if it is even achievable, within externally-led statebuilding.[6] At the root of the local ownership problem is the more fundamental 'operational challenge' of legitimacy.[7] With external demands, agendas and expectations driving the process, internal expectations and necessities are often marginalised or excluded. Within the liberal framework guiding statebuilding, there is also a distrust of indigenous structures, and local mechanisms of governance are viewed with scepticism or caution. There is a dilemma in the heart of statebuilding. Statebuilding is meant to be an endogenous process supported from the outside. However, with international dynamics and agendas driving the practice and its funding, statebuilding happening from the inside becomes impractical. The dilemma here is one centred on a gap in expectations: can both internal and external expectations be met within an externally-led process? Within this gap in expectations lies a gap in legitimacy as well, creating a dual faceted problem. If a state is not perceived of as acceptable or legitimate by external actors, that could have a detrimental impact upon its interactions in the global arena. At the same time, though, if domestic expectations are not met and the state is not legitimate from within, the sustainability of reconstructions or reforms, particularly

---

International Studies Perspectives 4.3 (2003), pp. 314–22; R. Paris and T. Sisk (eds), *The Dilemmas of Statebuilding: Confronting the contradictions of postwar peace operations* (London: Routledge, 2008); D. Chandler, op. cit.; B. Bliesemann de Guevara (ed.), *Statebuilding and State-Formation: The Political Sociology of Intervention* (London: Routledge, 2012).

5   M. Ottaway, 'Rebuilding State Institutions', op. cit., p. 248.

6   See T. Donais, 'Empowerment or Imposition? Dilemmas of local ownership in post-conflict peacebuilding processes', *Peace and Change* 34.1 (2009), pp. 3–26; R. Paris and T. Sisk, op. cit.

7   R. Paris and T. Sisk, op. cit.

those aimed at establishing liberal democracy, come under threat. Thus, balancing expectations and closing the legitimacy gap is key to successful statebuilding.

This is an area of focus largely because in previous interventionist statebuilding projects local ownership has been an elusive or distant desire, yet there is a necessary tangential link between local ownership, legitimacy and the chances of sustainable statebuilding that must be recognised. This chapter serves to address this gap first through a critical examination of statebuilding in order to identify it, and then offering a more complete understanding of the relationship between the state and society and its placement within statebuilding. Finally, this chapter explores internally-led statebuilding – a form of statebuilding more likely to show success in closing the gap – before turning to the case of Somaliland, where balancing the internal and the external is a key strategy of statebuilding.

Statebuilding, Take 2

Within externally-led statebuilding, the technocratic institutional approach prevails, and often local considerations are placed below external political or economic agendas and demands in order of importance. 'By the book statebuilding' is an externally driven project reflects external demands and requirements – a check list of sorts. At some point the state will be handed over to local leaders, at which point local ownership is supposed to take place. The ideas underpinning statebuilding vastly oversimplify the process, yet after a short period of time it is expected that a stable political entity will stay standing and the population will support it. As Larry Diamond notes, when Jay Garner, a proponent of the 'quick' and 'light' footprint approach to rebuilding Iraq, left for Baghdad, he stated that he intended to complete the transition to a permanent Iraqi government within four months. When challenged about the time frame and told that 'it takes a little longer to do democratization than three or four months in the summer in Baghdad', Garner responded by saying 'Oh yes we can, and we will'.[8] Statebuilding in Iraq is an extreme and exceptional case, and certainly a time frame of four months is unusually short. However, and perhaps Iraq is the best contemporary example of fallacies and potential dangers in the policy approach to statebuilding in this regard, it is presumptuous to assume that a quick approach will result in any lasting success. Political change, especially drastic political change such as statebuilding, is incredibly disruptive and unstable; democratisation just as much if not more so. Drastic political change requires drastic social change as well, and in an already contentious or volatile post-conflict or fragile society this social change is not as easy as imposing institutions with the idea that this will lead to the state providing the expected political and public goods of a modern 'good governance' state. Statebuilding tends to be approached as a step-by-step and relatively quick

---

8 L. Diamond, *Squandered Victory: The American Occupation and the Bungled Effort to Bring Democracy to Iraq* (New York: Times Books, 2005), pp. 32–3.

process – the state is imposed, or 'gifted', rather than negotiated or even tailored. This in itself creates its own complications and indeed fragility.[9]

As identified in the previous chapter, the approach to externally-led statebuilding is one dominated by building institutions as the means through which to build stability, security, development, peace and provision. However, in simplifying statebuilding to the practice of institution building, the complexity of the state is marginalised or ignored. The conception of the state within the practice of statebuilding is one that harks back to the Weberian understanding: a bureaucratic administration characterised by a collection of institutions that claim a monopolisation on legitimate authority and force within a given territory. The current approach to statebuilding assumes that in creating institutions the 'state' itself will follow. It assumes that the institutions define the state. However, the state is more than merely the existence of institutions, and an understanding of the state must also take into account the socio-political relationships existent within between the political community and the institutions; relationships that help define and shape the state, especially within a post-conflict environment. As noted by the Somaliland Academy for Peace and Development,

> state-building and peace-building are potentially contradictory processes – the former requiring the consolidation of government authority, the latter involving its moderation through compromise and consensus. The challenge for both national and international peacemakers is to situate reconciliation firmly within the context of state-building, while employing state-building as a platform for the development of mutual trust and lasting reconciliation.[10]

In maintaining a single-minded focus on building and strengthening institutions as its primary goal and as the path to peace, the current approach to statebuilding sets itself up for failure.

The fundamental problem with externally-led statebuilding is not the intended outcome of a legitimate, accountable, safe and secure state. Although much criticism can be placed on this set-in-stone end goal, without a paradigm shift away from the liberal framework in the international system the end goal is unlikely to

---

9   See, for example, R. MacGinty and O. Richmond, 'The Local Turn in Peace Building: a critical agenda for peace', *Third World Quarterly* 34.5 (2013), pp. 763–83. R. MacGinty, 'Indigenous Peace-Making Versus the Liberal Peace', *Cooperation and Conflict* 43.3 (2008), pp. 139–63; R. MacGinty, 'Routine Peace: Technocracy and peacebuilding', *Cooperation and Conflict* 47.3 (2012), pp. 287–308; R. MacGinty, 'Hybrid Peace: The Interaction between Top-Down and Bottom-Up Peace', *Security Dialogue* 41.4 (2010), pp. 391–412. See also, D. Roberts, 'Hybrid Polities and Indigenous Pluralities: Advanced Lessons in Statebuilding from Cambodia', *Journal of Intervention and Statebuilding* 1.3 (2007), pp. 379–402.

10   Somaliland Academy for Peace and Development (APD) and the War-torn Societies Project, *From Plunder to Prosperity: Resolving Resource-Based Conflict in Somaliland* (Nairobi/Hargeisa: Dialogue for Peace Somali Programme Report, 2006).

change whilst the policy option of statebuilding continues. The problem with the practice, rather, is the process through which this end goal is meant to be obtained. The rigid vision of state design and empirical expectations is a contributor to this problem, and the expectation of quick democratisation through the imposition of a defined set of institutions is not only indicative of external technocrats anxious to get to the point of a local leadership that can 'own the process' as soon as possible, but is also at the heart of the problem. Even more fundamental to this, though, is the exclusion of society from the statebuilding plans. Here is where the failure of local ownership and domestic legitimacy lies.

Although lip service is paid to statebuilding being a domestic process that is supported from the outside, external demands and expectations sideline local considerations, actors, structures and practices. As Woodward notes, statebuilding tends to be 'narcissistic'.[11] Design, assessment and evaluation are undertaken by external actors who

> view their actions as exogenous to local politics, but paradoxically assuming little influence while expecting much. Countries and local actors are viewed largely as aid recipients whose actions are relevant only in terms of outsiders' policies and expectations, as captured in terms such as 'political will', cooperation, obstruction and absorption capacity. We know very little about what Fortna calls the 'peacekept', that is, 'the decision-makers within the government and rebel organizations.[12]

With its emphasis on 'proven' institutional design and capacity building, often dependent upon the empowering of influential leaders or Western-educated reformers as the shortest way to capacity building,[13] the endogenous process must compete with the demanding, and sometimes forceful exogenous components. Sisk maintains that the 'international community's approach ... must balance the lofty goal of "local ownership" of statebuilding processes with an explicit and sometimes very assertive liberal interventionist agenda'.[14] It is interesting to note Sisk's choice to attach local ownership to the statebuilding process here rather than simply to the end result, as is common within discussion of local ownership. One must question, though, whether local ownership of the process is possible in external projects, and if not, is local ownership of the outcome an achievable reality.

---

11 Quoting Fortna. S. Woodward, 'State-Building and Peace-Building: What Theory and Whose Roles?' in R. Kozul-Wright and P. Fortunato (eds), *Securing Peace: State-Building and Economic Development in Post-Conflict Countries* (London: Bloomsbury, 2011), pp. 87–122: p. 88.

12 Ibid., pp. 88–9.

13 C. Call, 'Ending Wars, Building States', in C. Call and V. Wyeth (eds), *Building States to Build Peace* (London: Lynne Rienner, 2008), pp. 1–22: p. 9.

14 T. Sisk, *Statebuilding* (Cambridge: Polity, 2013), p. 2.

Statebuilding is seen as a project rather than a process. It is an imposition rather than a negotiation: it is imposing the apparatus of the state with little regard to how that apparatus meets the demands or expectations of society. Here the modern liberal state is something to be obtained rather than attained. Historically state formation and statebuilding in Western states was a highly political process during which the relationship between the state and the population evolved and was determined through war, victory and consent. Albeit often violent or repressive, the process itself fostered the socio-political change that ultimately resulted in the relationships now exhibited within those states. In imposing the state, the process of development and negotiation is skipped and the relationships that lay at the foundation of a strong state are absent. In post-conflict or fragile political environments, where peace may be unstable and where there may be little trust in the political processes of the state, failing to root the state in society and investing society in the state is problematic. There is a 'yawning gap' between what the idealised notion of and path to a modern state and the realities of governments on the ground in war-torn or fragile countries.[15] It is little wonder that local ownership is a problem.

The State and the Nation

Very often statebuilding and nation-building are used interchangeably. Interestingly, though, the 'nation' rarely factors into the very institutional and technocratic statebuilding design and process. As Fukuyama notes, much of this terminological conflation exists within US academia as the term 'nation-building' reflects the national experience in which 'cultural and historical identity was heavily shaped by political institutions like constitutionalism and democracy'.[16] Within European scholarship, however, there is an awareness of the distinction between state and nation, and a realisation that the creation of a community – 'nation-building' or the 'idea' of the state – cannot be undertaken by an outside power.[17] However, despite terminological recognition within European scholarship, in practice the distinction is significantly more ambiguous. Given the expectation that building institutions will lead to eventual social acceptance of the state and the processes surrounding it, it is assumed that the nation is complicit. This not only reflects the faith placed in the institutional approach, but it also reflects misgivings about the socio-political processes of the state. This view homogenises the nation, assuming a universal desire for state relationships that are found primarily where the evolution of the state has resulted in expectations for central democratic control through a set of defined institutions.

---

15 Ibid., p. 67.
16 F. Fukuyama, *State-Building: Governance and World Order in the 21st Century* (Ithaca: Cornell University Press, 2004), p. 134.
17 Ibid.

Within this is the assumption that in statebuilding there is not a need to 'reshape society or citizens'.[18] Call offers two reasons as to why this may perception may exist.[19] The first is that 'citizen identification with the state is no longer the *sine qua non* for successful stateness'. He claims that requiring nation-building with statebuilding is an idea that is trapped within the confines of Modernization theory and that in a globalised world with multicultural states, it is no longer necessary to assume that the population has to overcome ethnic or religious allegiances in order to form an allegiance with the state. In other words, the concept of the nation is outdated, so nation-building is not necessary. The second reason is that it believed that within statebuilding, it is 'self-defeating' and 'silly' in today's world for an outside actor to try to redefine a society's allegiances and identities. Although this reason seems to be implying that allegiance and identity within a state only exists in the context of ethnicity or religion not with a political identity, it also reflects the limitations of external actors to reweave social fabrics or reconcile societal divides.[20] It is fair to say that outside interveners are unlikely to be able to change ethnic or religious identities or allegiances. However, the assumption within this is that societal allegiance and identity does not have a role in building a state, and that is a limitation of the liberal prescription of statebuilding. Even if the identity being discussed is political in nature rather than ethnic or religious, it is presumptuous to assume that a state can be built without engaging with the social dimensions of the state, not matter how complex they may be.

Whilst the second reason given by Call is problematic, it easily falls under the criticism that assumptions about the processes of the state and therefore the process of change taking place during statebuilding are narrow and naïve. The first, however, warrants further examination and discussion. Whilst strict interpretations of the concept of the nation as an ethnic or religious grouping are often perceived as outdated, the concept of the nation as a political community is not. Existing within the territorial confines of the state, the population is the political community in question. In post-conflict or fragile environments this political community is not always unified, but the commonality is that it is the target and the subject of the exercise of governance and authority within the state. Thus, when discussing local ownership the concern is not only with ownership by the political elites, but also ownership by the political community. Within problems with establishing local ownership are concerns about the legitimacy of the state being built. With statebuilding being a means through which to obtain sustainable peace, certainly the institutions existing within the state must be accepted by the population in order for the state to have the legitimate authority to either mitigate

---

18 C. Call, op. cit., p. 10.
19 Ibid.
20 See R. Paris, *Building Peace After Civil Conflict* (Cambridge: Cambridge University Press, 2004); M. Ottaway, 'Rebuilding State Institutions', op. cit.; M. Barnett, 'Building a Republican Peace: Stabilizing States after War', *International Security* 30.4 (2006), pp. 87–112.

potential violence within society or to prevent violent contestation of the political settlement, the institutions or the regime. In his own criticisms, Call begins to recognise the fallacy of this categorisation in saying that a state is:

> an entity that represents a territorial political community over and above the government. This entity includes the institutions of government but goes beyond them, having its own character and (in some minimal way) speaking for the political community.[21]

Woodward goes further, noting that the crucial element of stabilised statebuilding is 'deference to the new authorities and compliance with their rules and decisions, in sum, the state's authority'. She discusses this in the post-civil war environment, arguing that nation-building is a compulsory for stabilised statebuilding in order to ensure that the state does not have to resort to military force to obtain compliance domestically, as 'no state survives' that.[22] She warns against confusing statebuilding and nation-building as if they were the same and maintains that 'discounting the importance of this process [of nation-building] (and thus the time needed for it and that only locals can do it) – all of which are common – repeats the outsider's misunderstanding of the particular nature of statebuilding after civil war'.[23]

The state being built derives its sovereign authority not from an external actor that empowers it, but rather from the legitimising acceptance of society. Legitimacy is the normative belief of a political community that a rule or institution ought to be obeyed.[24] States are legitimate when

> key political elites and the public accept the rules regulating the exercise of power and the distribution of wealth as proper and binding. Legitimacy implies that the political community views the goals pursued by the state, the means selected to pursue them, and the decision making process leading to both goals and means as proper.[25]

Because statebuilding operates under tight time constraints and with clear objectives and goals surrounding what is needed, lengthy negotiations 'aimed at achieving consensus among leaders about the role and structure of the state' are prevented.[26] Papagianni warns that this may result in a segment of the political elites not supporting the institutions, creating serious legitimacy deficits. Further,

---

21 C. Call, op. cit., p. 7.
22 S. Woodward, op. cit., p. 107.
23 Ibid.
24 I. Hurd, 'Legitimacy and Authority in International Politics', *International Organization* 53.2 (1999), pp. 379–408: p. 381.
25 K. Papagianni, 'Participation and State Legitimacy', in C. Call and V. Wyeth (eds), *Building States to Build Peace* (London: Lynne Rienner, 2008), pp. 49–71: p. 49.
26 Ibid.

though, concerns must also be expressed about support derived from the political community as a whole. In post-war and fragile environments, state legitimacy is difficult to maintain, especially if the state cannot provide public goods that are expected by the population, or if the state is or has been violent. During the statebuilding process the state violence is likely to be removed due to the presence of external actors, and external funding will change the negative balance of provisions. However, once external actors leave and sovereignty is exercised by the new institutions, those conditions are no longer guaranteed. In these conditions, the 'new' state will only survive if it is deemed legitimate by the political community, a community inclusive of not only the political elites but also society. If society is not accepting of or invested in the state – if the state is not domestically legitimate – the statebuilding process is unlikely to be successful or sustained. Society, defined within the concept of the political community or nation, is a vital legitimising component of the statebuilding process, as 'the state serves as an embodiment and guardian of society's shared principles and ideals'. These ideals are not based on a shared ethnicity or religion – traditional understandings of the nation – but on a 'shared understanding of and respect for the state's rules and institutions'.[27] As Woodward argues government effectiveness in terms of service delivery or provision will matter in the long-term stability of the state, 'but in the short run, the more important issue is trust: to what extend and how does the new political leadership and its institutions rebuild the trust of the population?'[28] Certainly, this is a complex component in any area where statebuilding is taking place as there was some form of a pre-existing divisive factor that not only potentially divided society, but also potentially created a situation of distrust between the state and the population; conditions dependent upon the situation of each state, but conditions that must be reconciled regardless. For this reason, assuming that nation-building is not needed is an erroneous conclusion that is detrimental to statebuilding.

One of the core principles of liberal democracy is the social contract, yet in externally-led statebuilding the social contract is assumed or absent. Chandler identifies a hypocrisy of liberal democracy within statebuilding that he identifies as being a hypocrisy of autonomy.[29] Within the proliferation of the liberal democratic state through development policies, including statebuilding, structures and practices familiar to leading Western states are reproduced, leaving very little room for alternative forms of state design or practice. Although some, such as Ghani and Lockhart, maintain that a future model for 'fixing' states must be flexible through 'stitching together local capabilities and resources and tailoring tactics to context', these solutions continue to depend upon pre-existing guidelines and frameworks and therefore do not go far in granting autonomy and independence that would

---

27 Ibid., p. 54.
28 S. Woodward, op. cit., p. 108.
29 D. Chandler, op. cit.

allow for deeper inclusion of individual contexts.[30] Whilst paying lip service to the importance of local considerations, underlying social structures that shape and determine the relationship between the people and the state are often disregarded in the political process. The institutionalisation of the ideal incorporates familiar and predictable institutions of governance into the statebuilding paradigm. This obsession with the known, predictable and controllable is symbolic of what Chandler notes is a fear of another core principle of liberal democracy: autonomy. In the quest to achieve the end goal of liberal democracy, a political system dependent upon autonomy of individuals and society, the autonomy of choice in states perceived to be failed or dysfunctional is a frightening prospect: What happens if the choices made to not comply with external expectations of how the state should be? To reduce the perceived threat of deviance or dysfunction, a clear shortcut to liberal democracy and good governance is laid out, removing domestic choice and voice for the sake of success in the larger project being undertaken. The assumption is that success will instil the conditions necessary for good choices, therefore shaping what societal and state autonomy will be. The problem with this is clear. Institutions are important, but institutions do not comprise a complete state. Excluding the population from the process of statebuilding isolates them from the political process that is the state. If the people do not have a voice in the institutions and mechanisms that will govern them, can there be the legitimising trust in the political process and relationships that is necessary for sustained success?

Legitimacy is difficult to assess and to determine, but it is even more difficult to install or impose. It is assumed that legitimacy comes through democracy. Whilst democratic choice can legitimise the authority of those occupying the institutions of government, it does not necessarily legitimise the state itself. As the embodiment or reflection of society's principles and ideas, the rules and institutions reflect the rules, or the political culture, of the state. Because of this,

> institutions cohere if they emerge out of existing social forces, if they represent real interests and real clashes of interest which then lead to the establishment of mechanisms and organisational rules and procedures which are capable of resolving those disagreements.[31]

Sisk claims that statebuilding constantly strives to balance a number of the exogenous and the endogenous, between external and internal expectations.[32] The challenge for external actors thus becomes balancing between external goals and agendas and internal expectations and socio-political structures, practices and consent, a balance that too often places the external before, if not above, the

---

30 A. Ghani and C. Lockhart, 'Closing the Sovereignty Gap: An Approach to State-Building', Overseas Development Institute Working Paper 253 (London: ODI, 2005).

31 D. Chandler, 'Editor's Introduction: Peace Without Politics', *International Peacekeeping* 12.3 (2005), pp. 307–21: p. 309.

32 T. Sisk, op. cit., p. 10.

internal. Building institutions and encouraging practices of good governance may have the best of intentions, but effective statebuilding must strategise around several key linkages, one of them being those between international interests and agendas versus national interests and legitimacy.[33] If statebuilding takes place without conscious strategies of how to balance the external and the internal, successful consolidation of the peace-bringing liberal state is questionable. Within statebuilding there exists a duality of legitimacy and therefore a duality of expectations. With external expectations and demands meeting internal expectations and necessities, a gap in expectations exists; a gap that leads to a gap in legitimacy. Balancing these expectations is important in statebuilding, not only for the success of the project, but also for success of the process.

Mind the Gap: Legitimacy and the Built State

The concept of the nation within the practice of statebuilding is a narrow one. It assumes no duality of identification or allegiance, something that can be proven false very quickly when looking at most liberal democracies, where identification with an ethnic group exists along with an identification with being part of an ethnically or religiously diverse political community (i.e. Irish-American, British Asian, Canadian First Nation, etc.). This is perhaps due to allegiance to the state being implicit rather than explicit within many Western states. Allegiance and a cohesive political community stemming from that is assumed in established democracies, and it becomes easy to overlook the importance of this in formulating plans for stabilising post-conflict or fragile situations. But as has already been discussed above, excluding the political community from the drastic socio-political transformation that is statebuilding creates a deficit of legitimacy and a gap in expectations. Based on a series of assumptions, it removes the autonomy and identity of the political community. It assumes a pre-existing identification of the population with what the state *should* be as determined by the external actors and within that, it assumes an identification with the mechanisms of governance to be created. It assumes a familiarity with, or at least expectation of, the institutions and practices being established and instilled within those mechanisms of governance. It assumes an automatic, or at least inevitable, societal acceptance of the political arrangement of the state. However, a state is not just the apparatus or the institutions. As such, statebuilding must include a consideration of the political relationship not only between the apparatus and the population, but also between the political community and what the state is or should be.

If we take the technocratic institutional component of the state as one end of the spectrum of what the state is, at the other end sits what Buzan considers the idea

---

33 See C. Call, op. cit., p. 3.

of the state.[34] In this, the state not a tangible entity that can be identified through the existence or functions of institutions, but rather it is an abstract that reflects and embodies the political culture of a territory and its population. Physically, the state can be identified by its foundations of territory and population. As Buzan identifies, the physical components of the state can exist without the state or without any particular state. And although the state can survive if the physical components are damaged, it cannot exist in the absence of them.[35] From this, it must be inferred that the state 'exists, or has its essence, primarily on the social rather than the physical plane'. It is more a 'metaphysical entity, an idea held in common by a group of people, than it is a physical organism'.[36]

When Anderson wrote of imagined communities, he wrote in terms of nationalism, arguing that a nation is 'an imagined political community' that is 'imagined as both inherently limited and sovereign'.[37] It is imagined 'because the members of even the smallest nation will never know most of their fellow-members, meet them, or even hear of them, yet in the minds of each lives the image of their communion'.[38] Extrapolated further, Anderson's ideas of communion and shared images within a political community ring true when discussing the idea of the state and the population's expectations of the political entity surrounding and encompassing it. In many ways, the idea of the state is akin to the nation in old concept of the nation-state. It is a form of identity or narrative of the state in that it is the 'essence' or character of the state: it is a reflection of the ideals and expectations of the political community over which it exists and it demands a shared idea of what it means to be 'us'. In this, the 'state' is where the people and politics meet. The institutions are a component of this, but they are best described as an embodiment of the people and politics coming together, reflecting political culture and domestic demands and expectations. As such, 'without a widespread and quite deeply-rooted idea of the state among the population, the state institutions by themselves would have great difficulty functioning and surviving' without resorting to brute force.[39] The idea of the state is what ties the population to the apparatus of the state, and is also what shapes societal expectations of how the state should be and how it should act: it is a component of the legitimising social contract. In this manner, a 'governing' state could exist even in the absence of bureaucratic institutions, what Buzan notes would be an argument of a purist

---

34 See B. Buzan, *People, States and Fear: An Agenda for International Security Studies in the Post-Cold War Era*, 2nd edn (Hemel Hempstead: Harvester, 1993), Chapter 2.

35 This goes back to basic Westphalian notion of statehood, as well as more recent understandings such as those expressed in the 1933 Montevideo Convention and the widely-used Weberian definition.

36 B. Buzan, op. cit., p. 38.

37 B. Anderson, *Imagined Communities* rev. edn (London: Verso Books, 1991), p. 6.

38 Ibid., p. 224.

39 B. Buzan, op. cit., p. 39.

anarchist.[40] A 'state' can also exist in the absence of external recognition of sovereignty, provided it exists within a defined territory. In this conception of the state the traditional Weberian notion of statehood, and indeed the dominant liberal understanding of the state prevalent within statebuilding, is inverted, with the idea of why and what the state should be predating the creation of physical institutions. It is a necessary component of state stability and, indeed, the state itself.

This component of the state does not assume an outcome of liberal democracy as it is possible that political culture leads to legitimate authoritarian rule if that is what the people expect or desire of the state or imagine it to be. Within any given state that is the subject of a statebuilding project, there may be a dream for liberal democracy and provision within the state, and there are almost certainly individuals within the state that have been shaped by external experiences and expectations. However, it is not guaranteed that this dream is a widespread one. Rather, the idea of the state is more likely to be shaped by a shared history, an area that undoubtedly impacts upon what domestic expectations are. In an area where there is 'deep social distrust of the state in the first place',[41] expectations of centralised power or strong institutions alone may invoke fear within a population that experienced political or state violence. Equally, expectations for liberal democratic provision may be much less of a priority than the provision of basic goods, services and stability. If the shared history is one of violence and oppression, domestic expectations might not expect the institutionalisation or provision of the kind that the liberal democratic state entails. History shapes political processes, but a shared history also shapes societal fears, expectations and necessities: a shared history shapes the idea of the state.

As a reflection of the relationship between the politics and society, the idea of the state is not homogenously applicable across all territorial states, and it is possible to have different ideas of the state within different communities within the same territory (this is likely to lead to political instability or turbulence). It is for this reason that it is an important consideration within statebuilding. In reflects the character of society and how that helps define the state, but the shared idea acts as a cohesive agent within society, creating a focus that helps shape and define the political community. It is something that can be utilised, constructed or even manipulated by elites, but because of this it possesses an incredible amount of power. In externally-led statebuilding, though, the internal idea of the state is overlooked in order for primacy to be placed on what external expectations of the state are. As a powerful agent within the political relationships found within a state, though, the absence or marginalisation of the ideas of the state not only creates the potential for instability and contestation, but also creates a gap in expectations of what the state should be.

---

40   Ibid.
41   T. Sisk, op. cit., p. 8; see also C. Call (ed.), *Building States to Build Peace* (London: Lynne Rienner, 2008).

Closing the Expectations Gap: Statebuilding in Unrecognised States

In today's international system, the state cannot exist on an idea alone, even if it existed within legally recognised sovereign boundaries.[42] But empirically the demands of liberal democracy – both its classical understanding and its understanding through the framework of liberal interventionism and liberal peace[43] – cannot be expected to be met through only institutions. This creates a fundamental problem within externally-led statebuilding. A mutual dependence between the empirical and the social exists, yet it is not acknowledged and is sometimes dismissed within statebuilding. Through this, externally-led statebuilding, with its limited yet dominating focus on institutions, creates gaps in expectations and legitimacy. On one side of the gap are internal considerations and demands of the political community. On the other are external interests and normative demands. In order to close this gap without resorting to force or military rule a balance between the internal and the external must be established and maintained. Whilst this is not overtly evidenced within externally-led statebuilding projects, it is apparent within another form of statebuilding: domestically-led statebuilding like that found in some unrecognised states.

Discussion of areas of separatist or extra-state governance within sovereign states is nothing new. These entities are often associated with civil war, ethnic conflict, rebel territories and criminality, particularly in relation to economic activity and resource wars. However, unrecognised states, also referred to as de facto states or states-within-states, are more specifically defined and identifiable than a territory controlled by a force other than the state apparatus. As King notes, 'the territorial separatists of the early 1990s have become the statebuilders of the early 2000s', creating territorial areas whose empirical attributes are 'about as well developed as that of the recognized states of which they are still notionally a part'.[44] Simply defined, they are state-like entities that have achieved de facto independence but have not gained international recognition of sovereign statehood.[45] Pegg, preferring the term 'de facto state', defines these entities as:

> entities which feature long-term, effective, and popularly-supported organized political leaderships that provide governmental services to a given population in a defined territorial area. They seek international recognition and view themselves as capable of meeting the obligations of sovereign statehood. They

---

42 For example, see Jackson's work on quasi-states.

43 For more on the contestation between the two, see D. Chandler, op. cit.

44 C. King, 'The Benefits of Ethnic War: Understanding Eurasia's Unrecognized States', *World Politics* 53.4 (2001), pp. 524–52: p. 525.

45 N. Caspersen and G. Stansfield (eds), *Unrecognised States in the International System* (London: Routledge, 2011): pp 1–2.

are, however, unable to secure widespread juridical recognition and therefore function outside the boundaries of international legitimacy.[46]

Kolstø and Caspersen specify further, maintaining that in order to be an unrecognised state an entity must not only have de facto independence over a territory which is controlled by the leadership, but must also have a leadership seeking to build further state institutions and demonstrate its own legitimacy; the entity must be seeking international recognition; and it must have existed in this manner for at least two years.[47] Although, as Pegg concedes, it is 'extremely difficult to discern what a movement's true goals really are',[48] the criterion for seeking recognition distinguishes between those entities within states that are seeking a degree of autonomy and those that are seeking statehood. Within these definitions is the recognition that statebuilding has begun and the process is a continuing one. These entities claim not only independence for a territory, but they claim independent statehood. Most simply put, these entities are 'states within states'.[49]

In many ways, statebuilding in unrecognised states is a form of modern state formation. Much of the academic work on state formation specifically references the formation of states in Europe, although translating those experiences to modern day cases and to the practice of statebuilding overall is not unheard of. One of the strongest arguments to come from these works is the importance of war and violence in the state-making process such as that put forward by Tilly.[50] Although Tilly maintained that his theories and observations were historically and geographically

---

46 S. Pegg, *International Society and the De Facto State* (Aldershot: Ashgate, 1998): p. 4.

47 P. Kölsto, 'The Sustainability and Future of Unrecognized Quasi-States', *Journal of Peace Research* 43.6 (2006), pp. 723–40: pp. 725–6; N. Caspersen, *Unrecognised States: The Struggle for Sovereignty in the Modern International System* (Cambridge: Polity, 2012): p. 6.

48 S. Pegg, 'From De Facto States to States-Within-States: Progress, Problems and Prospects', in P. Kingston and I. Spears (eds), *States-Within-States: Incipient Political Entities in the Post-Cold War Era* (Basingstoke: Palgrave Macmillan, 2004), pp. 35–46: p. 38.; S. Pegg, *International Society and the De Facto State*, op. cit.; C. King, 'The Benefits of Ethnic War', op. cit. Pegg and King both note that alternative motivations for maintaining de facto statehood may be political or regional stability or economic benefits from the 'illegal' status of de facto states. The difficulty of determining motivations is also apparent when discussing the criteria of actively seeking recognition. One such territorial entity, Kurdistan, is considered by some to be an unrecognised state but not so by others. The primary point of impasse here is Kurdistan's seeking of recognition is a latent rather than an overt action.

49 P. Kingston and I. Spears (eds), *States-Within-States: Incipient Political Entities in the Post-Cold War Era* (Basingstoke: Palgrave Macmillan, 2004).

50 See C. Tilly, 'War Making and State Making as Organized Crime', in D. Evans, et al. (eds), *Bringing the State Back In* (Cambridge: Cambridge University Press, 1985), pp. 169–91.

specific and that his work should not be transposed onto inappropriate historical or geographic cases, his foundational ideas of how the initial stages of state formation take place and how power is consolidated in a territory are often found in works on development and statebuilding today.[51] Indeed, King, Kolstø, Pegg and Lynch, among others, highlight the role of war and conflict as the foundation for the creation of unrecognised states; and scholars such as Collier identify the role of conflict in sustaining the secessionist or autonomous movements within some cases.[52] Whereas Tilly highlights the role of banditry in early European state formation, scholars examining contemporary cases often reference criminality (Eastern Europe) and corruption (Africa). Within Tilly's theory, however, is the allowance for these violent and corrupt elements to evolve into institutionalised political entities. It is then that the Weberian monopolisation of force shifts from purposes of territorial predation to those benefiting and enhancing the productive basis of society.[53] Even Weber recognised that building a state is a *process*: the often cited bureaucratic Weberian state is, in Weber's theory, the final stage of the evolution of state legitimacy.[54]

State-making through violence may have been vital state formation in Europe, and it may be the basis for claims of independence and the emergence of unrecognised states, but it must be remembered that European state formation did not take place in the short time frame that is commonly found in today's policy, and it did not take place in the normative complexity of today's international system. Because conflict and violence today are negatively perceived as contributing to state weakness rather than productively adding to the creation or stability of a state, the predetermined condition of modern 'stateness' does not include

---

51   See W. Reno, *Warlord Politics and African States* (Boulder: Lynne Rienner, 1999); I. Spears, 'States-Within-States: An Introduction to their Empirical Attributes', in P. Kingston and I. Spears (eds), *States-Within-States: Incipient Political Entities in the Post-Cold War Era* (Basingstoke: Palgrave Macmillan, 2004), pp. 15–34. See also, J-F. Bayart, S. Ellis and B. Hibou, *The Criminalisation of the State in Africa* (Oxford: James Currey, 1999); P. Chabal and J-P. Daloz, *Africa Works: Disorder as Political Instrument* (Oxford: James Currey, 1999); K. Holsti, *The State, War and the State of War* (New York: Cambridge University Press, 1996).

52   See P. Collier and A. Hoeffler, 'Greed and Grievance in Civil War', Oxford Economic Papers No. 56 (Oxford, 2004), pp. 563–95; P. Collier, A. Hoeffler, D. Rohner, 'Beyond Greed and Grievance: Feasibility and Civil War', The Centre for the Study of African Economies Working Paper Series Paper 254 (Oxford: Centre for African Economies, 2006); P. Collier, 'Economic Causes of Civil Conflict and their Implications for Policy', World Bank Working Paper 28134 (June 2000).

53   R. Bates, *Prosperity and Violence: The Political Economy of Development* (New York: W.W. Norton, 2001): p. 51.

54   See M. Weber, *The Theory of Social and Economic Organisation (1947)*, ed. Talcott Parsons (New York: Free Press, 1964); M. Weber, 'Politics as Vocation (1948)', in H.H. Gerth and C. Wright Mills (eds), *From Max Weber: Essays in Sociology* (London: Routledge, 1967), pp. 77–128.

a concession for force in the statebuilding process. Indeed, statebuilding, as a mechanism of peacebuilding, is antithetical to this, and it is perhaps unsurprising that most unrecognised states seeking recognition of sovereignty are relatively peaceful.[55] Throughout literature and policy on statebuilding, though, it is common to find short-cuts that are based on the state produced by the lengthy European state-formation process but excluding 'the war-induced development imperative European states did'.[56] There is a falsity in this, though, in that today's aspiring states must comply with a complex web of external expectations and demands that did not exist at the time of European formation.

Functioning within an international system dominated, and in many ways dictated, by Western norms and ideals, many unrecognised states have adopted a unique form of state formation that can be viewed as 'survival strategies',[57] in that in order to meet the demands of external actors the state itself incorporates and accommodates those external structural and empirical demands whilst at the same time being accountable to the governance necessities of the population and of political culture within the territory. This method of state formation – domestically-led statebuilding – reflects the preferences of external actors in a way that can best further the goals of recognition. At the same time, however, these strategies also often reflect or incorporate local preferences or demands needed to maintain the domestic legitimacy and justify the prolonged existence of the stateless state. Whilst some have noted marked similarities in the detailed recognition strategies employed by unrecognised states regardless of geographic region,[58] a lack of significant comparative research on this subject poses difficulties in marking any detailed specific or concrete consistencies. What can be noted, however, is the tendency for these territories to create what appear to be ideal modern states.

---

55 The obvious recent exceptions to this are Tamil Eelam in Sri Lanka and South Ossetia in Georgia, although the violence in the latter was instigated and prolonged primarily by Georgia and Russia rather than South Ossetia.

56 I. Spears, 'States-Within-States', op. cit., p. 18.

57 In his work on the state in Africa, Herbst notes what he terms 'survival strategies', or dependence on decentralised governance provided by sub-state actors. As a means of survival within a pre-determined centralised government structure, these strategies are not negative or undermining of the state, but are rather necessary to accommodate the necessities and circumstances of the states in which they take place. Similarly, in an international system that places primacy on modern liberal state structures and practices, finding ways to exist within that, and borrowing from Herbst, can be seen as survival strategies themselves. J. Herbst, *States and Power in Africa: Comparative Lessons in Authority and Control* (Princeton: Princeton University Press, 2000).

58 C. King, 'The Benefits of Ethnic War', op. cit.; N. Caspersen, 'Unrecognised States: Shadow Economies, Democratisation and Hopes for Independence', Lancaster University Seminar Series (24 January 2006); N. Caspersen, 'Self-Determination vs. Democracy? Democratization in De Facto States', Paper delivered at the 49th Annual ISA Convention, San Francisco (March 2008).

As Caspersen notes, external legitimisation is a key component of the recognition campaigns of unrecognised states; the governments of these territories demonstrate that they are self-sufficient and successful states in an attempt to increase their chances at gaining international recognition of their statehood by proving first what they can do.[59] Whereas claims to independence in these territories were once based on self-determination arguments, claims are now being made on the basis of exhibiting the empirical attributes of statehood consistent with both policy and literature.[60] Unrecognised states comply with the normative rules of statehood as accepted by their target audience. If seeking recognition from a single patron state, an unrecognised state can be expected to reflect the expectations of that state. If seeking broad international recognition of sovereign statehood, most posit themselves as 'good' states and exhibit 'acceptable' statehood in order to 'prove' their statehood. In many ways, they conform to what Ghani and Lockhart have identified as the 'way of the future' in statebuilding: states that fulfil their obligations of the right of sovereignty both externally and internally, where a compact not only between the state and its population exists, but a second compact between the state and the international community exists 'to ensure adherence to international norms and standards of accountability and transparency'. In this, strategies are 'inherently about "coproduction" because internal and external actors have to agree on rules, a division of labor and a sequence of activities'; although it must be noted the rules and activities referred to exist under the rubric of liberal good governance and interventionist statebuilding, meaning that the local considerations go not much further than how to meet the externally pre-determined expectations of legitimacy, governance and the obligations of sovereignty attached to that.[61]

Whilst Ghani and Lockhart are looking into the future of externally-led statebuilding, their identification of the two distinctive compacts is relevant when discussing unrecognised states. With the end goal being recognition of sovereign statehood and acceptance as a legitimate state, as opposed to state-like, entity, do unrecognised states *have* to exhibit these two compacts in order to stand a chance at recognition? Arguably, unrecognised states have a much greater pull on the necessity of domestic legitimacy. In projects characterised by direct engagement with the international community or external international actors it is expected that the expectations, demands or desires of those external actors will be

---

59 N. Caspersen, 'Unrecognised States: Shadow Economies', op. cit.
60 N. Caspersen, 'Unrecognised States: Shadow Economies', op. cit.; S. Pegg, *De Facto States*, op. cit.
61 A. Ghani and C. Lockhart, 'Closing the Sovereignty Gap', op. cit.; A. Ghani and C. Lockhart, *Fixing Failed States: A Framework for Rebuilding a Fractured World* (Oxford: Oxford University Press, 2008); A. Ghani, C. Lockhart and M. Carnahan, 'An Agenda for State-Building in the Twenty-First Century', *The Fletcher Forum of World Affairs* 30.1 (2006), pp. 101–23. Interestingly, within this there is recognition that a failure of legitimacy is a commonality in fragile states that either descend into conflict or fail, the discussion of legitimacy is confined to the very Weberian realm of 'legitimate monopolisation of force'.

reflected and met in both the statebuilding project itself as well as in the resulting state. In unrecognised states, though, there is something else at play. In external projects, some element of sovereignty is exercised by the external actors. In domestically-led projects, the exercising of sovereignty remains primarily within the borders of the territory and rests with local actors, and the continuation of this depends upon an acceptance by the local population; the state is propped up from within. In domestically-led statebuilding, domestic support for the state and the process of building it must exist in some capacity from the start. As a result, the state that is built in these self-led projects, particularly where there is a strategy for recognition of sovereignty, is one that must go beyond the seemingly nominal 'compact' and rigid liberal framework and instead must reflect the expectations of the local population. In these entities, statebuilding cannot be simply a technocratic exercise aimed at ticking boxes or meeting criteria, but also must reflect the idea of the state – connecting the people to the process – as a legitimising mechanism. Domestic legitimacy is integral the maintenance of these unrecognised states, but it does not stand alone as the demands of external legitimacy must also be met. Indeed narrowing, or even closing, the expectations gap and establishing a balance between internal and external legitimacy is arguably a defining characteristic of self-led statebuilding in unrecognised states.

Much of the discussion surrounding legitimacy and unrecognised states centres on the acceptance of these political entities into the club of states through acceptance of their 'statehood' and recognition of sovereignty. However, internal legitimacy and its impact on the creation and sustaining of unrecognised states are often overlooked. When approaching this from a statebuilding perspective rather than a legal or systemic perspective, though, the role of internal legitimacy and the burden of meeting that are difficult to ignore. Because of quests for recognition and the demands for acceptance of statehood, though, this cannot be examined in isolation. Indeed, in unrecognised states we must look at the interplay of internal and external legitimacy in the creation and maintenance of these political entities.

Unrecognised states exist outside of the legal international order and the formal international community. But they also create a new environment for the practice of statebuilding, one in which international recognition is sought but that also centres on a form of shared identity or political community. It is a practice of statebuilding that is influenced by the international community but is simultaneously beyond the direct input of its practitioners. In many ways, unrecognised states flip the problem of legitimacy found within externally-led statebuilding, largely because the process of creating a state is an internal process rather than an external imposition, creating stronger prospects for local ownership and domestic legitimacy. The linear progression with the technocratic institutional project sees institutions being built and then gaining legitimacy through their actions, with the expectation that the institutions will create governance that is accepted internally through practice and externally by design. The unrecognised state, through its struggle for external recognition, alters this path, beginning with internal legitimacy and governance and then creating the institutions that not only reflect internal acceptance, but that will lead to external acceptance as well. Within this form of statebuilding bridging the gap of expectations is not only desirable, but is necessary.

Conclusion

In unrecognised states, there is a need for internal control and legitimacy without a dependence on the war-making and criminality that was commonplace in European state making. Unrecognised states cannot take the European path; a new approach is necessary, yet the outcome is expected to be the same. Whilst this is especially the case in domestically-led statebuilding, it is also the same for externally-led projects. However, in externally-led projects, with the onus of statebuilding on institutions, there is less latitude for the socio-political transformation necessary for successful statebuilding.

To be clear, domestically-led statebuilding is a different form of statebuilding involving different actors, different pressures and different agendas to externally-led statebuilding. And just as externally-led statebuilding should not be a uniform practice, domestically-led statebuilding is not. Some unrecognised states, such as Tamil Eelam or South Ossetia, continue to be entrenched in or under threat of open conflict and do not meet the criteria of peace. Some, such as Kosovo and Timor-Leste, underwent externally-led statebuilding. Others may not desire international recognition of sovereignty, but may instead seek the recognition and thus support of a strong patron state. Or, in the case of Kurdistan, an unrecognised state may have latent rather than overt intent.[62] The target audience for some may be a single patron state whilst for others it is the wider international community. However, in these political entities statebuilding is taking place in various and specific forms, and the evident distinctions between not only the conditions of the entities but also the statebuilding processes themselves are no different to the contrasts seen within those states involved in externally-led projects. And although this type of statebuilding does have obvious differences from externally-led statebuilding, in both acknowledging the differences and recognising the similarities an analytical door opens and an expanded understanding of statebuilding can be obtained. It is a form of statebuilding, and as such should not be discounted in the quest to better understand and inform the policy option.

---

62 R.G. Smith, 'Kurdistan: The Road to Independence', unpublished manuscript (2013). Kurdistan is a grey area when it comes to identifying unrecognised states. With no official declaration of independence, it does not strictly fit the criteria as laid out by Caspersen and Kölsto. However, others, such as Smith, recognise the negative impact a declaration of independence would have on Kurdistan's economy, among other areas. Rather than viewing a lack of declaration as non-intent for independence, it is rather viewed as a strategic move beneficial to the Kurdistan state until recognition by at least one external state is certain. This 'latent intent' does not eliminate Kurdistan from consideration as an unrecognised state.

External support for statebuilding is a highly political process, made more complex by external agendas and dictates. But 'recreating states is more than technical assistance to government institutions; statebuilding is a function of state-society relations',[63] and as such cannot be reduced to building state institutions. As Fukuyama notes,

> [w]hile levels of social interchange and learning are far higher than they were three hundred years ago, most people continue to live in a horizon shaped largely by their own traditional culture and habits. The inertia of societies remains very great; while foreign institutional models are far more available than they once were, they still need to be overlaid on indigenous ones ... Modern institutions cannot simply be transferred to other societies without reference to existing rules and the political forces supporting them. Building an institution is not like building a hydroelectric dam or a road network. It requires a great deal of hard work to persuade people that institutional change is needed in the first place, build a coalition in favour of change that can overcome the resistance of existing stakeholders in the old system, and then condition people to accept the new set of behaviours as routine and expected.[64]

In the same way, legitimacy cannot be caged within the confines of the modern 'ideal' democratic state; a common problem as legitimacy continues to be presented as something that results from popular participation in democratic elections rather than popular participation and investment in the process and the resulting state. Statebuilding in practice 'needs to be much more oriented to building on what exists rather than transplanting foreign models and processes into ill-suited local environments'.[65] This should not be limited to institutions and practices, and certainly cannot be limited to only those institutions and practices that may conform to liberal expectations of the state. Indeed, when considering legitimacy and how best to 'legitimize' a state, looking beyond institutions is a necessity.

Statebuilding can be a form of peacebuilding, but it is much more than that. Statebuilding encompasses a political struggle among political actors over political power and the distribution of that power. This struggle takes place not only for the power to govern, but also 'between warring parties for international support and for domestic support, between those with economic power and those claiming political power in their mutual constitution of the state', and, importantly, 'between international preferences and local preferences'.[66] In maintaining a technocratic and institutional approach, externally-led statebuilding fails to recognise and accommodate these power struggles, thus creating obstacles not

---

63 T. Sisk, op. cit., p. 76.
64 F. Fukuyama, *The Origins of Political Order: From Prehuman Times to the French Revolution* (London: Profile Books, 2011): pp. 478–9.
65 T. Sisk, op. cit., p. 167.
66 S. Woodward, op. cit., p. 107.

only for legitimising the state, but also for sustained stability. Domestically-led statebuilding projects are not immune from these struggles, and in many ways are more susceptible to destabilisation because of them. As Migdal notes, 'state may help mold, but they are also continuously molded by, the societies within which they are embedded'.[67] In many ways, domestically-led statebuilding exemplifies this. They exhibit a degree of flexibility not seen in external projects; flexibility that, in combination with other powerful factors such as the quest for recognition, allows for the 'ill-suited' foreign model not to be discounted, but rather to be negotiated with local necessities, local institutions and local mechanisms of governance. And within this there are significant questions, and lessons, that pertain to the wider policy and concept of statebuilding.

Within self-led statebuilding projects, a balance must be reached between external expectations and internal necessities. In doing so, a duality of legitimacy is created: external legitimacy as an acceptable state, and internal legitimacy that, in domestically-led statebuilding, is vital for sustaining the process. Balancing external legitimacy with internal legitimacy is a prerequisite for 'success' not only in domestically-led projects, but in externally-led as well. The importance of popular trust and investment in the process of socio-political change that statebuilding brings should not be underestimated. In domestically-led statebuilding the process must be sustained from within, but at the same time, the process and the leaders would not have the rhetorical power needed to build the state if it were not for the need to 'comply to be recognized'; indeed, external recognition as a goal can maintain the domestic political and social cohesion needed to continue the statebuilding process. External demands can, and must, come together with internal necessities as a mechanism of stability.

Statebuilding also must be viewed as a process before it is a project in order to allow for and foster societal investment and the socio-political change needed for legitimacy and success. Building a state must be a flexible process that may encompass a project (or a defined end goal), but cannot be solely the technocratic project that is often seen, and is often referred to, within contemporary statebuilding. One paradox found within statebuilding literature and practice is that of long-term and short-term goals. Often contradictory, one of the most difficult problems to overcome is striking a balance between what is necessary in the short-term and what is beneficial in the long-term.[68] Long-term goals are more difficult to judge and to certify progress to donors; often the short-term is detrimentally favoured as the 'quick' stability helps tick off the criteria of the interveners' goals and agendas. With the long-term goals more encompassing of the nation-building process within statebuilding, the short-termism favoured focuses on the technocratic element of

---

67 J. Migdal, 'Introduction', in J. Migdal, A. Kohli and V. Shue (eds), *State Power and Social Forces: Domination and Transformation in the Third World* (Cambridge: Cambridge University Press, 1994), pp. 1–7: p. 2.

68 See, S. Woodward, op. cit.; C. Call, 'Ending Wars', op. cit.; K. Papagianni, op. cit.; T. Sisk, op. cit.; T. Donais, op. cit.; R. Paris and T. Sisk, op. cit.

statebuilding; the elements with clear and measurable goals and standards that strike a balance between external resource commitment and goals to be met. In doing this, however, statebuilding necessitates acting through a blueprint or a checklist and it becomes a project rather than a process; the state becomes something that is implemented rather than something that is fostered, negotiated or grown, posing obstacles not only for sustainable change but also for legitimising that change. Whilst a project can be at the centre of the process, it cannot exist alone, and this process must have the flexibility necessary to negotiate, rather than impose, the state as a means of mitigating potentially destabilising change. The state must be legitimated from the start, but it also must be re-legitimated throughout; what is accepted at one stage in the process may not be accepted at another, and the process and the state must be flexible enough to respond to this. If the state, the project, and indeed the process are not accepted as legitimate by the people, the bridge between short-termism and sustainable change will not be created.

One such unrecognised state in which lasting statebuilding 'success' is evident is Somaliland, the northwest territory of Somalia. The statebuilding process in Somaliland reflects the balance and mutual dependence between internal and external demands: it exhibits conforming to the norms of the ideal state, yet the survival of the externally valued democratic government in the territory is dependent upon stability provided by the domestic legitimacy. In creating and propelling a liberal democratic state, the founding fathers of Somaliland reflected the international preference regarding normative empirical attributes of statehood. As will be examined in following chapters, the creation of the democratic component of the government, whilst foreign to Somaliland society, was viewed as beneficial to obtaining recognition and the political and economic benefits that would bring. In the complex process of reacting to a multitude of demands, however, Somaliland deviated from the norm by including traditional governance structures as an institution in the central government. The creation of the Somaliland state did not follow the blueprint of statebuilding, but rather forged its own way by forming its own state. The remainder of this book will examine this process of statebuilding, focusing specifically on the utilisation of the clan to bridge the gap between external and internal demands and expectations. An obvious point of interest within this is the inclusion of traditional structures of governance in the central government of Somaliland. As identified in Chapter 2, the vital social and political functions of traditional social structures in weak, fragile, failed or even de facto states are often overlooked in favour of an attitude of incomprehensibility. Particularly true for a territory within Somalia, where the overriding perception of traditional structures of governance – the clan – will be negatively associated with the continuing violence and instability in the south of the country, the inclusion of traditional authority in the government of Somaliland was a risky proposition in a territory presenting itself as a state ready for recognition. The questions remaining, then, are why was the traditional authority included in the government in Somaliland, and what can be learned from this inclusion? The following chapters will examine these questions in more detail.

Chapter 4
The Clan, Governance and the Build-up to Breakdown

The 1991 coup that ousted long-term Somalia dictator Siad Barre resulted in the failure and fragmentation of the Somali state and the start of statebuilding in Somaliland. Much of the current literature on the state of Somalia focuses on the immediacy and the supposed anarchy created by the absence of a central government, as well as the successive failed attempts to rebuild the state. It is insufficient, however, to assess the current political situation in Somalia, and within that Somaliland, without examining first the social forces and historical legacies and developments that shaped the state and those that impacted upon its breakdown. By only focusing on the immediate, an incomplete account of this state is created. This is also true when discussing the circumstances surrounding the creation of the state in Somaliland.

As Bradbury notes, the current political situation in both Somalia and Somaliland cannot be examined without first understanding the pervasive Somali clan system, including the non-state based clan governance structures that exist within Somali society and territories and are a significant component of statebuilding in Somaliland.[1] The current political situation, including statebuilding projects, also cannot be understood without examining colonial and post-colonial governance structures. The place to start in examining contemporary Somaliland politics, therefore, is not with the history of Somaliland itself, but rather with the Somali and with the history of governance and government in the territories comprising Somalia, including that within the clan system. As the interest here is primarily on Somaliland, the historical focus inevitably will be directed there. However, Somaliland has a shared history with Somalia, and as such cannot entirely be treated in isolation. With a focus on the history of governance and governance structures, the background given here lays the foundations for understanding not only the Somali people and the Somali state, but also the systems of governance underpinning and guiding the creation of the Somaliland state. Whilst southern Somalia is not ignored here, the emphasis is on Somaliland.

The Basis for All: The Somali Clan System

As an indigenous source of structure and governance, the Somali clan system plays an important socio-political role in Somali society. The Somali population

---

1   M. Bradbury, *Becoming Somaliland* (Oxford: James Currey, 2008), p. 14.

inhabits the Horn of Africa, extending from the middle of Djibouti, into northern and eastern Ethiopia, throughout Somalia, and into northern Kenya.[2] Although some cite slight linguistic and cultural differences between the settled populations (*Sag*) and nomadic pastoralists (*Samale*), Somali society is not divided by ethnic, religious or significant cultural differences, and the Somali themselves often refer to the Somali 'race'. The Somali rarely view themselves as African, and identify more with their Arab heritage than their geographic placement. Despite their Arab heritage, though, the Somali do not consider themselves part of the Arab world. The Somali self-portrait is more of an exception than a component: neither African nor Arab, they are Somali.[3] However, there are divides within the Somali population despite the homogeneity. Many of these divides are based on geography or historical divergences and divisions.

The key to understanding Somali social, political and economic organisation is the clan system. These kinship relations binding the Somali are at the centre of Somali life; the clan not only provides a basis for identity but is also what Drysdale labels the Somali 'insurance policy' as each clan takes collective responsibility for its members, their losses and their security.[4] In his seminal works on Somali history, Lewis details these social, political and economic characteristics of the nomadic pastoral lifestyle and the role of the clans as an organisational system. In the sphere of politics, Somali genealogy holds importance in:

> it represents the social divisions of people into corporate political groups ... By virtue of genealogy of birth, each individual has an exact place in society and within a very wide range of agnatic kinship it is possible for each person to trace his precise connection with everyone else. Somali political philosophy is thus an evaluation of agnatic connection.[5]

As such, relations with others in Somali society, including the lines of political allegiance and division, are determined by these patrilineal genealogies. They also determine an individual's political, social, legal and economic status within Somali society. Some have argued, however, that increased attachment to territory or other social groups, together with damaging impacts of factors such as the emergence of a state, urbanisation, migration and harmful colonial or government

---

2 Saadia Touval defines the Horn of Africa as an indefinite territorial jurisdiction, but as a region 'inhabited mainly by Somalis'. S. Touval, *Somali Nationalism* (Cambridge, MA: Harvard University Press, 1963): p. 5.

3 Mohammed Hassan Ibrahim 'Gani', Mohammed Said Mohammed Gees, Abdi Aw Rabak, and Bobe Duale Yusuf. Conversations with author. (Hargeisa: August-September 2006).

4 I.M. Lewis, *Understanding Somalia* (London: HAAN Associates, 1993); J. Drysdale, *Stoics Without Pillows: A Way Forward for the Somalilands* (London: HAAN Associates, 2000).

5 I.M. Lewis, *A Pastoral Democracy*, op. cit., pp. 1–2.

policies, have lessened the impact of the clan system.⁶ Whereas this can be seen in Somali society, any rejection of categorisation by the clan takes place primarily in urban areas and within non-clan specific militias or religious movements such as the Union of Islamic Courts (UIC) and al-Shabaab. As indicated by many urban elite within northern Somalia, and summarised by Bradbury, though, 'the clan system remains an important feature of Somali social, political and economic life' despite drawn out statebuilding practices, urbanisation, industrialisation, civil war, and international migration.⁷ Although the clan is pervasive in all aspects of Somali life, the discussion here focuses on five key areas of clan provision: identity, governance, law and justice, co-existence and conflict resolution. Certainly, the clan and clan governance are more prevalent in some areas and less in others. Although in the area of focus – Somaliland – the clan system has been less disrupted and is thus more prevalent, what follows here should be read as a historical generalisation rather than a universally applicable description across all Somali inhabited territories.

Identity

As Bradbury notes, '[a]ll Somalis are born into this social structure and because it defines a person's relationship to other Somalis and non-Somalis, kinship is a critical source of an individual's identity'.⁸ Drysdale claims that although some non-Somalis view the clan as archaic, restrictive or unnatural, most Somalis accept the inevitability of adhering to traditional or traditional values through the clan; the Somali are not 'prisoners of the system' but are rather bound to the clan by necessity, both within the often harsh physical and political landscapes of Somalia as well as within and from the Diaspora.⁹ The complex Somali clan system is composed of six main structuring clan-families – the Dir, Isaaq, Hawiye Darood, Digil and Rahanweyn – and is further divided into numerous sub-clans, sub-sub clans, primary lineage groups and *diya*-paying groups. The Somali nation is one of nomads, with pastoral nomads making up a majority of the population.¹⁰ Touval's 1963 estimate that 80 per cent of Somalis are nomadic is commonly cited throughout the literature, although factors such as war, migration, modernisation and urbanisation have undoubtedly lowered this percentage.¹¹ Because of the dominance of pastoral nomadism, clans and their divisions became important

---

6   See A. Samatar, *The State and Rural Transformation in Northern Somalia, 1884–1986* (Madison: University of Wisconsin Press, 1989).

7   M. Bradbury, op. cit., p. 18; Interviews conducted by author (Hargeisa, August-September 2006).

8   M. Bradbury, op. cit.

9   J. Drysdale, op. cit., pp. 139–40.

10   I.M. Lewis, *A Pastoral Democracy*, op. cit.

11   S. Touval, op. cit., p. 13; I.M. Lewis, *A Modern History of the Somali* (Oxford: James Currey, 2002), pp. 1–2,7.

for the cohesiveness of the nomadic groupings as well as their physical security. Conflict over grazing land or access to water was frequent, and historically, war was not used to vanquish the enemy but instead became a way through which political ascendancy and access to resources could be established. As Bradbury notes, disputes over land or resources, although often violent, also involved negotiation and the formulation of political or social alliances. Because of this, the Somali have 'strong traditions of mediation, reconciliation and consensus-building alongside traditional institutions of law and order'.[12] Most of this is centred on the clan.

The segmentary nature of the clan system 'reflects the need for groups to be in constant motion, expanding and contracting as needs demand, while eking out a living from a harsh environment'.[13] Most certainly established as a means of control in the non-centralised pre-colonial Somali society,[14] the clan continues to influence a person's individual place as well as determining relations between members of competing or allied clans. Whilst the clan families define and bind large groups, but are too big to act as collective political units. Thus, the Somali sub-clans serve a more important function in daily life and society as the division of a clan into smaller sub-clan groupings allows for more comprehensive control and protection of clan members within geographical regions as well as creating a means of genealogical distinction that allows for linear identification.[15] Whereas a Somali may be a member of the Isaaq clan, his membership in his sub-clan distinguishes him and his family geographically, politically, economically and socially from the other Isaaq sub-clans. The clan creates basis for identity in Somali society, but the sub-clan creates a stronger sense of identity and placement within the clan itself. This form of identity and kinship does not stop at the borders of Somali inhabited territories, but continues to thrive within Somali communities elsewhere. Somali communities in the Diaspora tend to form themselves around clan or sub-clan groupings, and kinship relations with Somali communities outside of Somalia are strong within Somali inhabited areas. Indeed, much policy and scholarly attention

---

12 M. Bradbury, op. cit., p. 18.

13 M. Bradbury, 'The Case of the Yellow Settee: Experiences of Doing Development in Post-War Somaliland', ActionAid Draft Report (London: ActionAid, 1993); I.M. Lewis, *A Pastoral Democracy*, op. cit., pp. 4–7. Lewis labels the largest grouping within the structure as the 'clan-family', although common usage refers to it as the 'clan'. For purposes here, the common usage will from this point be used, with the largest grouping being the 'clan', the first level of sub-lineages as the 'sub-clan' and so on.

14 Historical studies of the pre-colonial Arab settlements found on the Somali coasts shows that an urban culture and civic identity rather than genealogy formed the basis of individual and communal identity. See L. Kapteijns, 'Woman and the Crisis of Communal Identity: The Cultural Construction of Gender in Somali History', in A. Samatar, ed., *The Somali Challenge: From Catastrophe to Renewal* (London: Lynne Rienner, 1994), pp. 211–31.

15 M. Bradbury, *Becoming Somaliland*, op. cit., p. 16; I.M. Lewis, *A Pastoral Democracy*, op. cit.

is made to the importance of financial remittances to the Somali economy. These remittances – payments sent to Somalia from the Diaspora – are kinship based; financial assistance is almost always sent to the family or the sub-clan, rather than any central governance structure. This is a means through which the clan takes care of its own, a modern form of practice that is not far removed from the original intent of protection associated with its nomadic origins.

Most Somalis adhere to Sunni Islam, and Sufism is commonly practiced. The close relationship between Islam and the Somali clans themselves has created a culture in which religion and the clan are so closely intertwined that they cannot be separated: both Somali and Islamic traditions, customs and laws remain distinct, yet are mutually dependent on each other within Somali society. The result is an amalgamation of Somali traditional practices and customs and those of Islam, with the two acting in conjunction to provide not only a socio-religious component of Somali identity, but also a moral and legal code upon which Somali society is based.

Governance

As Lewis notes, 'few societies can so conspicuously lack those judicial, administrative, and political procedures which lie at the heart of the western conception of government ... Yet, although they thus lack to a remarkable degree all the machinery of centralized government, they are not without government or political institutions'.[16] Much of the governance existent in Somaliland is abstract and unspoken; it is complexly ingrained in the social structures of the population. The Somali clans are predominantly non-hierarchical structures. Whilst some of the clans have titled leaders – a legacy of colonial rule – the inherited role does not grant executive power but rather bestows responsibility to act as arbiter.[17] Somali pastoralist society is traditionally not constituted on central institutional rule but it is not without governance or rules. As Lewis notes, the 'lack of any stable hierarchy of political units is characteristic of the Somali social system. In conformity with this, there is no formal hierarchy of political or administrative offices'. Historically, because of this, 'political leadership lies with the elders of the group concerned'.[18] Although altered through time, interactions, occupation and the creation of central government, much of the political association and of the governance provided by the clan continues to play an important role today. This is especially true in the nomadic population as well as in the north, where the clan system has been less disrupted than in the south and where clan governance

---

16   I.M. Lewis, *A Pastoral Democracy* (Oxford: Oxford University Press, 1961), p. 1.

17   Amongst the Isaaq the titled elders are known as *suldaan* or sultan. For the other clans, titled elders are called: *garaad, islaan and boqor* amongst the Darood; *ugaas* amongst the Hawiye and Gadabuursi; and *malaaq* amongst the Rahanweyn. M. Bradbury, *Becoming Somaliland*, op. cit., p. 17; I.M. Lewis, *Blood and Bone: The Call of Kinship in Somali Society* (Lawrenceville, NJ: The Red Sea Press, 1994).

18   I.M. Lewis, *A Pastoral Democracy*, op. cit., p. 196.

has been significantly invoked and incorporated in centralised structures. The 'ordered anarchy' that characterises this way of life maintains political and social order through 'collective social institutions and through reciprocal, rule-bound behaviour delineated in customary law'.[19] As the sub-clan is the 'upper limit of corporate political action' in Somali society these lineage groupings are central to governance in Somali inhabited territories.[20] As historically the majority of Somali society was not located within permanent settlements or subject to centralised government prior to colonisation, governance took place in community councils (*shir*) which were convened when need determined. These ad hoc councils were held primarily within the sub-clans, but clan *shir* and inter-clan *shir* also took place. It was at these meetings that clan or sub-clan affairs were controlled in what Lewis describes as a manner verging on anarchy. The traditional decision making process within the councils was not hierarchical but rather was a highly democratic system in which all adult males were allowed equal access and participation.[21] These councils provided a governing structure that acted as a means of enforcement of law and justice, as well as the decision and lawmaking body. The unit-wide binding contractual agreements made during these councils concerned everything from marriage practices to resource allocation, trade agreements, punishment for crimes and movement of the clans or sub-clans. It was through these *shir* that regular governing of the clan or sub-clan took place.

During times of conflict, crisis, disagreement between clans, when law had to be enforced or when negotiations within or between the clans were needed, a council of clan elders (*guurti*) met as a component of the *shir*. The *guurti* are traditionally the highest political council in Somali society, comprising titled and non-titled clan elders selected for their knowledge and wisdom.[22] With the clan elders being the most respected men within the clans and sub-clans, the *guurti* was the closest equivalent to hierarchical rule within Somali society and the decisions of the body bound the clans and sub-clans involved, creating a traditional legal system through a form of customary law (*xeer*). With power not being exercised by a chief, decisions were made through consensus and often the *guurti* and the *shir* lasted for months. These clan councils continue to function within Somali society, particular in the context of state collapse and in the absence of state institutions. In many areas of post-collapse Somalia the clan system provides a 'structure for inter-group relations and governance, for organising and managing violence and for organising trade' through *shir* and *guurti*.[23] As will be seen in later chapters,

---

19   M. Bradbury, *Becoming Somaliland*, op. cit., p. 16.
20   I.M. Lewis, *A Pastoral Democracy*, op. cit., p. 5.
21   I.M. Lewis, *A Modern History*, op. cit., p. 9. The age of adulthood for males in Somali culture is generally accepted to be fifteen years old.
22   I.M. Lewis and A. Farah, 'Somalia: The Roots of Reconciliation: Peace Making Endeavours of Contemporary Lineage Leaders in "Somaliland"', Report for ActionAid (London: ActionAid, 1993), p. 17.
23   M. Bradbury, *Becoming Somaliland*, op. cit., p. 15.

these clan and elder councils have also been instrumental in the establishment of peace and the establishment of a central government in the northern territory of Somaliland.

Law and Justice

As part of the governance provided by the kinship structure, agreements within and between clans provide a system of law and justice. In addition to kinship lines, Somali society is also divided into inter and intra-clan *diya*-paying, or blood-money, groups. Within these groups collective action is feasible; they are a means of policing the clans and enforcing the traditional legal system enacted by the *shir* and *guurti*. *Diya*-groups comprise a number of families who are typically united not only through genealogy but also marriage ties. Members of these groups are part of a 'self-help' justice system: they are obliged to protect each other and to pay and receive compensation for murder, injury or other forms of redress. The *diya*-groups are stable political units in 'a shifting system of agnatic attachment' in that within these groups, 'which [are] in effect the basic political and jural unit of pastoral society, contract and clanship meet' regardless of the relationship between the clans or the sub-clans of its members.[24] As Bradbury notes, the blood-money system 'provides a sanction against violence and reinforces collective responsibility'.[25] Largely based on Islamic law (*shari'a*) as well as customary contractual law (*xeer*) formed through clan agreements, the traditional Somali legal system defines the rules of collective rights and responsibilities as well as common interests.[26] Unwritten, these laws are the 'lynchpin of orderliness' and are handed down orally through the generations, binding members of a clan or *diya*-group to the agreements of the previous generations and forming a repository of customary law and practices.[27] Although the traditional Somali legal system emerged prior to the introduction of centralised governing structures, it continues to function in areas exhibiting central governance as well as those in which no government exists.[28] In Somaliland, broadly based contractual law not only forms the basis of the government being created, but *xeer* and *diya*-groups also supplement the codified legal and justice systems in the forming state.[29]

---

24   I.M. Lewis, *A Modern History*, op. cit., p. 15.
25   M. Bradbury, *Becoming Somaliland*, op. cit., p. 16.
26   I.M. Lewis, *A Modern History*, op. cit., pp. 4–5.
27   J. Drysdale, op. cit., p. 142; M. Bradbury, *Becoming Somaliland*, op. cit., p. 17. For more on the different types of *xeer*, see also I.M. Lewis, *Blood and Bone*, op. cit.; I.M. Lewis, *A Pastoral Democracy*, op. cit.; I.M. Lewis, *A Modern History*, op. cit.; A. Samatar, *The Somali Challenge: From Catastrophe to Renewal?* (London: Lynne Rienner, 1994).
28   K. Menkhaus, 'Kenya-Somalia Border Conflict Analysis', USAID Conflict Prevention, Mitigation and Response Program for East and Southern Africa Report (August 2005).
29   Firsthand experience of the functions of the customary legal system was gained during fieldwork conducted in Hargeisa. During my stay, there were thefts of money and

Co-existence

Although *diya*-groups and customary law act as important components of the legal and justice system in Somali society, they also play an important role in maintaining a balanced co-existence within and between the clans; these traditional values and codes are the 'secular lifejackets which keep Somalis afloat irrespective of formal systems of governance'.[30] Because the strong bond of kinship and therefore identity can both unify and divide society,

> [the] contract cements and temporarily stabilizes fission and fusion in the lineage system ... [*xeer*] denotes a body of explicitly formulated obligations, rights and duties. It binds people of the same treaty together in relation to internal delicts and defines their collective responsibility in external relations with similar groups.[31]

However, *xeer* is more than a contract between the different groupings within Somali society: '[i]t defines the basic values, laws, and rules of behaviour. It is the closest equivalent to the notion of a "social contract"', and thus plays an important role in establishing and maintaining forms of governance.[32] As these treaties and contracts are passed down through the generations, they bind a lineage to the agreements and laws and therefore become a form of custom found at every level of lineage segmentation and as the foundation of politics and legal relationships.[33]

---

clothes from people (non-Somali) in the house I lived in. The police, the owners of the house and representatives of the sub-clans of those suspected of committing the thefts were involved in lengthy discussions to determine the culprit and to resolve the matter. The person responsible – the house's cook – fled to Djibouti before she could be arrested. Members of her family's *diya*-group residing in Djibouti were responsible for returning her to Hargeisa, after which she was taken into police custody. The government's 'Westernised' legal system did not handle her case, however. Instead, elders from her sub-clan and *diya*-group and elders from the sub-clan and *diya*-group of the people she wronged (as the people she stole from were not members of a clan, it was determined that she had wronged the owner of the house and the person who had secured the cook her job) negotiated compensation to be paid. It was not until restitution was made between the sub-clans and the groups that the cook was released from jail. The police were involved because Westerners were involved; if it had been a dispute involving only Somali, the first call would have been to the elders rather than the police and the matter would have been settled through negotiation by the elders.

30   J. Drysdale, op. cit., p. 141.
31   I.M. Lewis, 'Clanship and Contract in Northern Somaliland', *Africa* 29 (1959), pp. 274–93: pp. 281–2.
32   M. Bradbury, 'Peace-enforcement, Peace-making and Peace-building: Options for Resolving the Somali Conflict', Exploratory Report for Oxfam (1993), p. 23; M. Bradbury, *The Somali Conflict: Prospects for Peace* (London: Oxfam Publishers, 1993), p. 23.
33   I.M. Lewis, 'Clanship and Contract', op. cit., pp. 282, 286.

The dual purpose of *xeer*, as both law and custom, is further highlighted by Lewis in his explanation of the word itself. He states that in the Somali language:

> [t]here are several other uses of the word which serve to elucidate its meaning. The rope placed over the top of the nomadic hut to give it stability, and either fastened to the ground on each side or secured by stones, is called *xeer*. Similarly the verbal form means 'to surround' as, for example, in the phrase 'we are surrounded by an enemy party'. Thus the implication of binding, fastening, and of securing, underlies each use.[34]

These customs not only bind society, but the legal framework created by *xeer* also underpins interactions in the inherently divided clan system; knowledge of and abidance by these customs and laws creates an overarching form of governance that facilitates co-existence between the clans and sub-clans in both areas with central government and those without. The agreements and treaties that become customs and laws form the stable grounding necessary to negotiate peace and balance between the clans, and as Somali society encounters new situations and conditions the contracts and customs are revised accordingly. Co-existence through customary law is particularly prevalent in the more nomadic north, where the clans have a long history of interaction, cooperation and competition stemming largely from contests over grazing land and water resources. As a result, 'the clans and sub-clans [in the north] have evolved a common *xeer* ... [t]he retention of such values helped later in resolving conflicts' during the lead-up to and following the 1991 collapse of the Somali state.[35] These customs and negotiated co-existence also played a significant role in establishing peace, stability and a government in Somaliland.

Conflict Resolution

Whilst the existence of *diya*-groups has always been the most effective sanction for redressing wrongs and resolving problems between small groups, they do not provide a framework through which to provide security to the clan or society as a whole. Divisions within the clan are essential to the organisation of Somali society, but threats to the clan unite the sub-clans in defence of the larger family group. The most common threat to the clan historically was, and in some areas still is, losing access to vital resources. Traditional notions of political power were therefore based in terms of physical strength and control of resources, as the more powerful clans were those that were able to capture and defend the best grazing lands and water sources;[36] thus, political power was 'won by the sword'. Co-existence between the

---

34 Ibid., p. 282.
35 M. Bradbury, 'Peace-enforcement, Peace-making and Peace-Building', op. cit., p. 78.
36 I.M. Lewis, *A Modern History*, op. cit., p. 11; M. Bradbury, 'Peace-enforcement, Peace-making and Peace Building', op. cit., p. 32.

clans depended upon conflict resolution mechanisms such as marriage agreements or *diya* paying groups for lesser, more personal crimes, and clan councils in the instance of inter or intra-clan warfare.[37] As Bradbury notes, 'Somali society works on a system of balanced oppositions between groups ... If peace is thought to exist where there is an equitable balance, anything which upsets the balance will continue the conflict'.[38] Because of this need for balance, conflict resolution mechanisms have become embedded in the clan structure itself, with clan elders through *guurti* being responsible for resolving conflicts. This mechanism most likely began in the early days of the clan system as a means to ameliorate bloody wars between the early clans. Negotiation became commonplace in resolving conflict most likely resulting from refusals of early sultans or other hereditary leaders to subordinate themselves to another or cede their clan as a spoil of war. Negotiation and compromise became essential tools in the resolution of conflicts; tools that continue to exist and are rich and powerful traditions in Somali politics and society.[39] It must be noted here, though, that negotiation in Somali society has its own character that is far different from that commonly found in Western society. It is a lengthy, loud and dynamic process, and often includes verbal abuse, quarrels and exchanging insults. Poetry writing and recitations, as well as storytelling, are often included, where heroic tales of previous accomplishments or moral stories are used to gain the upper ground or calm the discussions. Negotiations often involve chewing sessions where the stimulant *qaat* is used to loosen tongues and facilitate discussions. The negotiations process also often involves the exchange of compensation and ceremonial gifts as means of appeasement or restitution. Through all this, grievances are brought to the attention of all involved and the 'air is cleared'.[40] This dynamic process is central to conflict resolution in the Somali clan system, and many of these practices continue today.

Resolutions to conflict are typically negotiated by the most respected elders of the *guurti*, with the agreements binding lineages through the creation of customary law. As such, *xeer* becomes the first route for settling disputes and hostilities.[41] Because of the intricacies of *xeer*, clan elders are responsible for ensuring that conflicts are resolved rather than merely placating the parties involved, as future violations would be subject to *diya* compensation. Contemporary elders in Somaliland list other tools used in their peacemaking role as: age; *shari'a* law; proverbs and poems; *shir*; devotion to the public interest; impartiality; using clan resources as indication of commitment to process; compromise and consensus; and persistence. Significantly, the elders also list 'transparency, fairness, trust and

---

37 J. Drysdale, op. cit., p. 12, Chapters 9 and 10.
38 M. Bradbury, 'Peace-enforcement, Peace-making and Peace-Building', op. cit., p. 6.
39 J. Drysdale, op. cit., pp. 141–2.
40 Somaliland Academy for Peace and Development (APD), *Rebuilding Somaliland: Issues and Possibilities* (Lawrenceville, NJ: The Red Sea Press, 2005), p. 63.
41 M. Bradbury, *Becoming Somaliland*, op. cit., p. 19.

sincerity' as 'tools for the mutual trust and confidence building'.[42] Respect for the elders provides the basis for their abilities; without the respect and trust of the people their actions would be meaningless. Through negotiation, compromise and compensation in conflict resolution, the trusted clan elders ensure balance and co-existence within the volatile clan system. As Drysdale notes, in areas of southern Somalia 'where traditional value systems are bypassed in favour of show of force, continuing conflict is manifest'.[43] In places where the clan system is central to law and governance, though, the elders continue to constantly negotiate the balance within Somali society and to resolve conflicts when they arise.

Clan Elders: The 'Holders of Tradition'

Although throughout Somali history clan elders have played a vital role in the maintenance of society, Bradbury notes that it is misleading to talk about 'traditional' elders in Somali society, 'for this suggests an institution'. Instead, he notes, it may be more appropriate to consider elders as representatives 'holding the "traditions" of the clan'.[44] The dynamism of Somali society means that it is constantly adapting to changing circumstances, causing the clan elders to adapt as well to enable them to fulfil their roles in the changing environment. Regardless of these changes, however, clan elders continue to maintain importance in Somali society, largely in the arenas of governance and of peace and reconciliation. As long as the clan remains the primary ordering principle in Somali society, clan elders will continue to be of vital importance to stability.

As the egalitarian nature of Somali society means there is no hierarchy of authority in the clan or sub-clan other than the primarily symbolic position of the few titled elders, within the Somali clans and sub-clans it is the non-titled elders who hold the respect as leaders and guides. The position of clan elder can be confusing for a non-Somali, as there are no clear criteria for holding this position or choosing an elder. Likewise, there is no uniform standard for what authority an elder will possess and exercise. The only firm stipulation is that only men can be elders. Elders can be found at all levels of segmentation, from clan to nuclear family. Elders further up the segmentary line, however, hold the most respect as peacemakers, with elders of the main clan families held in the highest regard. As with any leader or negotiator, though, some elders are more respected than others,

---

42 Somaliland Upper House of Parliament, 'Somaliland: A Model, Indigenous Owned Peace and Democratic Governance Building in the Horn', Background report produced by the Upper House of Parliament (April 2006). This report also lists clairvoyance and telepathy as tools at the disposal of some elders, saying that some people believe that not obeying or going against the decisions of the elders will bring the wrath of Allah upon them.

43 J. Drysdale, op. cit., p. 13.

44 M. Bradbury, 'Peace-enforcement, Peace-making and Peace-Building', op. cit., pp. 81–2.

with respect largely tied to cultural and religious knowledge, trustworthiness, negotiating abilities and successes, and age.[45] The position of elder is not hereditary, although in some instances a particular line of lineage may be preferred to others for numerous reasons, including following a particular *xeer* or custom. Although the selection procedure varies from clan to clan or even sub-clan to sub-clan, the consistency across the clans is that 'an elder is a representative who is delegated authority, rather than assumes it. In council meetings they are delegates or emissaries of and for their clans, whom they represent and by whom they are supported'.[46]

Whilst elders have exercised numerous roles throughout Somali history and across clan lines, they are best known for their constant peacemaking or balancing role. Their position as 'professional negotiators and mediators in all clan matters'[47] makes them vital to maintaining balance needed to thwart the implosion or explosion of the clan system. As previously mentioned, much of this balancing act takes place through the *guurti*. These special councils composed of representatives chosen by all the involved clans were considered the highest authority in Somali society prior to the introduction of central government, and many maintain that the *guurti* continue to exist as such even with the presence of a central government.[48] Held at the local, regional or national level, the ad-hoc *guurti* exist only until a resolution is obtained thereby establishing *xeer*, or until an agreement for a further meeting is reached. In many ways, the *guurti* can be viewed as a type of judiciary – historically without a permanent institution or body – that maintains customs and establishes peace through upholding and creating *xeer*. These negotiating bodies, called upon when necessary and then disbanded when not, are vital in maintaining stability in the decentralised Somali clan system. As will be seen in later chapters, in Somaliland the social institutions of the clan, including the elders and the councils, together with traditional practices and traditions of mediation, arbitration, consensus decision-making and the upholding of *xeer* played a crucial role in the post-collapse peacebuilding and state building process in the territory.

Although potentially divisive, the complex Somali clan system not only provides a basis for identity but also acts as an ordering principle in all areas of life, including politics, economics, war and peace. These traditional forms of social and political organisation were not entirely lost during the disruptive

---

45 One of the most respected peace makers in Somaliland today, Haji Abdi Hussein, is reported to be over 100 years old, although his exact age is not known. Respect for him comes from his age and his experiences.

46 M. Bradbury, 'Peace-enforcement, Peace-making and Peace-Building', op. cit., p. 81.

47 Ibid. See also I.M. Lewis, *Blood and Bone*, op. cit.; I.M. Lewis, *A Pastoral Democracy*, op. cit.; M. Bradbury, *Becoming Somaliland*, op. cit.

48 Even after the introduction of central government in the Somali territories, *guurti* continued to be recognised as the highest authority, particularly during periods of violent or absent government. When the state was weak, the *guurti* assumed higher authority.

period of colonisation followed by the turbulent post-colonial era. Instead, the fundamentals of the clan system survived, albeit altered by experience, to exist in present day Somalia. As Lewis noted in his 1965 edition of *A Modern History of Somaliland*, 'in many respects, modernism provides new scope for the working of traditional social principles rather than creating entirely new circumstances to which the old order of society is irrelevant'.[49] The adaptable nature of the clan system has allowed for these mechanisms, procedures and customs to continue to provide governance and stability in the decentralised Somali inhabited territories for centuries. It would be inaccurate to suggest, however, that the clan system did not emerge from the colonial period or the post-independence governments unscathed. For this reason, the preceding sections will examine the impact of colonial rule on clan governance structures as well as that of the two different governments that ruled the state of Somalia prior to 1991.

Colonial Rule and Legacy

Throughout its history, Somalia experienced a host of foreign settlers entering and claiming possession of the territory. The most lasting of the pre-colonial influences were Arabian traders who established permanent trading posts along the coast as early as the seventh century.[50] It was not until European colonisation in the late nineteenth century, though, that the whole of the Somali population felt the influence of foreign rule and government. As previously stated, what is present day Somalia was colonised concurrently by two European powers: Italy in the northeast and the south, and Britain in the northwest. The ruling styles of these two colonising powers were drastically different, and both left lasting impacts on the modern political and social climate of Somalia and of Somaliland. Just as pre-colonial governance structures are important to understanding the basis of Somali society, the impact of colonial structures on that society is important for understanding Somaliland society today and the governance structures that exist within and above it.

Italian colonisation of southern Somalia was done with the intent of first expanding into Ethiopia and after failing that, establishing a settler colony in which plantations could be established and land acquired to solve a problem with a surplus population at home.[51] British colonisation in the Horn of Africa, on the other hand, was an accidental acquisition rather than a designed component of the

---

49 I.M. Lewis, *The Modern History of Somaliland: From Nation to State* (London: Weidenfeld and Nicholson, 1965), p. 17.

50 S. Touval, op. cit., p. 9. The first known Arabian settlement was an Arab sultanate established at Zeila on the Red Sea Coast. By the thirteenth century it had developed into the Adal Empire. Numerous Arabian sultanates were established in southern Somalia at Mogadishu and Brava in the fifteenth century.

51 S. Touval, op. cit., pp. 40, 90–97; I.M. Lewis, *A Modern History*, op. cit., p. 52.

expansive British Empire. Britain had an established military garrison at Aden, in what is today Yemen, which quickly became an important stopping point for traders going to and from India. Due to a lack of resources in the southern Arabian Peninsula the British were forced to look externally for supplies for the residents the troops stationed there. British interest in the Somali territory across the Red Sea, therefore, was not for territorial conquest or as a 'civilising mission', but instead was undertaken to protect and support British interests at Aden. Beginning in 1827 through a series of non-expansive treaties of protection made with the clan leadership of what is now northwest Somalia, a mutually beneficial relationship was established: the British gained provisions for the troops at Aden and at the same time guaranteed that no other foreign presence would be stationed across the sea from the British settlement; and the Somali clans were guaranteed a key market for selling fresh meat and other goods. British authorities at Aden did urge the government in London to use this territory in Somalia as a 'definitive British occupation of the Somali coast' to provide order to the feuding and 'lawless' Somali clans, but the response was that no occupation was to take place unless the coast was seriously threatened.[52] The opening of the Suez Canal in 1869 increased the importance of the Somali coast, but it was not until France, Ethiopia and Italy began seeking territory in the Horn of Africa that Britain formalised its territorial claim.[53] With the changing perception that northwest Somalia was strategically important in its empire and therefore necessitated a formal British presence in the territory, in 1886 Britain created the British Somaliland Protectorate and introduced British rule into the Horn of Africa.[54]

Instructions from the British government in London regarding the new Protectorate were to restrict involvement to the coastal areas and to make the occupation as 'unobtrusive as possible: there was to be no attempt to extend British control inland'.[55] The British officials initially employed methods of indirect rule, and the administrators within the Protectorate were instructed that 'no grandiose schemes were to be entertained; expenditure was to be limited to a minimum, and [it] was to be provided by the local port revenues'.[56] Britain's policy of ignoring the interior of the Somaliland Protectorate and running the territory 'on the cheap'[57]

---

52 I.M. Lewis, *A Modern History*, op. cit., pp. 40–41.
53 APD, op. cit., p. 11; S. Touval, op. cit., pp. 35–7. See also, I.M. Lewis, *A Modern History*, op. cit.; M. Bradbury, *Becoming Somaliland*, op. cit.; A. Samatar, *The State and Rural Transformation*, op. cit. In order for British possession of the Somaliland Protectorate to be recognised by other colonising powers in the colonisation of Africa in the late nineteenth century, Britain had to formally declare its intentions for colonisation of the territory. On 20 July 1887, Britain officially notified the European powers under the General Act of the Berlin Conference that the British Protectorate had been established.
54 APD, op. cit., p. 11; see also I.M. Lewis, *A Modern History*, op. cit., pp. 40–50.
55 I.M. Lewis, *A Modern History*, op. cit., p. 47.
56 S. Touval, op. cit., p. 47.
57 International Crisis Group (ICG), 'Somaliland: Democratisation and its Discontents', Africa Report No. 66 (Nairobi: ICG, 2003), pp. 2, 3. For more information

were disrupted in 1899, however, when the anti-British Dervish uprisings forced the attention of the British administrators as well as military forces inland.[58] The long and costly conflict caused the British to invest large amounts of financial and human resources in the Protectorate and moved the British authorities far from utilising the colony primarily as a meat supply.

After 21 years of clashes between British troops and the Dervish forces led by Sheikh Mohammed Abdullah Hassan (known as the 'Mad Mullah' by the British), the Dervish were defeated but the entrenchment of the British throughout the territory made a policy of limited engagement no longer possible. The conflict left the interior in 'violent turmoil', with 'nothing more tangible than a few ramshackle Ford cars and no decent roads or other means of communication' as the main legacy of the fighting.[59] The resources Britain committed to fighting the Dervish far exceed what the government in London had been willing to provide to the Protectorate, leaving no further funds for investment in the territory during the conflict. The twenty years of British neglect, however, did not mean that development of the territory did not take place as local economic, trade and development projects were initiated by Somalis in those areas not directly involved in the fighting.[60] The entrepreneurial Somalis in the western regions of the territory demonstrated the self-sufficiency of the Somaliland people, a trait that would again become apparent in the post-colonial era.

Following the defeat of the Dervish the British moved their administrative centre from the coastal port of Berbera to the interior city of Hargeisa, signalling their intention to shift their focus to establishing an authoritative presence throughout the entirety of the territory rather than only the coast. In the south, the heavily invested Italian colonisers ruled through both force and patronage, depending upon the Somali population for their plantation workforce. Through conscription, forced labour, displacement and financial incentives, the Italian administration disrupted pre-existing forms of social, economic and political control, especially that exercised by the clan. Infrastructural development deemed necessary for the economic benefit of the plantations was carried out, and rudimentary education enforced so as to ensure a trained pool of labour.[61] The British administration of the Protectorate, however, continued to resemble a form

---

on the Dervish War, see S. Touval, op. cit., pp. 56–7, 58–9; I.M. Lewis, *A Modern History*, op. cit., Chapter 3; E.S. Pankhurst, *Ex-Italian Somaliland* (London: Watts and Co., 1951), Chapter 3; APD, op. cit., pp. 11–12.

58 I.M. Lewis, *A Modern History*, op. cit., p. 85.

59 Douglas Jardine, Chief Secretary of the British Administration in the Somaliland Protectorate during the Dervish War, as quoted in I.M. Lewis, *A Modern History*, op. cit., p. 101; APD, op. cit., p. 11.

60 I.M. Lewis, *A Modern History*, op. cit., p. 102.

61 W. Reno, 'Somalia and Survival in the Shadow of the Global Economy', QEH Working Paper No. 100 (February 2003). I.M. Lewis, *A Modern History*, op. cit.; E.S. Pankhurst, op. cit.

of 'benign neglect' that was modestly focused on maintaining law and order and little else.[62] The colonial administration gradually introduced rudimentary social programmes in Somaliland, but little interest was shown in the development of the territory beyond building a few schools and clearing select roads between major population centres in the territory, all of which were paid for through a tax levied on livestock exports.[63] Haji Abdi Hussein recollects that under the British the clans were the primary social providers within the colony.[64] The minimalist policies in the area of development characterised the British colonisation of Somaliland, earning it the label 'the Cinderella of the British Empire'.[65]

The administrative structure of Britain's rule in Somaliland was based on similar structures found throughout British colonial possessions acquired during late colonialism in which traditional structures – in this instance the clan – were utilised in the administering of the territories, allowing for a minimalist British presence. At the beginning of colonial rule in the Somaliland Protectorate, only three British Residents, each in charge of one district, were present in the territory. At the time of independence, five residents were responsible for the administration of six districts.[66] As the clan system was not ruled by chiefs, though, there was not a strong basis for a true system of indirect rule. Like their counterparts in the south who bought compliance through the creation of titles,[67] the British administrators also fabricated titles, empowering titular clan leaders and elders of lineages to function as 'chiefs', thereby creating a structure of hierarchical rule. In addition, paid elders appointed by the British (*Akil*) were granted limited judicial powers and thus furnished a rudimentary system of subordinate courts based on a combination of English Common and Statute Law and customary Somali law. Separate courts run by Muslim magistrates (*Kadis*) were given authority over cases involving personal status or *shari'a* law.[68] In establishing these courts and in utilising and strengthening the system of *diya*-groups as enforcement mechanisms, the British

---

62 ICG, op. cit., p. 3; I.M. Lewis, *A Modern History*, op. cit., p. 105.

63 APD, op. cit., p. 12; ICG, op. cit., p. 3; I.M. Lewis, *A Modern History*, op. cit., pp. 101–3.

64 Haji Abdi Hussein, Member of Somaliland House of Elders. Interview with author (Hargeisa, September 2006).

65 I.M. Lewis, *Blood and Bone*, op. cit.; J. Drysdale, op. cit.

66 I.M. Lewis, *A Modern History*, op. cit., pp. 49, 133.

67 W. Reno, 'Somalia and Survival', op. cit.; I.M. Lewis, *A Modern History*, op. cit., pp. 98, 100. In the seven provinces and thirty-three districts, Italian Resident Commissioners were assisted by Somali 'chiefs'. The men who held this invented title were appointed by the Italians but did not necessarily hold positions of authority or influence in their clan. These men were highly paid by the Italians to be tools of the Italian administrators, and they were rewarded with financial incentives for cooperation and loyalty.

68 I.M. Lewis, *A Modern History*, pp. 105, 133–4, 170. These courts were replaced in 1945 by a new system of Subordinate Courts which consisted of a judge and assessors expert in Islamic and customary law as the previous system was seen as inefficient for the non-hierarchical Somali society.

administration ruled through an elaborate and exaggerated interpretation of Somali traditional governance that offered more control to the British administrators. Despite the intention of indirect rule and the utilisation of indigenous structures, as Lewis notes, the system in Somaliland closely resembled a more direct style of rule, although 'with lighter hand and more restricted purview' than their contemporaries in the Italian colony of Somalia.[69] The system of direct-indirect rule administered in Somaliland was difficult to execute and maintain, largely due to the continued British attitude of ambivalence towards the Protectorate but also because of the social structure of the Somalis themselves. The pervasiveness of the clan system continued to dictate social organisation through the clan system itself rather than through the British-created 'traditional' structure. Because of the continued practices of benign neglect and moderation, even with the newly created 'traditional' structures the clans were able to remain semi-autonomous throughout most of Somaliland provided they did not cause problems for the British. As a result, the clan continued to be the primary 'insurance policy' and agent of provision within British Somaliland, particularly in the areas outside of Hargeisa and the main port of Berbera.

Colonial rule in Somaliland was not consistent throughout the territory and an effective system of administration was difficult to establish. This was largely due to the minimalist British involvement and the nature of that involvement, but was also because of the nomadic lifestyle of the majority of Somalis in the territory. As they were not bound to permanent settlements and they were not forced or enticed away from their pastoral lifestyles as many Somalis were in the Italian colony, many Somalis had little or no contact with the British or those employed by the administration. As Lewis states, 'any radical changes would have required a much more strongly established administrative machine', which was something the British were not willing to provide to a territory that did not provide enough natural and commercial resources to cover the costs of the administration.[70] Because of the weak and inconsistent nature of British administration of the territory, the dominance of the clan governance system persisted in many areas, and many of the traditional practices continued relatively uninterrupted throughout the colonial rule.[71]

---

69 Ibid., p. 105. See also M. Bradbury, *Becoming Somaliland*, op. cit., Chapters 1 and 2; APD, op. cit., Chapter 1.

70 I.M. Lewis, *A Modern History*, op. cit.

71 Colonial newsletters from Somaliland indicate that amongst other things, in many cases peacemaking was still under the purview of clan elders rather than the British administration. For example, the October 1957 Protectorate Report discusses the ongoing work of local elders in resolving a conflict between the Habr Toljaala and the Habr Yunis near Burco. According to the report the negotiations also included elders from Berbera and were funded by local merchants. Although one British representative appears to have been present, the report shows that negotiating a peaceful settlement was left to the clans. UK Government, 'Peace Talks at Burao: No Agreement Reached but Discussions Continue', Protectorate Report No. 125 (19 October 1957).

Despite Britain's expressed policy of preparing possessions for eventual independence,[72] the British administrators in the Somaliland Protectorate practiced a relaxed and slow approach to decolonisation up to the day of independence on 26 June 1960. In July 1947 the British administration established the Protectorate Advisory Council which was composed of 'chiefs' and other clan representatives, representatives of the religious community, members of the Arab and Indian populations in the territory and British colonial officials. This council was the 'first step in the process of associating the Somalis with the government of the country'.[73] Somaliland political clubs were also formed, being parties in all but name.[74] In Somaliland, more autonomy was granted to the future Somali leaders than those under Italian rule experienced, where political association was closely guarded and controlled by the administrators. Despite relative freedom of political association and practice, though, executive and legislative power remained solely vested in the British Governor of the Protectorate until 1957.

Although the British administration did not have a scheduled independence day for the Protectorate, a United Nations established independence date for the Italian colony, together with increasing nationalistic pressure for quick post-independence unification of the Somali colonies, led to increasing demands for independence for the British Protectorate.[75] In 1956 the British government agreed to an accelerated schedule for self-government to coordinate with that in the south, and in 1957 preparations for self-government in Somaliland increased and executive and legislative councils were formed. A finalised independence date for Italian Somalia of 1 July 1960 adopted by the UN in December 1959 created increased pressure and haste to complete preparations in the north.[76] Although the British attempted to leave lasting democratic reforms in Somaliland during these rapid preparations, the short time frame and restricted resources, the legacy of neglect that had accumulated throughout the colonial period and the knowledge that Somaliland's independence would be short lived as it would unify with Somalia under the banner of Somali nationalism upon the latter's independence, led to few significant reforms.[77] Because of this and the general ambivalence

---

72 R. Johnson, *British Imperialism* (Basingstoke: Palgrave Macmillan, 2003), pp. 1–5.

73 UK Secretary of State for the Colonies, 'Report of the Somaliland Protectorate Constitutional Conference Held in London', Report presented to Parliament (May 1960), p. 3.

74 I.M. Lewis, *A Modern History*, op. cit.

75 I.M. Lewis, *A Modern History*, op. cit., p. 163; ICG, op. cit., p. 3. See also, G. Reece, 'Despatch to the Right Honourable Oliver Lyttelton, Secretary of State for the Colonies', Despatch No. 161/52 (9 March 1952).

76 UK Secretary of State for the Colonies, op. cit., pp. 3–4.

77 There was a small increase in educational provisions in Somaliland, primarily to educate future leaders in the ways of democracy, and there were some improvements to physical infrastructure. The British also created a legislative body that governed Somaliland for its five days of independence. Aside from this, however, impacts made in the sprint to

characterising the British rule of the territory, at the time of independence the traditional structures of governance in Somaliland, although certainly altered by the colonial experience, were not completely replaced by a foreign state structure. Thus there remained a level of autonomy between the small 'imposed' state and the traditional Somali structures and institutions of governance. This contrasted sharply with the experience of Italian Somalia, where a mixture of force and co-existence characterised colonial rule. The Italian administration relied much more heavily on bribery, enticements and patronage than the British did. Itself rooted in patronage based political and economic system, the Italian administration ruled through selective patronage backed by military force, and the administration on the whole was significantly disruptive to traditional Somali practices. This, coupled with a highly centralised and bureaucratic practice of governance typical of many settler colonies as well as Italy at the time, became a strong legacy of the Italian administration on southern Somalia.[78] The Italians also left southern Somalia with political, social, economic and physical infrastructures that were not consistent with those in the north.[79] Following the 1960 creation of Somalia, the physical, social, economic and political legacies of the Italians starkly contrasted to those of the British, and these divisions would arise as an obstacle to a successful and lasting unification of the two territories.

As early as 1943, calls for unification of the Somali people were being made within the Somali inhabited areas. The desire for unification was closely linked with the nationalist ideal of transcending 'tribalism' and abolishing 'wasteful' clan rivalries in order to allow for all the Somali populations to come together as a nation under one sovereign flag. Somali nationalists desired all the Somali inhabited territories to join together,[80] but British Somaliland and Italian Somalia were the only two to seek a union. The calls for Somali unification and the strengthening nationalist movements in both colonies were eventually supported by the colonisers and the United Nations.[81] Even with the knowledge that the

---

independence were minimal. For details of specific programmes, including the creation of a Protectorate Advisory Council that acted as a pre-independence legislative body, see I.M. Lewis, *A Modern History*, op. cit., Chapter 6. See also ICG, op. cit.; APD, op. cit.

78 S. Touval, op. cit.; W. Reno, 'Somalia and Survival', op. cit.; I.M. Lewis, *A Modern History*, op. cit.; E.S. Pankhurst, op. cit.

79 I.M. Lewis, *A Modern History*, p. 148. Although the two colonies had experienced different styles of rule, and both colonial powers had knowledge of the intentions for unification, there was little cooperation between British and Italian authorities prior to independence and unification.

80 On the flag of Somalia, each of the five points of the star represent a Somali inhabited territory: northern Kenya, the Ogaden in Ethiopia, Djibouti, Somalia and Somaliland.

81 The British were initially hesitant about unifying the Somali territories. As late as January 1960 British administrators continued to express concern over extreme nationalist calls, particularly in regards to inclusion of the Somali in Ethiopia and French Somaliland (Djibouti), where the British believed very little interest in a unified Somalia existed. They were also hesitant about the Somali inhabited areas of Kenya being absorbed into

differing colonial experiences and legacies would pose structural and logistical problems, a quick unification was pushed for by all parties involved with the expectation that the differences in the administrative traditions and experiences of the two territories would 'sort themselves out afterwards'.[82] The British Somaliland Protectorate was granted independence on 26 June 1960. Following Italian Somalia's independence on 1 July 1960 the two united to form the state of Somalia.[83] The nationalistic motivations behind the unification, however, recognised little more than the aspiration for a unified Somali nation. The union of two former colonies with varied histories proved to be unstable, despite the commonality of ethnicity, and within the first year exhibited signs of the eventual break-up of Somalia. The collapse of Somalia progressed through two distinct eras: the initial period of unification and democratic government; the rule of Siad Barre; and the 1991 coup. The subsequent collapse of the state will be discussed in the following chapter. Experiences during these eras not only impacted upon mechanisms and expectations of governance, including sub-state governance, in the state, but also laid the foundations for an emerging Somaliland identity.

The Acts of Union, Democracy and Clan Politics

Three weeks following the unification of the two former colonies a central state government was in place in Mogadishu in the new state of Somalia. The new state's dual colonial heritage posed numerous problems, however. Indeed, 'the process of unification was anything but smooth … the former Italian colony and trust territory in the south and the former British protectorate in the north were, from an institutional standpoint, two separate countries',[84] meaning the 'mechanics of establishing a unitary administration were daunting'.[85] Leading up to 1 July, important logistical and technical questions pertaining to the unification of two

---

Somalia. The British administrators did, however, agree to the union between Somaliland and Italian Somalia. P. Carrel, 'Ministry of Defence and External Affairs Internal Memo Hargeisa to London', Memo SD/EA/18/8/6 (3 March 1960); D. Hall, 'Inward Telegram to the Secretary of State for the Colonies from Somaliland Protectorate', Telegram No. 34 (16–17 January 1960); D. Hall, 'Inward Telegram to the Secretary of State for the Colonies From Somaliland Protectorate', Telegram No. 50 (25 January 1960); W. Luce, 'Colonial Office Internal Memo Aden to London', Memo GH/8/21/2/54 (23 January 1960); J. Selwyn Lloyd, 'British Consulate General Mogadishu Despatch to London', Despatch No. 6 (21 January 1960).

82 I.M. Lewis, *A Modern History*, op. cit., p. 162.

83 The Somali nationalist cause aspired for a unification of all the Somali inhabited territories in the Horn of Africa. Following the independence of Kenya and Djibouti, and the defeat of Somali forces in the Ogaden region of Ethiopia, it was apparent that the Somali state would consist only of the former British and Italian colonies.

84 ICG, op. cit., p. 4.

85 J. Drysdale, op. cit., p. 76.

vastly different territories were 'suppressed rather than worked out openly'.[86] In addition to differing legacies resulting from the different colonial administrations, the unified state was also facing problems resulting from logistical and institutional variations such as unequal economic, social and political infrastructures; a lack of roads and communications links between Hargeisa and Mogadishu; and even different operating languages of English in the north and Italian in the south. The nationalist motivations for unification were consistent with post-independence Pan-African movements, but the consequences of the immediate unification of significantly differing territories had lasting impacts on the state as unification never fully occurred. The powerful drive of Somali nationalism was not enough to ensure the survival of the state, and problems soon became apparent.

Prior to independence, colonial and Somali leaders from the north and the south met in Mogadishu to formulate a plan for unification and to create the framework for a unified government and two separate Acts of Union – one specific to the north and one to the south to be ratified by respective parliaments – were drawn up. The result of these negotiations, a new democratic system of government, was considered to 'represent a reasonable balance of northern and southern interests'.[87] For six months following unification, the two separate Acts of Union constituted the only legal binding between the two territories. Although both territories had agreed to the negotiated balance between north and south in the new government, what emerged after unification heavily favoured the south in not only representation in the Somalia parliament, but also in terms of logistical infrastructure as the administrative and economic centre of state was in the extreme southern city of Mogadishu.[88] Because of the different practices of the two colonial powers, few transportation and communications links existed between the north and south, making the new capital of Mogadishu distant and difficult to reach from the main northern city of Hargeisa.[89] It was difficult to overlook that politics was centralised in Mogadishu, and coupled with northern marginalisation in allocation of government spending, the unparalleled economic and social opportunities

---

86 M. Brons, *Society, Security, Sovereignty and the State in Somalia* (Utrecht: International Books, 2001), p. 161.

87 I.M. Lewis, *A Modern History*, op. cit., p. 165.

88 The immediate post-independence government was a unitary republic based on parliamentary democracy. Of the 123 members of the new unicameral Somalia parliament, only thirty-three represented the former British Protectorate. Of the initial fourteen ministerial posts, only four were held from men from the 'Northern Regions'. I. Kaplan, et al. (eds), *Area Handbook for Somalia* (Washington DC: Foreign Affairs Studies, 1969); APD, op. cit., p. 9; I.M. Lewis, *A Modern History (2002)*, op. cit., p. 164. Lewis notes that in the newly unified state, the former British Protectorate was referred to as the 'Northern Regions', whilst the former Italian colony was the 'Southern Regions'.

89 APD, op. cit., p. 12; ICG, op. cit., p. 4; I.M. Lewis, *A Modern History*, op. cit., pp. 165, 170–72; M. Mukhtar, 'Somalia: Between Self-Determination and Chaos', in H. Adam and R. Ford (eds), *Mending the Rips in the Sky: Options for Somali Communities in the 21st Century* (Lawrenceville, NJ: The Red Sea Press, 1997), pp. 49–64: pp. 51–3.

created in the southern city led to a social and economic decline in the cities in the north, especially Hargeisa.[90] The former northern capital 'had declined to a mere provincial headquarters remote from the centre of things ... northern pride found it hard to match this reduction in prestige'.[91] Whilst inequality of representation and participation, as well as the distance between north and south were not seen as problematic in the period immediately following unification, the significant benefits given to the south at the expense of the north would become a contentious issue in the future and would contribute to a sense of isolation in the former British Protectorate. With the majority of political seats being held by southern Italian trained politicians, coupled with economic and social marginalisation, it was not surprising that the former Somaliland Protectorate – the only Somali territory that 'heeded the nationalist call' from the south to relinquish sovereign independence – was frustrated by the lack of benefits received compared to what many believed was their sacrifice.[92]

The two separate Acts of Union were significant in highlighting the division between north and south in the new state as the two separate Acts were just that – two separate Acts. Upon unification, the new Somalia parliament did not ratify an amalgamated act.[93] When this oversight was discovered in 1961, the legislature in Mogadishu repealed the previous two Acts of Union and a new, single and retrospective act was created. However, its acceptance by the southern dominated legislature did not reflect the extreme opposition to it from the north. When a referendum was held on the new act in June 1961, despite a northern boycott of the vote 100,000 votes were cast in the former Protectorate, of which more than 60 per cent were against it. The 'union between the two countries quickly lost its bloom' as northern discontent over the unfair unification became increasingly apparent.[94] The referendum thus became a test of confidence in the new government and, by extension, in the union itself. As the initial euphoria created by Somali nationalism faded and the realities of the uneven distribution in the new state became more apparent, and codified in the new Act of Union, the population of the former Protectorate gained a 'more sober appreciation of the true situation' of southern

---

90 Haji Abdi Hussein, Member of the Somaliland House of Elders. Interview with author (Hargeisa, September 2006); Mohammed Said Mohammed Gees, Executive Director, Somaliland Academy for Peace and Development/Former Somaliland Government Minister (various posts). Interview with author (Hargeisa, September 2006); APD, op. cit., pp. 9–11.

91 J. Drysdale, op. cit., p. 78; I.M. Lewis, *The Modern History*, op. cit.; APD, op. cit., p. 9. Distance measured on a map between Hargeisa and Mogadishu equates to roughly 1500 kilometres through Somali territory (shorter if travelling through Ethiopia). The distance, according to Drysdale, is roughly equivalent to the distance between Berlin and Rome.

92 Haji Abdi Hussein, Interview with author (Hargeisa, September 2006); I.M. Lewis, *The Modern History*, op. cit., p. 172.

93 ICG, op. cit., p. 4.

94 APD, op. cit., p. 14; D. Laitin and S. Samatar, *Somalia: Nation in Search of a State* (Boulder, CO: Westview Press, 1987), pp. 70–71; J. Drysdale, op. cit., p. 77.

dominance in the new state.[95] The vote in the north thus reflected 'widespread discontent in the Northern Region over the economic decline there, and over the growing political influence in Mogadishu'.[96] This northern dissatisfaction was further emphasised in December 1961 when northern army officers, unhappy with the dominance of southern leaders in the Somalia military, attempted a coup aimed at ending the unification.[97] The dissatisfaction of the army officers who staged the coup mirrored the dissatisfaction of the people of Somaliland, and according to Lewis, the coup attempt was widely regarded as a signal of extreme disapproval of the union and as an attempt at secession.[98] As the uneven distribution of government power became more apparent, many in the north became more disenchanted and feelings of neglect and isolation grew.

Bringing together the two Somali territories had 'at once a profound effect on Somali politics'.[99] Prior to unification, both territories had discussed the problem of 'clannism', and the new leaders of the state identified clan association as an obstacle to Somali unification as it was believed that a strong association with particular clans would prevent the creation of a unified Somali identity. The reaction to this was an attempt to separate clan politics from national politics. In trivialising and sometimes vilifying clan politics the new leaders attempted to remove the intrinsic method of identification for the Somali from the political arena. As the anti-clan movement intensified, the traditional nature of Somali politics and social control became increasingly targeted. Rather than eliminating the 'clan problem', though, this created a realisation on an unofficial level that 'there could be no doubt of their [clan associations] continuing importance in the political life of the new state'.[100] Politicians soon learned that they had to utilise bonds of kinship to achieve desired political aims and to maintain their positions, and as a result clan politics became inseparable from the running of the Somalia government. As Lewis notes, there was danger in enmeshing party politics in the contentious Somali clan system in that personal or clan gain would be put above the best interests of the state, resulting in a corrupt system with an abundance of clan dominated political parties dependent upon ancient clan allegiances for

---

95 APD, op. cit., p. 14.
96 S. Touval, op. cit., p. 121.
97 I.M. Lewis, *A Modern History*, op. cit., p. 172.
98 Ibid., p. 174; J. Drysdale, op. cit., p. 77. The eighteen officers who led the coup were arrested shortly afterwards and put on trial for treason. The British judge presiding over the trial dismissed the case on the grounds that there was no legitimate Act of Union at that point in time, thereby raising questions as to the legality of the southern presence in the north. Although this ruling was not regarded as significantly important at the time, contemporary calls for recognition of independence in Somaliland refer back to this early decision.
99 Ibid., p. 166.
100 Ibid., p. 167.

political gain.[101] Further, this changed the role of the clan from one of mostly social control over a limited population linked by kinship to that of state-level control over a vast and diverse population.

This new large-scale system of centralised clan association had a significant impact on the power balance between the clans, as the new democratic system politicised them in a way never previously experienced. As Lewis notes, 'despite the patriotic fervour ... the all-pervasive element in politics remained the loyalty of the individual to his kin and clan'. The unification of the two territories into one political entity 'entailed significant, and in some cases quite drastic changes in the political status of the various clans and lineages within the state'.[102] Despite what were believed to be modernising influences, such as the establishment of national political parties and the proliferation of education, identification with the clan remained the primary allegiance and the centre of life for the majority of the population. In the north, a considerable majority belonged to the Isaaq clan, making it a powerful force in the former Protectorate. However, the Isaaq are a very small minority outside of the Protectorate, meaning that in a unified Somalia they were significantly overpowered by the southern clans. The reduction in political status of the Isaaq clan impacted upon the position of the north in the increasingly clan-based political realm.[103] Clan and regional animosities arose as certain clans were able to exert more control than others, creating instability within the new government, the state and society. As power centralised in Mogadishu and as politics and the government became increasingly nepotistic and inseparable from the clans, the north became increasingly isolated.

During the nine years of the democratic government in Somalia, unification of the two former colonies was never fully achieved and perceptions of northern inequality added to the mix of dissatisfaction throughout the state. In the attempt to rid Somalia of clan identities and to replace them with the idea of a Somali nation, what was instead created was a system of politics plagued by nepotistic clan-based party politics that left the new state with a 'morass of poverty, insecurity and inefficiency'. Throughout Somalia the democratic government was viewed as a 'sordid market-place' where politicians openly engaged in bribery and embezzlement and who bolstered their own personal and clan coffers by

---

101   I.M. Lewis, *A Modern History*, op. cit., p. 166; I.M. Lewis, 'The Recent Political History of Somalia', in K. Barcik and S. Normark (eds), *Somalia: A Historical, Culture and Political Analysis* (Uppsala: Life and Peace Institute, 1991), pp. 5–15: p. 5. See also, M. Mukhtar, op. cit., pp. 52–3.

102   I.M. Lewis, *A Modern History*, op. cit., p. 166.

103   Ibid.; M. Brons, op. cit.; M. Bradbury, *Becoming Somaliland*, op. cit.; M. Bradbury, 'Somaliland Country Report', Report for CIIR (1997); A. Samatar, *Socialist Somalia: Rhetoric and Reality* (London: Zed Books, 1988); A. Samatar and A. Samatar, 'International Crisis Group Report on Somaliland: An Alternative Response', *Bildhaan* 5.1 (2005), pp. 107–24.

funnelling state funds and resources into personal accounts.[104] Disenchantment was no longer limited to the former British Protectorate, as people throughout Somalia grew increasingly frustrated by the corruption of the government.

Even though the democratic government in Somalia was short lived, the isolation of the north under this government would not soon be forgotten. Because of the fragmented and decentralised nature of the Somali population, the north and south were not a unified entity prior to colonisation, and when the two territories came together following independence it was an artificial unification based on nationalistic motivations rather than a historical claim or political cohesiveness.[105] Combined with corruption, nepotism and divisive clan politics, post-independence Somalia was a volatile entity. Whilst the separation between north and south that became apparent in the early years of the new state was not enough to end the unification, it did lay the foundations for the eventual division of the state. This is not to say that the isolation of the north was a pre-requisite for the state's collapse, but rather the continuation of these divisions was 'sowing the seeds of growing Northern discontent with the union ... leading, nearly three decades later, to its dissolution'.[106] The break-up of Somalia, whether inevitable or not, was certainly hastened by the rule of Siad Barre and the impacts of that on northern Somalia.

Siad Barre and the Manipulation of the Clan

In October 1969 the Somalia army staged a coup, after which rule by a Supreme Revolutionary Council headed by army commander General Mohammed Siad Barre was established. Rather than offering solutions to the problems that plagued Somalia, though, Barre's increasingly repressive rule, nationalistic motivations for conquest and unsound economic policies exacerbated the cracks already apparent in Somalia. In addition, Barre's twenty-two year rule had a lasting impact on the placement of the clans in society, and his practices also significantly widened the gap between the north and the south. As Dool states, under Barre, 'Somalis in the North were made second-class citizens in their own homeland'.[107]

---

104   I.M. Lewis, *A Modern History*, op. cit., pp. 205–6.
105   See H. Adam and R. Ford (eds), op. cit.; H. Adam, et al. (eds), *War Destroys, Peace Nurtures: Somali Reconciliation and Development* (Lawrenceville, NJ: The Red Sea Press, 2004); I.M. Lewis, *Blood and Bone*, op. cit.; M. Bradbury, *Becoming Somaliland*, op. cit.; P. Gilkes, 'Descent into Chaos: Somalia, January 1991–December 1992', in C. Gurden (ed.), *The Horn of Africa* (London: UCL Press, 1994), pp. 47–60 ; G. Prunier, 'Somaliland: birth of a new country?' in C. Gurden (ed.), *The Horn of Africa* (London: UCL Press, 1994), pp. 61–75; J. Drysdale, op. cit.
106   APD, op. cit., p. 10.
107   A. Dool, 'Good Governance: Self-Administering Regions within a Democratic Union', *Somalia* No. 4 (June 2001), pp. 5–36: p. 9.

Following the experience of corruption under the democratic government, Barre swept into power vowing the cleanse Somalia's political realm of corruption and nepotism and vowing to establish a 'just and honourable society' in which attention would be given to 'real economic and social betterment for all'.[108] A major component of Barre's rule was the revival of notions Somali nationalism, reiterating calls for a unification of all Somalis under a single flag free of clan and territorial divisions. Many Somalis welcomed the coup, but within a year Barre had eliminated the democratic structures of government, turning Somalia into a one-party state based on his own style of Scientific Socialism.[109] It was through this that he established an environment of fear and repression, drawing on language and practices that were reminiscent of Stalin, Mao and Kim Il Sung.[110] Under Barre, Somalia quickly transformed from a state plagued by corruption in the democratic government to a state plagued by corruption and violence in the one-party regime. As much of the history of Somalia in current literature begins with a detailed account of the 1969 coup,[111] a detailed history of Barre's rule is not offered here. What needs to be examined, however, is the impact of his rule on the clan and governance structures within Somali society and within the north.

Barre's solution to the destructive clannism plaguing the previous government was detribalisation, or ridding Somalia of clans and clan associations.[112] The stated desired outcome of this policy was similar to that of the democratic government in its own attempt to remove the clan from politics: a united Somali society. Barre's policy differed, though, in that he enforced detribalisation with an iron-fist rather than through legislation. Barre viewed the Somali clans as a 'perversely persistent force',[113] and any mention of clan association or membership was outlawed as a political offence punishable by death. High levels of surveillance became prevalent throughout the state, monitoring the Somali people for treasonous acts such as clan loyalty or even mentioning clan names. Barre's vision of a Greater Somalia 'demanded the dismantling of the traditional clan-based social order, economic networks and political institutions upon which the majority of Somalis still depended' in order to change the object of loyalty in Somalia from the clan to the whole, and later to him alone.[114] By forcibly dismantling and outlawing

---

108 I.M. Lewis, *A Modern History*, op. cit., p. 207.
109 ICG, op. cit., p. 4.
110 APD, op. cit., p. 15; I.M. Lewis, *A Modern History*, op. cit., pp. 210–11. The population of Somalia was issued blue and white pocket manuals similar to the Little Red Book of Maoist China, Barre's sayings were prominently displayed and spread, and Barre portrayed himself as the 'Father' of Somalia. His public appearances were full of pomp and circumstance, adoration, and the sense of fatherly love. Barre even went as far as creating a new 'holy trinity', placing himself in the ranks with Marx and Lenin.
111 See I.M. Lewis, *A Modern History*, op. cit., Chapter 9; ICG, op. cit., pp. 5–6; APD, op. cit., pp. 15–16.
112 The exception to this was for those lineages associated with Barre's close family.
113 I.M. Lewis, *A Modern History*, op. cit., p. 220.
114 APD, op. cit., p. 15.

clan association and identification, Barre further altered traditional systems of governance and control. The system of forced nationalistic loyalty did not erase divisions within society, but it did create a means through which Barre could enforce his rule.

Even though Barre publically and legally demonised the clan, personally he still heavily relied on the politicisation of the clan as a means of social and political control. He increasingly elevated his own lineage and placed his own clan members into high positions, drawing on family allegiance and patronage politics to ensure loyalty from the top members of his regime. Those who were not loyal or were suspected of being subversive were killed or imprisoned and replaced with another member of Barre's lineage, or with a member of a clan that needed to be appeased.[115] In addition to using clan politics to maintain his regime, Barre also used links through his maternal Ogadeni lineage to rally Somali nationalism in Ethiopia, eventually leading to Somalia's involvement in the Ogaden War, and used his son-in-law's northern lineage to contain friction between the north and south of Somalia.[116] Forcibly co-opted clan elders – renamed 'peacemakers' – were placed within the state bureaucracy to be used as a means of further societal control.[117] Whereas the clan was outlawed for ordinary Somalis, for Barre manipulating its structures was a vital tool with which to sustain his regime. Rather than ridding Somalia of destructive clannism, Barre's manipulation, similar to that practiced by the Italian colonisers, depended on bribery, brute force and fear to control the population. Interestingly, though, as Barre became more brutal, the influence of kinship re-emerged in many areas as people turned to the clan for provision and protection. This was especially true in the north where the brutality of Barre's regime was disproportionately felt, but also where, because of geographical distance, the population was more isolated from the day-to-day activities of the regime than those living closer to Mogadishu.

Despite calling for a Greater Somalia, Barre did not aim to unite all the Somali territories but instead focused specifically on annexing the Ogaden region of Ethiopia.[118] In this quest Barre involved Somalia in the separatist struggles of two Somali movements in the Ogaden: the Somali-Abo Liberation Front (SALF) and the Western Somalia Liberation Front (WSLF). With one of the largest and best equipped armies in Africa, Barre exercised his nationalistic plans almost solely through force, and by 1977 a full-scale war had broken out between Ethiopia and

---

115 I.M. Lewis, *A Modern History*, op. cit., pp. 207–8; W. Reno, 'Somalia and Survival', op. cit., pp. 18–20.
116 W. Reno, 'Somalia and Survival', op. cit., p. 22.
117 M. Bradbury, 'Peace-enforcement, Peace-making, Peace-building', op. cit., p. 10.
118 I.M. Lewis, *A Modern History*, op. cit., p. 221. Desire to place this region under Somali control can be traced back to 1886, and was once again brought into contention during the 1960s at the height of Somali nationalism. Lewis speculates that Barre's focus on the Ogaden was largely due to his kinship link to the region through his maternal lineage.

Somalia.[119] Somalia lost the war, and the defeat 'decisively buried the dream of a pan-Somali state'.[120] Devastating to the ethos of a single Somali state that had brought the former Protectorate into the union, the Ogaden War not only marked the beginning of the end for the Barre regime and the Somali state, but it also aggravated those existent feelings of mistrust between the north and the south.[121]

All of Somalia felt the impacts of the Ogaden War, but due to its geographical proximity to the fighting the northern region experienced the majority of the physical and human destruction. It also absorbed large numbers of Somali refugees fleeing Ethiopia, overwhelming the population of the region. Approximately a quarter of a million refugees were settled in the north by the United Nations High Commissioner for Refugees with the approval of the Somalia government, and overflow from designated refugee camps spilled into the major cities creating chaotic conditions.[122] As international aid was funnelled into the area, aid resources earmarked for the refugees became a source of envy and resentment for local residents as no compensation was given to them for bearing the burden of the war. To further problems and resentment, following the end of hostilities Barre heavily favoured the Ogaden refugees, most of whom were members of his lineage. In addition to government and aid resources, the refugees also enjoyed preferential access to social services, business licenses and even government posts.[123] As expressed animosity and discontent in the north grew, refugee militias were created and armed by the Barre government to quell any rebellion and to protect the refugees, thereby creating a dangerous and hostile situation in the northwest.[124] In what was essentially buying off the Ogaden refugees through continued preferential treatment and protection, Barre was ensuring their loyalty to his regime at the expense of the Isaaq who were not only bypassed for economic, social and political advancement, but in many cases were also forcefully suppressed by both the Somalia army and the refugee militias. This practice gave Barre a power base

---

119 W. Reno, 'Somalia and Survival', op. cit.; Haji Abdi Hussein, Interview with Author (Hargeisa, September 2006), op. cit.; Abdirahman Aw Ali Farah, Former Somaliland Vice President (SNM Administration)/Former SNM Commander, Interview with author (Hargeisa, September 2006). By the time of the military coup that brought Barre to power, the Somali state was already heavily dependent on foreign financial assistance. Barre's regime further entrenched this need for aid and from the beginning was heavily dependent on support from the Soviet Union. With Soviet assistance, Barre was able to build a very large and well-equipped army, making it one of the largest military forces in Africa.

120 APD, op. cit., p. 11.

121 G. Prunier, 'A Candid View of the Somali National Movement', *Horn of Africa* 14.1–2 (1991), pp. 107–20; G. Prunier, 'Somaliland Goes It Alone' *Current History* 97.619 (1998), pp. 107–20; APD, op. cit., p. 11.

122 ICG, op. cit., p. 12.

123 Ibid., p. 5; For a more complete explanation of the impact of the Ogaden War, see I.M. Lewis, *A Modern History*, op. cit.; A.M. Issa-Salwe, *The Collapse of the Somali State: The Impact of the Colonial Legacy* (London: HAAN Associates, 1996).

124 APD, op. cit., p. 12.

in the northwest, a region of Somalia where he had never been able to fully exert his power. However, it also exacerbated the division between the north – primarily the Isaaq – and the southern regime and led the population in Somaliland to begin taking steps to fight back.

The increased militarisation through the formation of refugee militias complemented Barre's already violent handling of the northwest region and the 'rebellious' Isaaq, as well as his increasingly centralised regime which depended largely on kinship and bought loyalties.[125] During and following the Ogaden War, Barre had suspected the Isaaq of supporting and assisting Ethiopian forces, even though many in the northwest initially and enthusiastically backed Somalia's war effort.[126] This suspicion was a key factor in Barre's often violent treatment of the northwest, and after its defeat in the Ogaden the regime became 'even more repressive' as the primary method of exercising power in the northwest.[127] As such, '[t]ensions between the local inhabitants and the refugees were just a symptom of the government's cynical manipulation of kinship divisions within Somali society for the purposes of divide and rule'.[128] In the case of the north, this tactic was characterised by brutality and violence targeting the Isaaq and carried out by those benefiting from Barre's patronage practices.[129]

By early 1978, the regime had concentrated Somalia's economic resources, including large amounts of foreign aid, in its hands, 'using selective redistribution to ensure loyalty to the regime'.[130] By the end of his rule Barre had isolated himself in his small resource-rich inner circle, turning the one-party Somali state into a one-man state.[131] Increasing economic neglect and deprivation, stringent controls on trade, increasing centralisation of administrative functions in Mogadishu, and the growing brutality of the Barre regime, both from the army as well as from the Barre-supported refugee militias, again exacerbated the widening gap between the north and the south. Exacerbated by the political, social and economic isolation and maltreatment of the north, reliance on the clan increased in the former Protectorate, and as relations between the government in Mogadishu and the former British Protectorate worsened following the Ogaden War and during Barre's well-documented violent campaign in the territory prior to and during the

---

125 Somaliland Academy for Peace and Development (APD), *A Self-Portrait of Somaliland: Rebuilding from the Ruins*, Centre Report (December 1999), p. 17; W. Reno, 'Somalia and Survival', op. cit., p. 17.

126 ICG, op. cit., p. 2; APD, *Rebuilding Somaliland*, op. cit., p. 11.

127 G. Prunier, 'Somaliland Goes it Alone', op. cit., p. 226.

128 APD, 'A Self-Portrait', op. cit., p. 17.

129 Many Somalilanders, as well as some scholars, claim that between the end of the Ogaden War and the end of the Somali civil war, Barre engaged in a genocidal campaign against the Isaaq in the northwest. Although this has never been officially labelled genocide, physical evidence of torture and mass killings of Isaaq have been found in Somaliland, particularly in and around Hargeisa.

130 APD, 'A Self-Portrait of Somaliland', op. cit., p. 17.

131 I.M. Lewis, *A Modern History*, op. cit., p. 248.

civil war, clan identification became a vital tool in the struggle against the dictator. Amongst other factors, the resurgence of the clan system added to stability in the north creating a basis for a clan-based liberation movement as well as for the eventual establishment of governance and government. This re-emergence of the clan system will be examined in greater detail in the next chapter.

Conclusions

Almost immediately from unification the fragility of the state of Somalia was apparent. As Menkhaus simply states, '[t]he Somali state was a castle built on sand'.[132] Colonial legacies, nationalist aspirations, corrupt government and politicisation of the clan system contributed to the rise of Barre, which in turn led to increasingly militarised and violent government and a further demonisation of the clan. However, despite attempts to repress it, the centrality of the clan in many areas persisted throughout the colonial and post-independence eras. As Luling identifies, politicians could not manipulate clan divisions if those ties were not a 'reality in peoples' minds and lives'.[133] It is interesting to note that in both the colonial and the post-colonial regimes, the clan was used as a component of social and political control. More so, in both pre-1991 post-colonial regimes, clannism was discouraged or outlawed, yet in both instances there was a heavy investment and entrenchment of the clan in politics and as a mechanism of governance, arguably out of necessity for the establishment and maintenance of political and social control. Attempts to divorce it from either politics or its larger embodiment, government, failed. As will be seen in the next chapter, this was especially the case in the former British Protectorate during the Barre regime. Indeed, coupled with a sense of persecution and an intense divide between north and south, the clan provided fertile ground for the establishment of armed reaction to Barre; action which would eventually lead to the establishment of an independent Somaliland.

On 18 May 1991, the former British Protectorate of Somaliland declared its independence from the troubled state of Somalia and has since functioned as an unrecognised state, balancing the demands of international expectations of statehood with domestic necessities for stability. Although Somaliland officially declared its intention to separate from Somalia in 1991, the build-up to this action began almost from the outset of the unification that created the state. States and territories do not simply break-up often, and lasting claims of independence are rare. Whilst this chapter addressed the broad, overall problems with the union itself and the placement of the clan in society and governance leading up to the 1991 breakup of Somalia, the next chapter continues in focusing on the specifics pertaining to Somaliland in the context of its declaration of independence and its

---

132 K. Menkhaus, op. cit., p. 220.
133 V. Luling, 'Come Back Somalia? Questioning a Collapsed State', *Third World Quarterly* 18.2 (1997), pp. 287–302: pp. 289–90.

process of statebuilding. Whilst undeniably a historical offering, the following chapter also establishes the foundations upon which the state of Somaliland are laid; foundations that not only have supported the long statebuilding process, but that have also supported a stable and growing state out of the political chaos that characterises the archetypal failed state: Somalia.

Chapter 5

The Emergence of the New State

The extreme militarisation of society and the collapse of Somalia's central government have garnered much attention in contemporary literature, particularly within those works concerned with failed states. Somalia is often regarded as the archetypal case of state failure, as since 1991 no lasting or legitimately accepted government has existed to organise and run what are considered to be normal state affairs. Even though Somalia lacks a central government, the state does not persist in anarchy as pockets of governance have emerged from the clan system, religious movements and even the militarised movements to provide public and political goods within and throughout Somalia.

By the time of the 1991 collapse and failure of the state, a significant change in Somali society was the channels through which the clans interacted. Competition over political and economic resources determined interactions, just as they had done in the pre-colonial era when grazing and water resources were the point of contention. With insertion into the international system of states and with a highly militarised society, though, the methods and objectives of these contests, and the role of the clan within them, had changed. Once primarily an agent of societal stability and governance maintained through negotiated co-existence and appeasement, in post-1991 Somalia many of the clans in the south became associated with the existence of warlords who had played on clan divisions for their own rise, even though the warlords were not necessarily a component of the clan. In parts of Somalia, particularly in the south-central regions where the clan system had been most disrupted through the previous eras of rule, the warlords and subsequent militarised movements became the substitute for the state. In other areas, particularly Somaliland, Puntland and northern regions in southern Somalia, however, the clan system remained more intact and therefore maintained more of a position of power within society. Within and below the large-scale struggles for power in Somalia, the traditional clan system provide Somali society with traditional forms of governance in a 'stateless' state.[1]

In spite of attempts at or success in disrupting clan control, outside of the central political realm Somalis throughout most of the country continued to turn to their clans for survival and protection when life got tough. Menkhaus identifies a 'radical localisation' of the political landscape within Somalia, with collective security ensured through local structures such as the clan as well as through *shari'a* courts in neighbourhoods and villages, and even through locally

---

1 K. Menkhaus, 'Somalia: Political Order in a Stateless Society', *Current History* 97.619 (1998), pp. 220–24: p. 223.

created and supported police forces.[2] In the economic sector, the 'wide-ranging kinship system that facilitates personal contacts and strategic relationships' helped establish a 'second economy' within Somalia.[3] Grassroots developmental projects in large cities such as Hargeisa and Borama, largely funded by clan-associated remittance money from members of the Somali Diaspora, provide development of physical infrastructure as well as social services such as health care and education within those northern cities.[4] In many areas of Somalia, including areas where violent contestation between both intra-Somali parties as well as between external actors and Somali parties continues to be violent and destructive, the clan system has filled the vacancy left by the absence of government and uncontested political and social control. In most instances these are isolated pockets of governance. However, clan governance does play a large role in larger organised governments as well.

Just as the political situation in Somalia and Somaliland cannot be understood without first understanding the social and political forces that shaped it, neither can the statebuilding process in Somaliland be understood without first examining the circumstances surrounding the declaration of independence forces surrounding and underpinning the creation of the new state. States and territories do not simply break-up often, and lasting claims of independence are rare. The creation of a new, and especially stable or peaceful, state is even rarer. This chapter focuses on the period of Somaliland's declaration of independence during a time of collapse in Somalia, the foundations for the institutional state and the initial stages of institutional statebuilding. Central to this process was bringing together the 'old' and the 'new' mechanisms of governance – balancing the internal and external demands – within the emerging government. Doing this, however, resulted not only in the establishing of institutions, but also a locally owned state. Whilst this chapter focuses on the institutional component of statebuilding, the following chapter has a specific focus on the clan as a stabilising and facilitating actor in the legitimising of the state during the statebuilding, and indeed nation-building or identity-building, process. The role of clans in Somaliland is central to understanding the development of the state in Somaliland.

The Rise of the Somali National Movement and the Fall of Siad Barre

In response to the increasing centralisation of resources and power under Siad Barre, as well as increasing governmental brutality against anyone suspected of being disloyal to the dictator, the Somalis turned to their clans for not only basic needs, but also for protection from Barre's government troops. A number of

---

2 K. Menkhaus, op. cit.
3 See P. Little, *Somalia: Economy Without a State* (Oxford: James Currey, 2003), quote at p. xv.
4 ICG, op. cit., p. 7; APD, op. cit., Chapter 3; K. Menkhaus, op. cit., p. 223.

failed coup attempts after the Ogaden War caused Barre to tighten his hold on the population through heightened reprisal violence and pre-emptive persecutions.[5] To counter the well-armed military, many clans and sub-clans formed their own militias for the protection of their people and resources, and armed resistance groups emerged throughout the state. These bands of militias were a key component of the overthrow of Barre as they actively sought regime change in the state. In the former British Protectorate, the largest and strongest militia was the Isaaq-led Somali National Movement (SNM).

The liberation struggle in Somaliland began with the April 1981 formation of the SNM in London. Formed from a succession of various political organisations created by Isaaq businessmen, students, former civil servants and former politicians who were living in the United Kingdom, the SNM emerged following the merger of the UK organisations with similar groups from Saudi Arabia and the United Arab Emirates. The initial intent of the political organisations preceding the SNM was not to become an armed liberation front. Rather, these groups formed in response to new policies enacted by Barre which were viewed as direct attacks on Isaaq living abroad. Following a meeting of the newly formed SNM Congress in October 1981, however, the official position changed to one of liberation, with the expressed aim of ridding Somalia of Barre and instituting a democratic government in Somalia that would be inclusive of and based on the clan system.[6] According to Lewis, upon its formation the SNM 'articulated Isaaq grievances ranging from inadequate political representation, neglect in development, and the frustration of local businessmen and exporters chafing at economic controls'.[7] These grievances also included violent and repressive tactics used by the Barre regime in the north. From the outset, the SNM conveyed that even though it was primarily an Isaaq movement and at the start membership and leadership of the SNM was almost exclusively limited to the Isaaq clan,[8] it was fighting for all of Somalia and as such it would eventually coordinate its efforts with its counterparts in the south. The SNM was fighting for the overthrow of Barre, not the independence of Somaliland.

The SNM was one of two political units to emerge from the clan militias, the other being the Hawiye-based United Somali Congress (USC), led by General Mohammed Farah Aideed. Structurally and logistically, the SNM was both a political and military organisation formed within the Isaaq population. The movement consisted of two separate wings: a political wing tasked with making necessary political decisions and garnering logistical and physical support for

---

5 Mohammed Said Mohammed Gees, Executive Director, Somaliland Academy for Peace and Development/Former Somaliland Government Minister (various posts). Interview with author (Hargeisa, September 2006).

6 Somaliland Academy for Peace and Development (APD), *Rebuilding Somaliland: Issues and Possibilities* (Lawrenceville, NJ: The Red Sea Press, 2005), p. 59.

7 I.M. Lewis, *A Modern History of the Somali* (Oxford: James Currey, 2002), p. 252.

8 I.M. Lewis, *Blood and Bone: The Call of Kinship in Somali Society* (Lawrenceville, NJ: The Red Sea Press, 1994), pp. 191–3.

the movement; and the military wing responsible for fighting Barre's forces. For many involved in the SNM, the military wing was necessary for the struggle, but the political component was of primary importance and the focal point of the movement and its goal of giving the government back to the people.[9] Largely because of the existence of a separate political wing, the SNM had the 'ability, capacity and interest to form an effective government' in Somalia.[10] The political wing itself acted as a quasi-government for the movement, making important decisions concerning the actions of the movement as well as functioning as a diplomatic entity for the SNM. The practice of participatory democracy in the SNM's Central Committee brought traditional Somali decision making practices into the body, and the institutionalisation of a council of clan elders (*Guurti*)[11] into the political wing established a system of checks and balances to constrain the actions of the military movement and to give the SNM the social and political capacity necessary to promulgate its stated aim of a democratic government. This focus on consensus politics and the inclusion of the familiar and traditional clan system secured support from a majority of the people affected by Barre's retaliatory campaigns. The actions of the SNM during the campaign not only created trust in the movement, but also facilitated the political foundations that would emerge following the military victory.

In February 1982 the SNM moved its base of operations from London to Ethiopia where the movement gained assistance from the Ethiopian government and rooted its support in the Isaaq in the country.[12] From there the SNM waged open rebellion against the Barre regime through incursions, attacking army positions in

---

9 Hassan Issa, Somaliland Vice President (SNM Administration)/ Former Vice Chairman of the Somali National Movement. Interview with author (Hargeisa, September 2006); Abdirahman Aw Ali Farah, Interview with author (Hargeisa, September 2006).

10 M. Bradbury, *Becoming Somaliland* (Oxford: James Currey, 2008), p. 60.

11 For purposes here, to distinguish between the institutionalised body and the traditionally ad hoc clan council, the institutionalised body will be referred to as *Guurti* whereas *guurti* should be read to mean the traditional non-centralised and ad hoc council of elders.

12 In late 1981 the arrest of the members of an action group determined to improve social services in the northwest sparked open retaliation in Hargeisa. Following this, senior Isaaq military officers in the Somalia army defected to the SNM, providing the political movement with military leadership and signalling its start as a militarised liberation group. The rebellion in Hargeisa also marked the start of the war between the north and Barre, causing Barre to attempt to tighten control in the north through force. The result of this was increasing support for the SNM within Somaliland. The movement began operating in Ethiopia shortly after. Dr Aden Abokor, Progressio Country Representative. Interview with author (Hargeisa, September 2006). Dr Abokor was a member of this group, which he refers to as the 'Hargeisa Group'; I.M. Lewis, *Blood and Bone*, op. cit., p. 206; Somaliland Government, 'Policy Document for the Government of Somaliland: Demand for International Recognition', (Hargeisa: Somaliland Ministry of Information, 2001), p. 23.

Somaliland before returning to Ethiopia. Barre responded to this campaign with 'disproportionate violence' against the population in the north and in particular the Isaaq, marking the start of the movement's involvement in Somalia's civil war.[13] The mounting repression against the Isaaq in the northwest that had started during the Ogaden War and increased following the emergence of the SNM was documented by Africa Watch:

> [t]he government exploited the emergence of the SNM to justify indiscriminate violence against individuals and groups that criticized government policies and leadership, or merely because of clan affiliation ... Whenever the SNM launched an attack ... that area was subject to harsh reprisals, including summary execution, the burning of villages, the destruction of reservoirs, the indiscriminate planting of landmines and the killing and confiscation of livestock, the lifeline of the nomads.[14]

In spite of the violence waged against the Isaaq within Somalia, because of its base in Ethiopia the SNM was able to escape prolonged direct confrontation with Barre's forces. In April 1988, however, Barre and Ethiopian leader Mengitsu Haile Mariam agreed to halt support to Somali armed movements based within the two states. As a result, the SNM lost support from the Ethiopian government and lost its base of operations. If the campaign was to continue, the SNM had no choice but to go into Somalia and fight.[15] In May 1988, the SNM forces began their move into Somalia by taking control of Hargeisa and Somaliland's second city, Burco. Barre's response to these actions was a new level of violence to handle the 'Isaaq problem',[16] ordering the shelling and aerial bombardment of the major cities in the northwest and the systematic destruction of Isaaq dwellings, settlements and water points. These reprisal attacks forced an estimated 300,000 Isaaq and non-Isaaq to flee to Ethiopia.[17] With assistance from clan elders from all the Somaliland clans and sub-clans affected by Barre, the SNM garnered enough physical and logistical support from the influx of refugees to enable its continuing move into Somalia.

---

13   M. Bryden, 'State-Within-a-Failed State: Somaliland and the Challenge of International Recognition', in P. Kingston and I. Spears (eds), *States Within States: Incipient Political Entities in the Post-Cold War Era* (Basingstoke: Palgrave Macmillan, 2004), pp. 167–88: p. 170.
14   Africa Watch, *A Government at War With Its Own People* (New York: Africa Watch, 1990), pp. 8–9.
15   Dr Aden Abokor, Interview with author, op. cit.
16   Major General Mohammed Said Hirsi 'Morgan', 'The Somali Democratic Republic Ministry of Defence Report ('The Morgan Report')', Report to the President of Somalia, Siad Barre (23 January 1987). Translated by Mohamoud Sheikh Ahmed Musa. Potential problems with the Isaaq were identified early by the Barre regime, and in 1987 initial actions to address the 'Isaaq problem' were outlined by General Morgan.
17   ICG, op. cit., p. 6.

The Isaaq in the north, facing further isolation and exploitation in addition to violence from the Barre regime, had long since turned to the clan for protection, and the emergence of the SNM offered this on a larger scale. Whereas military action initially concentrated on the Isaaq, other clans were not immune to large scale attacks and bombardments. Broad hard-won support for the SNM throughout the territory and amongst the different clans meant that although still dominated by the majority clan, the SNM became a Somaliland movement rather than just an Isaaq movement. As this happened, almost the entirety of Somaliland became the target of increasing state violence. The disillusionment with Somali unity that had emerged during the democratic government became cemented in the northern mindset. As the war intensified and the violence increased, though, the stated aim of the SNM continued to be the overthrow of Siad Barre rather than independence for Somaliland.

In January 1991 the USC ousted Barre from Mogadishu and the SNM began its final campaign in the north. After continued fighting and a bloody campaign,[18] the SNM claimed victory over the army of Somalia in the territory in February 1991.[19] The SNM took no part in fighting that took place in Mogadishu following the overthrow of Barre and it was excluded from the post-Barre political arrangement in the south. Being omitted from political occurrences in post-conflict Somalia, although viewed as disastrous at the time because of the political ideals espoused by the SNM and the sense of ongoing exclusion, would prove to be an advantage to the people of Somaliland. Whilst the south continued to descend into chaos, the people of the north began the long process of reconciliation and reconstruction. The end of Barre's regime brought the beginning of state collapse and central government failure for the south, but also brought promise to the north.

The road to peace in Somaliland was not bloodless, and the end of the civil war did bring retributive acts against those who had supported Barre or those who were in opposition to the SNM. Because of actions of the SNM, however, this violence was kept to a minimum. Once Hargeisa was liberated, the SNM Chairman of the Central Committee, Abdulrahman Ahmed Ali 'Tuur', immediately sent SNM commanders and clan elders throughout Somaliland with instructions for the SNM and the people to not seek revenge against those in the north that had supported

---

18 Somalilanders and many human rights groups claim that Barre's targeting of the Isaaq clan and his systematic massacres account to genocide.

19 For a more detailed and complete history of the SNM, see D. Compagnon, 'The Somali Opposition Fronts: Some Comments and Questions', *Horn of Africa* 13.1–2 (1991), pp. 29–54; D. Compagnon, 'Somali Armed Movements: The Interplay of Political Entrepreneurship and Clan-Based Factions', in C. Clapham (ed.), *African Guerrillas* (Oxford: James Currey, 1998), pp. 73–90; I. Samatar, 'Light at the End of the Tunnel: Some Reflections on the Struggle of the Somali National Movement', in H. Adam and R. Ford (eds), *Mending the Rips in the Sky: Options for Somali Communities in the 21st Century* (Lawrenceville, NJ: Red Sea Press, 1997), pp 21–38; I.M. Lewis, *Blood and Bone*, op. cit.; G. Prunier, 'A Candid View of the Somali National Movement', *Horn of Africa* 14.1–2 (1991), pp. 107–20; M. Bradbury, op. cit.

Barre.[20] This was not wholly successful in stopping revenge attacks, but it did succeed in preventing many of them. Although the civil war had created divisions in Somaliland society, the majority of the population had in some way supported the SNM. Because of this and the non-violent post-war stance of the SNM, even though a level of animosity existed between the Isaaq and other communities the cessation of hostilities was expedited.[21] The fact that the SNM were the 'victors', a place of respect and political power in Somali society, helped with this process. In addition to its immediate efforts, the SNM leadership allowed for a reconciliation process led by the elders of the Somaliland clans rather than asserting its authority in the territory through force; this step helped bring about an end to the fighting and laid the foundations for the envisaged democratic government.[22] The bottom-up road to peace and reconstruction was the first and only avenue taken.

In February 1991, the SNM and the elders of Somaliland began the peacemaking process by convening the first of many national *shir* (see Chapter 6). This process of national conferences aimed to reconcile the fractured Somaliland society, with reconciliation efforts falling primarily on the shoulders of clan elders. At the second of these national conferences held at Burco in April and May 1991, the representatives of the Somaliland people resolved to create a new and independent state, and the agreement reached there established the 'cornerstone of the peace' that allowed for the creation of a government in Somaliland.[23] A succession of national conferences and local initiatives has continued since 1991, working for further reconciliation as well as a strengthening of governance and government – institutional statebuilding – in the territory.

Going It Alone: The Declaration of Independence and the Beginnings of the State

Although the creation of a government is only one component of Somaliland's statebuilding process, as an unrecognised state the style and functions of government are important in the strategy to obtain recognition of sovereign statehood. Indeed, if recognition had been the goal from the start, the style and function of government would have been predetermined. However, the roots for the style of government chosen in Somaliland existed prior to any irredentist or secessionist claims. Indeed, the political leadership brought ideas of Western democracy and liberal government to Somaliland through the SNM its inception in London, and it was these desires that provided not only a starting point, but also a goal for what would be the new institutions of state.

---

20 Hassan Issa, Interview with author, op. cit.
21 APD, op. cit., p. 14.
22 M. Bradbury, op. cit., p. 79.
23 APD, op. cit., pp. 14–15; APD, 'The Somaliland Parliament: A Case Study', Report for UNDP (2004), p. 2.

The initial goal of the SNM was realised when Siad Barre was driven from power in January 1991, but the exclusion of the SNM from the newly formed interim government in Mogadishu created concerns of further repression of the north if the union were to continue.[24] Under popular pressure the SNM leadership was compelled to consider and then formulate plans for secession. On 18 May 1991 the representatives at the Burco Conference revoked the 1960 and 1961 Acts of Union and declared the secession of the Republic of Somaliland from Somalia. Based on the territorial boundaries of the British Protectorate of Somaliland at the time of its independence, the creation of the new Republic was a 'pragmatic stance to distance the north from the factional fighting in the south', as well as a recognition that the people of the north, particularly the Isaaq, had minimal physical, economic, social or political stake in Somalia. According to Bradbury, it was also believed that the foundations of security and stability in the north would attract much needed international aid that would not be linked with or conditional upon occurrences in the south.[25] Declaring independence was a relatively simple task. The creation of a state, on the other hand, was a monumental undertaking as the new leadership needed to prove both to its people and the international community that it was not going to be another Somalia.

Following the declaration of independence, the SNM quickly established a government based on the structure of and formed from the leadership of the movement. The SNM had always advocated that the clan could not be ignored in Somali politics as 'the clan system lay at the root of political stability, social cohesion and economic activity'.[26] The previous two governmental eras had proved that the clan and politics were inseparably intertwined. Within the SNM there was a realisation that the clan was the centre of not only individual but collective identity, and the strength derived from that drove through the centre of all social and economic activity, including politics. Thus, the intention of the leadership was not to remove that force from political life, but instead to create a modern democratic government that also included traditional Somali practices, including customary social contracts (*xeer*) and the moderating roles and practices of clan elders, as 'without the traditional sector protecting the integrity of its values, a reversion to authoritarian rule over the democratic essence of the body politic could not be excluded'.[27] The hybrid government that resulted is specifically

---

24 M. Bradbury, 'Somaliland Country Report', Report for CIIR (1997); APD, 'The Somaliland Parliament', op. cit., p. 2.

25 M. Bradbury, 'Somaliland', op. cit., p. 18. Somaliland's quest to be treated separately from the south in regards to aid or international assistance became apparent almost immediately when the leaders rejected UN assistance through the UN Operations in Somalia II (UNOSOM II). As the aid would be received as part of the UN's nation-building project for a united Somalia, this assistance was refused.

26 M. Bradbury, 'Somaliland', op. cit., p. 21.

27 J. Drysdale, *Stoics Without Pillows: A Way Forward for the Somalilands* (London: HAAN Associates, 2000), p. 160.

tailored to Somaliland, and this is often credited with the establishment of peace and stability in the territory. As Abdirahman Aw Ali Farah notes, the hybrid system 'began from when we [the SNM] were in the bush' when a council of clan elders (*Guurti*) was incorporated into the political operations of the SNM.[28] The fusion of this stabilising clan governance structure with the stated democratic desires of the SNM carried over into the immediate post-independence statebuilding period and into Somaliland's government.

Following the declaration of independence the SNM did not automatically assume control over the territory. Instead, the first government that was formulated at Burco was mandated to the SNM by the clan elders at the conference, thereby legitimising the rule of the movement through the sanction of the elders. The political-military separation established by the SNM during the liberation struggle eased the transition between liberation movement and ruling regime as the political structures were already in existence and were translated into the government structure. The political wing of the SNM, which had acted in the role of the executive during the liberation struggle, assumed leadership of the territory under former chairman of the SNM cum interim president, Abdulrahman Ahmed Ali 'Tuur'. The legislative branch of the new government also came from the SNM: one house of the new bicameral legislature came from the SNM Central Committee, whilst the other was filled by the elders (*Guurti*) who had assisted the SNM during their military campaign.

Tuur's interim administration was tasked with two key issues. First, peace needed to be established throughout the territory and fighting between those who had supported Barre and those who had not, as well as between clans attempting to profit from the chaotic situation, had to be stopped. The institutionalised *Guurti* together with local clan elders were instrumental in achieving this. Second was building a functioning government in the new state, which proved to be fraught with difficulties. As Lewis notes, Somaliland's initial years were testing and Tuur struggled to generate the income needed to finance the government. In addition, the continued existence of militias undermined public security and the government's attempts at reconciling the rifts created by the war.[29] Tensions within the SNM also quickly became apparent as factional pursuits emerged in the absence of the common and unifying enemy, Barre. As a result, lasting support for Tuur's administration was difficult to obtain; his ability to complete the tasks was questioned and lack of cohesion within the SNM threatened to derail the interim administration.

In 1992, fighting again broke out in Somaliland between Tuur's government forces and a coalition of militias loosely based on clans and linked with opposition factions within the SNM. The violence that started in Burco and quickly spread

---

28   Abdirahman Aw Ali Farah, Interview with author, op. cit.
29   I.M. Lewis, *A Modern History*, op. cit., p. 283; APD, 'The Somaliland Parliament', op. cit., p. 2.

to Berbera and Hargeisa 'reduced [Somaliland] to a state of near-anarchy'.[30] Throughout the Somalia civil war clan elders had been vital to gaining popular support for the SNM, and in the post-war return to fighting the SNM leadership and the population again turned to the clan elders, this time the now permanent *Guurti*, for guidance and assistance with reconciliation. In October 1992, at the town of Sheik, the *Guurti*, as a body of the government, negotiated a cease-fire to end the conflict. Another national reconciliation conference, the 1993 Grand Borama Conference, was convened to address the causes of the violence.

The Borama Conference was an important milestone in the formation of the government in Somaliland. It was a 'make or break event' in the creation of the state for on the agenda were two vital items: reconciliation and security, and statebuilding. A national committee of 150 Somaliland elders representing all the Somaliland clans and sub-clans comprised the voting delegation at the conference, and during the four months of the conference more than 2000 Somalilanders attended or participated.[31] Significantly, the Borama Conference, as with most of the national *shir*, was funded almost entirely by Somalilanders and members of the Diaspora. Without the pressures exerted by external donors, the people of Somaliland, which included the Diaspora community, were able to establish what they perceived of as best for the territory at that given time. In the words of Gerard Prunier, Somaliland '[went] it alone'.[32]

Rejecting 'Anarchy': Peace, Reconciliation and Making Somaliland

Whilst the international community was present in Somalia under the guise of the United Nations Operations in Somalia, the leaders in Somaliland clearly expressed their desire for the UN to stay out of the northern territory. Somaliland's quest to be treated separately from the south in regards to aid or international assistance became apparent almost immediately when Somaliland's leaders were offered UN assistance through UNOSOM II. As the aid would have been under the auspices of the UN's statebuilding project aimed at reconstructing a unified and functioning Somalia, this assistance was refused. As Abdullahi Duale recalls, when UNOSOM commander Admiral Jonathan Howe met with leaders in Hargeisa they told him, 'thank you, but we don't need your help'. He continues in his reflection in stating, '[w]e appreciated Operation Restore Hope, or whatever it was called, but we were busy with institution building'.[33] In rejecting international assistance, Somaliland also rejected internationally led mediation and reconstruction efforts; instead depending on conflict resolution mechanisms present in the clan system

---

30   APD, *Rebuilding Somaliland*, op. cit., p. 15.
31   M. Bradbury, 'Somaliland', op. cit., p. 21.
32   G. Prunier, 'Somaliland Goes it Alone', *Current History* 97.619 (1998), pp. 225–8.
33   Abdullahi M. Duale, Former Minister of Foreign Affairs. Interview with author (Hargeisa, September 2006).

and clan governance structures to create the foundations for the state. Starting with Burco, a series of national *shir* took place aimed at ending the violence and, following Borama, establishing the framework and guidelines for the procedural and institutional structure of a new state. The agreements made at Burco ended the violence resulting from the Somalia civil war and began to lay the foundations for the introduction of a new government. The 1993 Borama Conference continued these processes.[34]

At the Borama Conference two significant agreements were made: the National Charter and the Peace Charter. Together these formed Somaliland's first interim constitution and served as the basis for continued peacemaking and state formation during the transition period. In addition, at Borama the clan elders serving as representatives of the communities transferred power from the SNM factional rule to a civilian system characterised by community-based governance (*beel*) and power-sharing between the clans. Remarkably, in accordance with the agreement established by the elders at the 1991 Burco Conference, after two years of rule the SNM leadership peacefully stepped down in order to allow the civilian administration appointed by the elders at the Borama Conference to take control of the territory and continue the creation of a state. Mohammed Ibrahim Egal, the first prime minister of Somaliland in 1960 and the last civilian prime minister of Somalia in 1969, was appointed as the first civilian president and was tasked with leading the transition to the *beel* based government.[35] Although not chosen through a national plebiscite but rather by the council of clan elders, Egal was a highly respected and experienced leader who was regarded as the 'right person for the job' of guiding the territory through the period of state formation.[36] The Borama Conference not only succeeded in establishing a legal framework for the government and transferring power to civilian rule, but it also marked the start of the local efforts undertaken to establish a modern Somaliland state.

The establishment of the Peace Charter and the National Charter laid constitutional foundations upon which the new government would be built. The Peace Charter was created as a direct response to security issues that arose after independence was declared, in particular the fighting that had broken out in 1992. The Charter not only recognised the importance of the clan elders in ending that conflict and emphasised their position in reconciliation and peacemaking, but also officially regularised and institutionalised the role of elders in establishing and strengthening security in the territory. As an agreement between clans and therefore binding customary law (*xeer*), the Peace Charter established a structure in which demobilisation of the militias and the remaining SNM factions could take

---

34 These conferences will be discussed in greater detail in Chapter 6.

35 APD, *Rebuilding Somaliland*, op. cit., pp. 15–16.

36 Dr Aden Abokor, Interview with author, op. cit. Although, as with any leader, Egal is not considered to be faultless, he remains highly regarded by the people and politicians of Somaliland.

place, and in which law enforcement and the judicial system could be established.[37] It therefore 'set out a clear code of conduct, which the council of elders and people of Somaliland were to follow, so that harmony and security could exist as desired at independence'.[38] This legal acknowledgment of the importance of clan elders in establishing a secure environment conducive to the creation of a state not only tasked the elders with the maintenance of stability, but it also constitutionally sanctioned the institutionalisation of the previously ad hoc *guurti* as a governmental body.

Whereas the Peace Charter was concerned with establishing and maintaining a stable and secure environment, the National Charter addressed the need for state institutions founded on that stability. Ratified with a two-year mandate, the National Charter outlined the framework for the new government institutions and mandated the creation of a permanent constitution under which a democratic government would develop. The government outlined by the National Charter was not only to be a modern democracy, but it also allowed for every clan and subclan to be represented in the parliament. It also promoted consensus politics, a type of decision making with a long history in Somali society. In essence, the National Charter 'established a government rooted in a clan system with a fusion of the western system'.[39] The fusion of the 'old' – the Somali clan system – with the 'new' – modern democracy – is regarded as the cornerstone of stability in the Somaliland government. When Somaliland turned its attention to seeking sovereign recognition, that fusion of the 'old' and the 'new' became one of the 'internal' and the 'external'.

With the Peace Charter firmly identifying the need for peace and stability upon which a government could be created, and with the National Charter establishing the foundations for a hybrid government tailored to Somaliland, the intentions of those involved in creating these two documents were clear. Bradbury notes that within both Charters there are clear links to the original vision of radical governance reform proposed by the SNM, who envisioned a democratic government rooted in the clan system.[40] As Lewis notes, the most novel feature of the new government structure was its hybrid nature:

> an imaginative innovation in the shape of a bicameral legislature, with a non-elected upper house of traditional elders (the *guurti*), and an elected lower house of representatives: a kind of compromise between the old clan-based SNM and the exigencies of modern administration.[41]

---

37   I.M. Lewis, *A Modern History*, op. cit., p. 283; APD, 'The Somaliland Parliament', op. cit., p. 3.
38   APD, 'The Somaliland Parliament', op. cit., p. 3.
39   Ibid.
40   M. Bradbury, 'Somaliland', op. cit., p. 22.
41   I.M. Lewis, *A Modern History*, op. cit., p. 283.

Starting with the first national conference at Berbera, the clan elders had played a vital role in the establishment of peace in the territory and in laying the foundations for the government. As such, many involved in the creation of Somaliland's government claim that the clan elders provided the bedrock for the establishment of Somaliland and the spine for the continued stability of the emerging state.[42] The importance of the clan system in the new government was enforced in the institutionalisation of the clan elders as the upper house of parliament – a house responsible for the maintenance of peace and stability as well as mediating and guiding the statebuilding process. Because of their respected position both within and outside of the emerging political structures, the elders became the impartial and selfless 'King Makers'[43] who were responsible for sanctioning the new government and appointing its members. The prominent placement and power of the clan elders in the central government not only confirms the importance of the clans in the territory, but also reflects the recognition that the inclusion of the clan system was essential to the success of creating the new state.

With the foundations laid at the Borama Conference, President Egal began constructing the state in Somaliland. With the assistance of the clan elders and starting with the basic foundations of security, the Egal administration was able to make advances in moving from existing as a break-away territory to creating a separate state. The first step in this was the demobilisation of the militias begun in 1993 and undertaken primarily by the upper house of parliament through negotiations and agreements with local clan elders. Although complete demobilisation and disarmament did not take place, as early as February 1994 an estimated 5000 militias had been disbanded and disarmed.[44] While demobilisation was not as effective in the eastern Sanaag and Sool provinces, the main population centres in the west as well as the route from the port of Berbera to Hargeisa were secured. In addition, through his clan associations Egal was able to gain control of the port of Berbera, the primary import-export centre and a major source of revenue for Somaliland.[45] With the improved security situation and control of the port, Egal was able to drastically increase financial resources available to the government as taxes could be levied throughout the territory and customs duties were collected.[46] In addition, increased security brought more investment

---

42 Interviews by author. Hargeisa. August-September 2006.

43 Dr Aden Abokor, Interview with author, op. cit.

44 M. Bradbury, 'Somaliland', op. cit., p. 23. Many of the former militia members were integrated into the policy and customs forces, and later into the national army.

45 Ulf Terlinden, Researcher for Somaliland Academy for Peace and Development/ Institute for Development and Peace (INEF). Conversations with author (Hargeisa, August-September 2006); Mohammed Hassan Ibrahim 'Gani', Lead Researcher for Academy for Peace and Development. Conversations with author (Hargeisa, August-September 2006). It is widely acknowledged that Egal's clan associations are to credit for the reclaiming of the port of Berbera, as Egal's clan dominates the area in and around the city.

46 M. Bradbury, 'Somaliland', op. cit., p. 24.

money from the Diaspora community which funded projects such as improving infrastructure and establishing businesses.[47] Under Egal security in the territory drastically improved and the economy boomed.

Whereas Tuul's rule was characterised by inadequacy, Egal's administration was able to ride the 'wave of euphoria after Borama' and oversaw remarkable progress in establishing the institutions and functions of a state.[48] Key to this progress, though, was Egal. In his discussions on statebuilding, Call identifies three resources that are crucial for consolidating state power and for statebuilding success: coercion, capital and charisma.[49] In Somaliland, Egal provided the resource of charisma. A career politician, he was both a revolutionary and had a reputation tainted with failure and corruption. He had been educated in London, campaigned for Somaliland's independence from the British, was Prime Minister of Somalia at the time of Barre's coup, had ambiguous links with Barre's regime, and had not been a part of the SNM. However, he had connections with wealthy merchants who valued his clan ties to the port of Berbera, and he was the leader of Somaliland during its few days of post-colonial independence. As a seasoned politician, he was well-known and had an international reputation as a statesman.[50] He was popular and trusted. Throughout his rule his charisma and influence, as well as his popularity and veneration from the people, greatly benefited the emerging state. Egal was the 'man who made the base foundation for Somaliland. He knew the culture of the elders, he knew the culture of the people, he knew the culture of the west. He knew how to bring them together'.[51]

Although Egal was revered, his clan connections and political savvy cannot be overlooked: in many ways he was an opportunist, not necessarily for himself but for the project, and he utilised numerous avenues to press the statebuilding project further. Egal maintained tight control over Somaliland, not in a dictatorial manner but as a strong leader managing the creation of the government and the infrastructure of the state. Under the guidance of Egal, state ministries were established, government buildings were built or restored, the central bank of Somaliland was re-opened, a new currency was printed and introduced, regular business working hours were established and a civil service agency was created. A national army, customs offices, local and regional judicial systems, a legal system and a police force were also established. The infrastructure of the major population centres was repaired and work began on improving transportation

---

47 APD, *Rebuilding Somaliland*, op. cit.; I. Ahmed, 'Remittances and their Economic Impact in Post-War Somaliland', *Disasters* 24.4 (2000), pp. 380–89.
48 M. Bradbury, 'Somaliland', op. cit., p. 22.
49 C. Call, 'Ending Wars, Building States', in C. Call and V. Wyeth (eds), *Building States to Build Peace* (London: Lynne Rienner, 2008), pp. 1–22: p. 11. See also C. Tilly, *Coercion, Capital and European States* (Oxford: Blackwell, 1992).
50 M. Bradbury, *Becoming Somaliland*, op. cit., pp. 109–10.
51 Ahmed Yusuf Yassin, Vice President of Somaliland. Interview with author (Hargeisa, September 2006).

links between the major cities. Communications links were improved and links were made to domestic and foreign NGOs and the UN through the newly created planning ministry. Schools were set up, hospitals were re-opened and sanitation services were established. A minimum wage was introduced and civil servants were paid regularly. A working relationship was also begun between the central government and regional authorities within Somaliland.[52] In addition, the government institutions first mandated by the National Charter began to function and to govern. Laws were passed and the legal system, comprised of both 'modern' and customary laws – was updated. The Egal administration was building the attributes of statehood – the public goods articulated by Rotberg – concurrently with building the institutions of a state from the ground up. All the trappings of statehood were beginning to emerge, even those often overlooked such as the printing of postage stamps and the composition of a national anthem. Building on the extraordinary security measures accomplished with the help of the Somaliland clans, the Egal administration began ticking the boxes of acceptable modern statehood.

Although considerable progress was made establishing the institutions of government in the first two years of Egal's rule, the state remained politically fragile and was increasingly vulnerable to a shift in power between clans and politicians.[53] The potential for instability and return to conflict is reflected in the high cost of security in the first year: 50 per cent of government spending went to defence and the police, whereas health and education received only 17 per cent jointly.[54] This fragility was exposed when fighting again broke out in the territory in 1994. Largely sparked by opposition to the government and fuelled by desires for personal gain, this return to conflict was a substantial setback for the new state.

A combination of factors, including inter-clan hostilities, continuing dissatisfaction from SNM factions that felt the government had 'slipped from their hands',[55] the clash of powerful egos, unremitting struggles over control of Hargeisa airport, and a backlash against attempts at expanding government control outside the capital city came to a head when 'the Borama process moved from the conference hall to the proving grounds of Somaliland'.[56] The return of fighting first broke out in Hargeisa and quickly spread to Burco. It was seen by many non-Isaaq clans as an Isaaq problem that concerned only the political and economic elite. Despite this belief, the conflict involved the heaviest fighting since

---

52   APD, 'The Somaliland Parliament', op. cit., p. 3; M. Bradbury, 'Somaliland', op. cit.
53   M. Bradbury, 'Somaliland', op. cit., p. 24.
54   I.M. Lewis, *A Modern History*, op. cit., p. 285.
55   Mohammed Hassan Ibrahim 'Gani'. Interview with author (Hargeisa, August 2006).
56   See M. Bradbury, 'Somaliland', op. cit., p. 25; APD, 'A Self-Portrait of Somaliland: Rebuilding from the Ruins', Hargeisa, APD and Interpeace/War-torn Societies Project Report (1999), p. 15; APD 'The Somaliland Parliament', op. cit., p. 3; I.M. Lewis, *A Modern History*, op. cit., p. 286.

the civil war, with tens of thousands of people fleeing Hargeisa and Burco and with widespread destruction of property.[57] The war also damaged confidence in the new government and its ability to maintain order and security within the territory. As Bradbury notes, 'the war threw Somaliland's viability into doubt'.[58] In order to resolve the conflict, the *Guurti* opened negotiations and mediation efforts and another national conference was convened in Hargeisa beginning in 1996. At the conclusion of this five month conference a peace agreement was reached, ending Somaliland's last major conflict to date. The grievances of those in opposition to the government were also addressed and the reconciliation process was expanded beyond the clans, resulting in greater inclusion within the government as well as peaceful means through which to address opposition opinions and groups. Just as importantly, though, were the endorsing of a new provisional constitution to replace the National Charter and the establishment of a schedule for the transition to a multi-party democracy.[59] Egal was re-elected as president by the delegates and a new vice president, Dahir Rayale Kahin, was chosen. Faith in the government and its ability to end conflict and maintain the peace had been severely damaged by the conflict, but after steps taken at Hargeisa confidence was partially restored and the next step in creating a multi-party democracy was taken.

Codifying the Hybrid: The Constitution and Democratic Elections

The founders of the state made it clear that the government structure and functions must be mandated and defined by a constitution and thus it became a priority to make Somaliland a constitutional state. Creating the Somaliland Constitution was a lengthy and difficult undertaking, but as Abdullahi Duale states, '[you] can't draw a constitution overnight and say this is it'.[60] With the new interim constitution drafted at the Hargeisa Conference in place, in 1997 work was begun on a permanent constitution. The final product was then adopted in 2001 following a national referendum.[61]

The National Constitution of Somaliland is a compromise between two separate drafts: the interim constitution and a draft proposed by Egal. After lengthy negotiation and compromise between the two drafts, the final constitution was ratified by a margin of one vote in Parliament and a national referendum was prepared.[62] Even with a completed document to put before the people, Egal faced significant opposition as the document mandating democratic elections potentially threatened the political positions of those already in the government. With this as well as public uncertainty

---

57 M. Bradbury, 'Somaliland', op. cit., p. 25; APD, *Rebuilding Somaliland*, op. cit., p. 15.
58 M. Bradbury, 'Somaliland', op. cit., p. 25.
59 APD, *Rebuilding Somaliland*, op. cit., p. 16.
60 Abdullahi M. Duale. Interview with author, op. cit.
61 APD, *Rebuilding Somaliland*, op. cit., p. 16.
62 Abdirahman Aw Ali Farah. Interview with author, op. cit.

following the lengthy process, the Egal administration needed to push hard to gain popular support for the document. Thus the president very publicly linked a yes vote for the constitution as a yes vote for independent statehood, implying that the democratic practices to be established by the constitution were a pre-requisite for international recognition of statehood.[63] The campaign was successful: the 2001 national referendum returned public approval for the constitution and it was quickly ratified by Somaliland's parliament. The power of the new constitution and the stability of the new government were put to the test, however, when in May 2002 Egal died suddenly. Upon hearing the news, one government minister is reported to have wept 'not because Egal died, but because of what will happen to [Somaliland]'.[64] These fears were unfounded, however, when the constitution was closely followed and Vice President Rayale peacefully took office.[65] The first of many tests for the Somaliland Constitution was passed, and opposition to the process of introducing democracy was diminishing in Somaliland.

The structure of the government found in the constitution mirrors that established by the National Charter: an Executive led by a president, a bicameral legislature, and a Supreme or Constitutional Court.[66] The constitution mandates that the president, vice president and lower house of parliament be elected through popular elections, and that government ministers and court justices be appointed by the president and confirmed by both houses of parliament. The lower house of parliament is the House of Representatives and is comprised of 82 members chosen through popular elections and representing geographic regions. The upper house of parliament is where the institutional inclusion of the clan in Somaliland's hybrid government is found. Codified in the constitution, the House of Elders (*Guurti*) is the continuation of the permanent clan council that first emerged within the SNM leadership, and its membership is drawn solely from clan elders. The membership of the House of Elders continues to be nominated by their respective clans and officially appointed by the president, and the 82 appointed voting members[67] of

---

63 Abdullahi M. Duale. Interview with author, op. cit.

64 Ibid.; Mohammed Said Mohammed Gees. Interview with author, op. cit.

65 APD, *Rebuilding Somaliland*, op. cit., p. 17; Somaliland Government, 'Somaliland Constitution (2001)'. Copies of English translation obtained from Somaliland House of Elders and Somaliland Ministry of Information, Hargeisa. Article 89 of the Somaliland Constitution stipulates that the vice president shall act as temporary president upon the death of the president, with elections for the president to follow within six months. Rayale, as Vice President, filled the vacancy and although more than six months elapsed before an election was held, the extension of this period was sanctioned by the *Guurti*.

66 The judicial branch of the government is called both the Supreme Court and the Constitutional Court. Similar to the Supreme Court of the US, it has appellate power in criminal cases, and is also responsible for interpreting the Constitution.

67 The Constitution also allows for the appointment of honorary non-voting members to the *Guurti*. These honorary members are: up to five members selected by the president based on their significance to the nation; any person who has served as the Speaker of either House of Parliament; and any person who has served as president or vice-president of

the upper house technically represent their clans, although many members of the House claim they represent all of Somaliland.[68] The membership of Somaliland's *Guurti* functions both as a clan council and as a parliamentary body.

Although the House of Representatives 'forms the first part of the country's legislature, passing laws and approving and overseeing the general political situation and the direction of the country', the upper house also holds significant powers.[69] The House of Elders also holds legislative powers, and all legislation passing through the lower house except for those pertaining to the budget and finance must be passed by the upper house before being signed into law by the president. The *Guurti*, as the representation of the clan, also has sole jurisdiction over legislation concerning religion, traditions and culture. Whilst the legislative duties are important, more crucially the *Guurti* continues to be responsible for the maintenance of peace and security in the territory as well as reconciling between the people and the government and within the government itself. As the general secretary of the *Guurti* states, 'the *Guurti* is both legislative and cultural. It still plays an important role in linking the two. You can't just impose democracy. The *Guurti* acts as a link between the old and the new'.[70] The *Guurti* also acts as the key advisor to the government, and as such has a wide purview of powers that are rarely checked. As part of this role, the upper house has the exclusive power to extend the terms of any member or branch of the government, a power that has been exercised on a number of occasions when it was deemed that the territory is not capable of holding elections due to lack of resources, instability, or war.[71] As the physical as well as symbolic inclusion of the clan and the traditional practices of clan governance, the House of Elders is seen by many as the spine of the Somaliland government, a position which grants it broad power.

Powers of the other two branches of government are also defined by the constitution. As expected, the Supreme Court is the highest appeals court in Somaliland and is responsible for interpreting the constitution. Powers granted to the president, on the other hand, are broad and highly interpretable. The constitution is often referred to amongst government officials and members of civil society as 'Egal's suit' as it gave the first civilian president wide latitude with which to create the state.[72] Given Egal's esteemed status in the territory and

---

Somaliland. At the time of writing there were six honorary members. Source: 'Somaliland Constitution (2001)', Article 60.2.2; Abdullahi Habane, General Secretary Somaliland House of Elders. Interview with author (Hargeisa, August 2006).

68 Interviews conducted by authors with members of Somaliland House of Elders (Hargeisa, August and September 2006).

69 'Somaliland Constitution (2001)', Article 38.1.1; Article 39.

70 Abdullahi Habane. Interview with author, op. cit.

71 The *Guurti* has extended the mandate of the National Charter, the term of office for Egal, the term of office for the current president, the term of office for the House of Representatives (prior to the 2005 elections), and the term of office for the *Guurti* itself.

72 See 'Somaliland Constitution (2001)', Articles 90–92. The label 'Egal's suit' was widely used during interviews conducted in Hargeisa (August-September 2006).

his political prowess, these broad powers benefited the stability of the territory and the government as they paved the way for quick reform as well as creating a means through which security and stability problems could be immediately addressed.[73] Although seen as problematic by some both within and outside of Somaliland, without giving Egal this wide purview it is likely that the early years of statebuilding would have been significantly more difficult for the state.[74] With the strengthening of institutions and practices, and with the popular election of both the president and the House of Representatives, however, the 'suit' no longer fits the purpose, and the broad powers given to the President are beginning to be checked by the representatives of the people. The resultant changing dynamics of the government are exposing the holes in the Constitution that had allowed for the growth of the government, but are now 'creating more problems than solving'.[75] However, the government, civil society and the Somaliland population continue to address these problems and negotiate lasting solutions to them, thus continuing the process of institution building and statebuilding.

Although the Somaliland government is grounded in the clans, safeguards have been put in place to protect against the destructive clan politics that plagued the 1960–1969 government of Somalia. These measures primarily restrict political parties and electoral practices. The constitution allows for only three political parties which cannot be clan based and must be representative of all the Somaliland clans. These parties were officially confirmed following local elections held in 2002, with the three parties obtaining the largest number of votes in that election – Ururka Dimugraadiga Ummadda Bahawday (UDUB), Kulmiye and Ururka Caddaalada iyo Daryeelka (UCID)[76] – becoming the official parties. An elaborate practice of party-list proportional representation is another means through which to protect against clan politics. In this system, theoretically the party becomes more important than the clan in determining representation, although in reality the backing of clan leadership of often needed for a person to become a candidate.[77] With the clan as the dominant organised social community

---

73 M. Bryden, 'The Banana Test: Is Somaliland Ready for Recognition?' *Annales d'Éthiopie* 19 (2003), pp. 341–64. For more information on Egal's role in the early formation of the government see also I.M. Lewis, *A Modern History*, op. cit.; M. Bradbury, 'Somaliland', op. cit.; H. Adam and R. Ford (eds.), *Mending the Rips in the Sky*, op. cit.; APD, 'A Self-Portrait', op. cit.; APD, *Rebuilding Somaliland*, op. cit.

74 Mohammed Said Mohammed Gees. Conversation with author (Hargeisa, September 2006); Mohammed Hassan Ibrahim 'Gani'. Conversations with author (Hargeisa, August-September 2006).

75 Dr Aden Abokor. Interview with author, op. cit.

76 UDUB, translated into English, is the United Peoples' Democratic Party. Kulmiye is the Peace, Unity and Development Party. UCID is The Party for Justice and Development.

77 Mohammed Hassan Ibrahim 'Gani'. Interview with author (Hargeisa, September 2006). Each vote cast in the election acts as one 'cast twice', with the same vote being for the candidate and the party at the same time rather than just the party. This system theoretically prevents stacking the top positions on the party lists with members

in Somaliland, it continues to play a role in the political process, but limitations placed on its infiltration into the party realm have thus far eliminated the one clan-one party practice that plagued Somalia's democratic government.

On its path to creating a modern democracy, Somaliland has so far held four national elections. Voter education drives have been consistently held during which the purpose and procedure of democratic elections have been explained both through community meanings and individual action as well as through pamphlet distribution.[78] The first democratic election was the 2002 local elections which also determined the three official political parties. In 2003 presidential elections were held in which President Rayale, representing the UDUB party, was narrowly elected for another term in office by a margin of 80 votes.[79] Despite the close result, the runner-up refused calls from his party, Kulmiye, to establish a rival government in the territory and instead chose to respect the electoral process. This election marked the first peaceful contest over leadership of the forming state. Deemed relatively free and fair by international observers, the 2005 parliamentary elections were also conducted peacefully.[80] Problems arose following the vote, however, when the popularly elected majority comprising the two opposition parties was incorporated into a government that had previously

---

from a single clan, as the candidates are ranked in order of number of votes received. Allocation of seats is then proportional to the percentage of votes the party received. As Gani explains, '[e]ach clan has to vote for their man rather than getting a free ride' through a clan controlled candidates list.

78 Somaliland National Election Commission, 'Voters Manual: Parliamentary Elections 29 September 2005', Hargeisa, Voter Education Manual (2005). These pamphlets utilise a mixture of words and pictures to tell the 'story' of democratic elections. The pictures are an important component as illiteracy rates are high, especially amongst the rural and nomadic populations.

79 Progressio cites this number to be 217 votes, which is the final figure approved by the Supreme Court after the original 80 vote announcement by the Somaliland National Electoral Commission. A. Abokor, S. Kibble, H. Yusuf, and G. Barrett, 'Further Steps to Democracy: The Somaliland Parliamentary Elections, September 2005', Progressio Report (London, January 2006), p. 8.

80 Catholic Institute for International Relations (CIIR), 'Somaliland Elections to House of Representatives, 29th September 2005', International Election Observation Team Interim Report (7 October 2005); A. Abokor, et al., op. cit.; R. Hollekim, S. Hansen and G.M. Sorensen, 'Somaliland: Elections for the Lower House of Parliament September 2005', NORDEM Report (March 2006); ICG, op. cit.; International Republican Institute, 'Somaliland September 29, 2005 Parliamentary Election Assessment Report', (Washington DC: IRI, 2006); APD, 'A Vote for Peace: How Somaliland Successfully Hosted its First Parliamentary Elections in 35 Years', Dialogue for Peace Somali Programme Report (September 2006); Somaliland NAGAAD and COSONGO, 'Parliamentary Elections: Domestic Election Observers' Report', (Hargeisa, November 2005); Somaliland National Electoral Commission, 'Report of the Parliamentary Election', Hargeisa (December 2005); IRIN News, 'Somaliland Elections Peaceful Say Observers', Somalia News Report (3 October 2005); Freedom House, 'Somaliland Country Report', 2007 edition, http://www.freedomhouse.org.

been dominated by Egal's party (UDUB). Contention over leadership of the newly elected House of Representatives emerged, but was resolved peacefully through negotiations moderated by the House of Elders and with the opposition parties maintaining the power and influence associated with their electoral victories. The next rounds of local and presidential elections were scheduled to take place in early 2008, but instead took place in 2010, after which Somaliland experienced its first transfer of party power at the executive level. Work has begun on creating a national electoral roll, and voter turnout is high. Although the election process in Somaliland has not been flawless, as one Somali researcher states, '[t]his country is a lab ... We're still going through the process, still experimenting'.[81] Despite the minor problems encountered, beginning to introduce and establish the democratic component of the hybrid government was a milestone in the statebuilding process in Somaliland.

Although much has been accomplished in Somaliland, those involved in creating the state realise that the framework, both on paper and in practice, is not perfect, and as of yet many functions of the emerging state are still weak. The framework for the government and the wording of the constitution indicate that a greater provision of public goods is aspired to, but the government of Somaliland does not yet have the resources or the institutional capacity to expand upon those provisions begun by Egal. Accusations of corruption or abuse of power have been rare, but have still arisen. There is some discontent with the three current parties, with groups arguing that because of a maturing of the system the option of choosing new parties should be made available. Some also argue that the constitutionally mandated three party limit is exclusionary and should be eliminated.[82] Curtailing freedoms expected in a liberal democracy, particularly freedom of the press, has also been a concern.[83] What has been successful, however, is establishing peace and security within the territory, which is not a small accomplishment when compared with the chaotic and violent situation that exists in most of southern Somalia. The nascent state in Somaliland has the foundations for further political and social development and provision, but has yet to fully realise them.

State-Democracy-Recognition

As Bryden argues, Somaliland 'fulfils the principle criteria' for statehood.[84] The aspiring state reflects the normative values of acceptable statehood, an attribute that makes it complicit with the pressures of the international community even

---

81 Mohammed Hassan Ibrahim 'Gani'. Interview with author (Hargeisa, August 2006).
82 Conversations with author (via email, 2008–2009).
83 See, for example, editorials and reports in *The Somaliland Times* 2008–2011, available at www.somalilandtimes.net.
84 M. Bryden, 'The Banana Test', op. cit. Bryden is basing this assessment on the principles of statehood found in the 1933 Montevideo Convention. These principles are

in the absence of direct international action. From the beginning, the process of statebuilding in Somaliland has been propelled by a group of self-socialised elites within the territory who push for compliance with the norms of statehood that are seen as necessary for recognition, but who also strive to ensure that the state being created is one that reflects the needs of Somaliland. The result of this is the hybrid reconciliation between the 'old' Somali governance and the 'new' liberal democratic practices in the Somaliland government; a reconciliation that also works to balance the demands between the external and the internal. Initially composed of SNM political leadership, this group continues to evolve as the statebuilding process continues, and is increasingly becoming composed of Diaspora members and Diaspora returnees with experience of European and American government systems; the 'old guard' of the SNM is being replaced by the 'new' and the internal is being increasingly supplemented by the external. Both the old and the new – the internal and the external – however, continue to strive to prove to both the international community and the Somaliland people that Somaliland can be a successful and acceptable state.

The crux of meeting normative demands and creating the hybrid state in Somaliland was the introduction of a multiparty democratic system. The original objective of the SNM was the establishment of a democratic government as a means of returning the government to the people, and the introduction of democracy in Somaliland goes back to the democratic practices of the SNM at its inception.[85] Although the stated aim of the SNM was to give the government back to the people, it is unclear if a Western-style democracy was the intended aim, or even if how to introduce this new form of government to the population had been considered. As the intention of the SNM was not the creation of an independent state in Somaliland, though, it can be assumed that democratic government was not proffered to appease the international community but was instead was what the SNM leadership thought was best for Somalia. However, the emphasis on recognition now places the modern democratic government in a new context and it is at the centre of Somaliland's claims for statehood.

Regardless of whom one speaks to in the government of Somaliland, whether it is a top ranking cabinet official or an elected member of parliament, the conversation consistently begins with the story about the SNM struggle and then the formation of Somaliland. The story almost always includes mention of the success of the most recent democratic elections and concludes with a strong statement about how Somaliland deserves to be recognised. It would be rare for anyone involved in the creation of Somaliland or those in the current government to publicly state

---

reflected in the conceptions of empirical statehood found in Chapter 2, as well as the definition of statehood provided by Brownlie.

85 Interviews conducted in Hargeisa (August-September 2006); M. Bradbury, *Becoming Somaliland*, op. cit., p. 63. This intention is also apparent in a 1981 political manifesto published by the SNM in which the leadership calls for a return to a representative form of democracy that would guarantee human rights and freedom of speech.

that Somaliland's push for democracy is propelled, at least in part, by the quest for recognition. Whilst direct statements are not likely, however, there is much that indicates that democracy and the quest for recognition have become linked. Much can be taken from statements, particularly early speeches by President Egal that indicate that democracy had obtained a second purpose other than returning the government to the people. In a speech prior to the 2001 constitutional referendum in which Egal had linked democratic government with recognition, the president stated, '[w]e could only be accepted as a member of the world community if we move to a new stage of nationhood ... The international community does not recognize congregations of clans, each remaining independently separate'.[86] Current government actions continue to link style of government with recognition. Reflecting this, a former elected vice president indicates that today the primary goal of the government is for Somaliland to be recognised, with 'all other problems [being] secondary'.[87] Former Minister of Foreign Affairs Abdullahi Duale goes further in recognising that although necessary, democracy was unknown to the majority of the population of Somaliland and '[t]eaching and introducing the democratic process itself was a huge challenge ... We put the package together and sold it to the people. It's a miracle it happened'.[88] There is a sense from some that Somaliland is merely imitating democracy, with the institutions and practices being created because of the importance placed on the appearance of a democratic government.[89] Regardless of the initial motivations, however, with recognition being the primary objective and with a connection being made between style of government and recognised statehood, the push for continued democratisation cannot be separated from the quest to be a legally recognised state.

It is very difficult to discuss Somaliland in any capacity without some mention of recognition. As Bryden appropriately notes, the pursuit of international recognition has become a 'sort of national obsession' in Somaliland.[90] Whilst for many Somalilanders the benefit of legal statehood would be improved economic opportunities, the recognition campaign is driven by the political. The existence of a democratic government within the territory, whilst created as part of the bigger scheme to give the government back to the people, is now utilised as the central focus of the campaign and the primary evidence of deserving legal statehood. In other words, the argument being made is that the territory has *earned* sovereignty through exhibiting preferable and acceptable empirical statehood. Whereas a strong legal justification for recognition can be made based on brief period of sovereign independence in 1960, the campaign for statehood has

---

86 Egal as quoted in APD, *Rebuilding Somaliland*, op. cit., p. 16.
87 Ahmed Yusuf. Interview with author, op. cit. Yusuf was vice president under President Rayale.
88 Abdullahi Duale. Interview with author, op. cit. Duale held this office under President Rayale.
89 Interviews conducted in Hargeisa (August-September 2006).
90 M. Bryden, 'The Banana Test', op. cit.

grown to encompass this acceptableness, and as such the style and appearance of the state and the government has become a vehicle through which recognition is sought. With sovereign statehood being a pre-requisite for the acquisition of resources and entry into international frameworks, organisations and legal codes, the statebuilding process and the democratising government in Somaliland have become part of a complex and very politically rooted strategy for recognition and extraversion. As such, the growth, strengthening and modern practices of the Somaliland state must be viewed not only as part of fulfilling the initial desires of the founders of Somaliland, but also as fulfilling international normative demands for acceptable statehood.

The institutional components of the state in Somaliland are not perfect, and Somaliland is continuing to 'learn' democracy. The newness of this system of government cannot be overlooked. Those who were involved in creating the state recognised that the introduction of democratic practices would not be easy as they could not 'jump from point A to E without going through B, C, and D'.[91] This challenge was met through hybridity: using the old to introduce the new and depending on the old to foster cooperation in the hybrid system.[92] Although this system also creates particular obstacles, the hybrid Somaliland democracy is often credited with maintaining the foundational peace and stability necessary for the creation of the state. As Bobe Yusuf Duale recognises, the people of Somaliland 'live in two worlds, the west and the clan', and the government reflects this duplicity of life.[93] It is this duality that will be the focus of the following chapters.

Conclusions

When in 1991 long-term instability resulted in the collapse of the state, the people of the north seized upon the opportunity to remove themselves from the Somalia union. It was at this here that the state of Somaliland was born.

As will be further explored in the following chapter, the methods employed by the statebuilders in Somaliland were more than just institution building; they were nation-building and statebuilding, with legitimacy coming from within rather than from the outside. Instrumental to both – institution building and the legitimisation of the statebuilding process and the resulting state – was the clan, specifically the *Guurti*. Indeed, the clan and traditional practices – the 'old' – themselves became

---

91 Abdullahi Duale. Interview with author, op. cit.
92 Abdikadir Mohammed Hassan 'Indho', Member of Somaliland House of Elders. Interview with author (Hargeisa, September 2006). An example of this comes from Indho, a ranking member of the House of Elders, who notes that the most important role the *Guurti* has had since the end of fighting in 1996 was reassuring the people about the democracy process and keeping the peace during elections.
93 Bobe Yusuf Duale, Former member of the SNM Central Committee and current Programme Coordinator for APD. Interview with author (Hargeisa, September 2006).

institutions throughout this process, incorporated into the formal structure of the state with traditional practices both underpinning and existing in tandem with 'modern' state practices. The purpose-driven and permanent institutionalisation of the traditional *guurti* granted recognition to the elders. This acknowledged the historical debt owed to the clans by the SNM while simultaneously recognising their continued importance in the political process. This recognition brought the once non-centralised and ad hoc clan governance structure into the central government of the forming state. The inclusion of the traditional leadership brought an immediate legitimacy to the statebuilding project; the *Guurti* provided a stable base for the new structures, meaning the new state would not face the accusation of being 'built on sand'. Throughout the statebuilding process, the institutionalised *Guurti*, acting as a clan body, was used in lieu of international mediators and statebuilders to carry out and oversee conflict resolution and the formation of a government. In the national *shir* reconciliation conferences, the clans of Somaliland came together in discussion and negotiation and the agreements reached became customary law (*xeer*), thereby binding all of the clans to the outcome. Throughout this series of national *shir* the clan system, clan elders and traditional practices were used by the SNM, including its institutionalised *Guurti*, to negotiate a state. At the same time, the clan system, the clan elders and the traditional practices were serving to domestically legitimise the resulting state, setting the stage for the continuation of the statebuilding process within society rather than primarily within the *shir*.

Mohammed Said Gees articulates that the attitude at the time of the creation of the government was 'we don't want to be old', reflecting not only a desire to rid Somaliland of the corrupt practices that plagued the Somalia governments, but also a desire for something progressive.[94] For Somaliland, this meant a move towards a modern democratic state. As strong as the push for something new was, however, the value of the old Somali practices and customs were not discounted. Thus, the clan governance system and the social, political and economic control that the clan elders held became integral to creating the foundations upon which a democratic government could be introduced. Although the new was believed to be necessary to return the government to the people as well as in the active quest for recognition of sovereign statehood, its existence within the government would not be possible if it did not exist in tandem with the old.

The people involved in creating the state in Somaliland acknowledge that the democratic system that is in place in Somaliland today is not perfect, but that what has been created is 'the best there is' at this point.[95] However, that does not exclude, but rather allows for, a continuing process of statebuilding. As a high ranking civil servant succinctly notes, '[w]hen we were writing that constitution we were trying to kill one bird with thousands of stones in order to assert our separation' from the south.[96] Many of the obstacles present in Somaliland today stem from

---

94 Mohammed Said Mohammed Gees. Interview with author, op. cit.
95 Interview with author (Hargeisa, September 2006).
96 Interview with author (Hargeisa, September 2006).

the constitution and its ambiguities. Regardless of the real or potential problems, though, what has taken place in Somaliland since 1991 is remarkable. Out of a violent conflict resulting in the failure of one state, a new state is emerging; one that is overcoming obstacles that have derailed its neighbours for many years. The establishment of a secure and stable environment in which a new style of governing is being introduced is a testament to the devotion of the Somaliland people to this project of statebuilding. That this is domestically driven and is being done almost entirely in the absence of international involvement contrasts sharply to the 'cookie cutter' approach to statebuilding that was attempted and failed in Somalia. The success in introducing and establishing components of the acceptable state, though, was dependent on forming a state the Somaliland way. That is, the success in introducing these structural components and practices of the state were dependent upon grounding the state in the Somaliland clans.

Interestingly, though, Somaliland's key deviation from the preferable or the acceptable is something that has been a vital component of the statebuilding process: the inclusion of traditional or traditional authority in the central government. This inclusion in Somaliland is not an anomaly. Indeed, attention paid to hybrid governance is increasing, and hybridity occurs within many existing states.[97] However, hybrid governments, although not unheard of, are rarer. Hybrid government are those in which differing mechanisms of governance, such as traditional and modern norms and practices, exist within a single political order. Clements defines these political orders, such as that in Botswana, as 'characterised by a contradictory and dialectic co-existence of forms of socio-political organisation that have their roots in both non-state indigenous social structures and introduced state and societal structures'. They emphasise both liberal ideals and power relations outside of the Western liberal model, and as some argue, are a means through which to secure government legitimacy within complex post-conflict or fragile societies.[98] However, establishing hybrid government as an externally-determined policy option or process would be atypical. Although elements of hybrid governance exist in Afghanistan, especially when considering the role of the *Jurga*, these continue to exist outside of the realm of the formalised state: hyridity in Afghanistan is a tool of governance in Afghanistan rather than a component of

---

97 This is not to be confused with hybrid governance, a term often associated with amongst others the work of Beatrice Hibou, where there is a blurring between the public, the private and the voluntary in the economy or the provision of public services. Hybrid governance in this regard is most often exhibited in the economic sector and is often a consideration within studies of political economy. See, for example, B. Hibou, (ed), *Privatising the State* (London: Hurst and Co., 2004).

98 See D. Roberts, 'Hybrid Polities and Indigenous Pluralities: Advanced Lessons in Statebuilding from Cambodia', *Journal of Intervention and Statebuilding* 1.3 (2007), pp. 379–402.

the government.[99] Incongruent with the normative liberal model of government, hybrid government is not a path taken within externally-led statebuilding projects. For an unrecognised state seeking for sovereign statehood and therefore striving to comply with normative demands, it seems counterproductive to establish such a deviation in its government structure. The perception of unpredictability and uncertainty that accompanies the inclusion of the traditional signifies that it should not be preferred in such an important position, yet for Somaliland it is a vital component not only in creating the institutional state, but also in creating and domestically legitimising the state and its identity.

---

99   R. Lamb, 'Political Governance and Strategy in Afghanistan', Center for Strategic and International Studies Report (April 2012).

Chapter 6
The Institutionalisation of the Traditional

The clan and the *Guurti* in Somaliland added much needed legitimacy to the newly forming state. The deviance from the norm stemming from this has not been ignored, though. In a June 2005 report commissioned by the World Bank, Ahmed Mohammed Hashi identifies the central inclusion of the clan in the government as the point of potential instability in the Somaliland state. He argues that if the clan continues to be part of the central government Somaliland will be plagued by the same clan struggles and warfare found in Somalia.[1] Although this is only one report, it reflects the distrust and deviance associated with the inclusion of the unknown into a central government; in this case it is specific to Somaliland. To be clear, the inclusion of the clan in the central government is not the cause of Somaliland's continued non-recognition; complex regional considerations, peace initiatives for Somalia and policies of the African Union as well as non-African actors have thus far prevented recognition of Somaliland. However, the notable inclusion of the clan in the government of a Somali state is perceived of as a significant risk factor for instability and violence. With the continued volatility in the south of Somalia, and with the clan, until very recently, being targeted as a key component of this instability, it is curious that in Somaliland the clan has had and continues to have such a place of prominence within the modern democratising government.

It is common in literature on Somaliland to see the clan and the *Guurti* referred to as the 'spine' of Somaliland. Often this is discussed in terms of the *Guurti* in its institutional capacity; its role in the building of the institutions of the state and in the transition to democracy. However, this role extends beyond the institutional. In Somaliland, the clan and the *Guurti* also guide and underpin the process of legitimising the state and, indeed, the process of socio-political change that is vital not only to building a Somaliland identity but also to aspects of nation-building. As Lewis notes,

> The Somali clan system serves as a mechanism of solidarity and fragmentation as well as competition and coalition building. It is this enigma of the functions of the clan system – its capacity to serve as a mechanism of solidarity and warfare, its vulnerability to fragmentation and the weakness of its mechanism of leadership accountability – which needs to be understood. Somaliland adapted

---

1   A. Hashi, 'The Implication of Traditional Leadership, "Guurti", and Other Non-State Actors in Local Governance in Somaliland', Study Report for the Traditional Structures and Local Governance Project of the Community Empowerment and Social Inclusion Program of the World Bank (June 2005).

these features and functions of clan organisation in its strategies of organising resistance to the regime, resolving conflicts within the movement during the struggle, as well as in postwar reconciliation and in building political consensus.[2]

Building the institutions of the state can take place without nation-building, but in order to be successful and to be legitimately accepted, it has to take place concurrently with nation-building. As the nation is not only reflective of a popular collective defined by ethnic, religious or cultural identity but is also defined by and reflective of political culture – expectations of governance and the state – the nation plays an important role in the legitimisation of the state; the institutions and the nation must be reflective of and embedded within each other. In Somaliland, statebuilding and nation-building are taking place concurrently. Initially invoking a separate Somaliland identity brought about through common political experiences and separateness within the Somali ethnicity and originally rooting the state within common understandings and expectations of governance, the SNM began to build the state on foundations within the community and the burgeoning Somaliland nation. As the statebuilding process progresses, nation-building also progresses concurrently; as governance changes, the expectations for that governance and the identity of Somaliland are also changing. As Sisk notes, consolidating peace and building a state is 'not simply a matter of rebuilding state capacity based on what was there before, or 'recovery'; statebuilding is about transformation of both state and society'.[3] Although certainly not the only actor or factor involved, the clan and clan governance have been an instrumental component of these tandem processes. In Somaliland, the clan has facilitated a link between state and society and a reciprocal investment of one in the other.

Ironically, though, despite Somaliland's success in building a strengthening state that has strong domestic legitimacy, for many who study statebuilding or many in the policy realm, and reflected in Hashi's report, Somaliland's methods would be questioned because of the dependence on and centrality of the clan and the *Guurti*. As identified previously, there is an inherent distrust of unfamiliar mechanisms of governance within the liberal state and thus statebuilding. Whilst it is common practice within development and statebuilding projects to utilise traditional or indigenous actors and structures, those are rarely incorporated into the central structure of the state and, as Ghani and Lockhart acknowledge, are used as intermediaries between the local population and the interveners.[4] However, this relationship is not characterised by autonomy of the domestic but rather the domestic as a subject to external sovereignty. As Woodward identifies, however,

---

2 M. Jama, 'Somalia and Somaliland: Strategies for dialogue and consensus on governance and democratic transition', Paper prepared for the UNDP Oslo Governance Centre (January 2003).

3 T. Sisk, *Statebuilding* (Cambridge: Polity, 2013), p. 67.

4 A. Ghani and C. Lockhart, 'Closing the Sovereignty Gap: An Approach to State-Building', Overseas Development Institute Working Paper 253 (London: ODI, 2005).

'the crucial element of stabilised statebuilding is deference to the new authorities and compliance with their rules and decisions, in sum, the state's authority'. In this aspect of statebuilding, 'the period of transition from civil war to peace has particular characteristics unrelated to other statebuilding conditions – the required complement of nation-building'. An internal process central to statebuilding success, it is necessary to create a political community and its implied obligations. Indeed, the creation of a new state's authority is a 'symbolic contest of nation-building',[5] and in Somaliland the clan, and trust fostered in and by the clan, was central to this.

Throughout the campaign of the SNM the Somaliland clans were integral to the success of the liberation struggle as well as post-conflict reconciliation and state formation. Although the clans were vital to the emergence of an independent Somaliland, out of the SNM campaign and rule emerged not an absolute dependence on the clan, but rather a democratic government rooted in traditional Somali practices, including customary laws and the moderating roles and practices of clan elders; the clan intrinsically underpins the government and the state.[6] The result was intertwining of the modern and traditional, physically within the legislative branch and as a mediation body, and practically and symbolically as a link between the state and society, the 'old' and the 'new' and the external and the internal. Somaliland's *Guurti* is a legislative body within the government, but it is also a clan body and as such its responsibilities reflect democratic demands as well as both traditional and symbolic expectations of the *guurti*.[7]

In institutionalising the *Guurti*, Somaliland established a hybrid political order as a key component of its statebuilding strategy. But Somaliland's hybridity went beyond just the composition and practice of the institutions; the utilisation, integration and dependence on the clan and clan governance mechanisms makes both practical and symbolic traditional governance part of the statebuilding process and part of the state. Whilst the aim of the SNM had been creating a democratic government in Somalia, after the declaration of independence this goal became one for Somaliland. As Abdullahi Duale articulates, however, '[y]ou just cannot impose democracy. It has to come from within'. He goes on to argue that Somaliland had to create a government from the bottom up, and they had to 'do it [their] own way'.[8] For Somaliland, this meant including traditional structures

---

5 S. Woodward, 'State-Building and Peace-Building: What Theory and Whose Role?' in R. Kozul-Wright and P. Fortunato (eds), *Securing Peace: State-Building and Economic Development in Post-Conflict Countries* (London: Bloomsbury Academic, 2011), pp. 87–112: p. 107.

6 J. Drysdale, *Stoics Without Pillows: A Way Forward for the Somalilands* (London: HAAN Associates, 2000).

7 R. Richards, 'The Road Less Traveled: Self-led statebuilding and non-intervention in Somaliland', in B. Bliesemann de Guevara (ed.), *Statebuilding and State Formation: The political sociology of intervention* (London: Routledge, 2012), pp. 149–64: p. 154.

8 Abdullahi Duale, Minister of Foreign Affairs. Interview with author (Hargeisa, September 2006).

of governance in what would become a democratic government, not only for the sake of stability but more importantly for legitimacy of the ongoing process of statebuilding, of the government and of the state itself. Whilst certainly not the only actor in Somaliland's statebuilding project, the clan acts as not only an actor but also a foundational structure, making it central to the overall project.[9] This chapter examines the foundational role and evolution of the clan as a political and legitimising actor as well as the process of 'locally owning' the state. Beginning with the role of the clan during the liberation struggle, this chapter examines the foundations of the state and nation-building processes, focusing on the inclusion of the clan and traditional practice, building the state from within and the legitimising functions those served.

The Clan and the Council of Elders: A Pillar of the SNM

For Somali society, '[t]he clan is everything. It is the basis of all. Social, economic, political, all'.[10] Historically, '[c]ollective action through kinship' provided physical, political, social and economic security.[11] As power increasingly centralised in the country under Barre, Somalis turned to the clan for provision and protection. In Somaliland, where the clan system had been less disrupted by events such as colonisation and government practices than other areas of Somalia, this clan allegiance and dependence, together with the influence of elders over their clans, contributed to the success of the liberation movement throughout the long campaign against Barre. It is during this period that the institutionalised *Guurti* emerged as a mechanism of centralised governance, a role that would become a component of centralised government. It was also during this period that the social foundations for the Somaliland state were laid.

The first SNM constitution, created in 1981, mandated that clan units should be respected in any new government and that cooperation between the clans should be based on customary law (*xeer*) rather than through government mandates or force.[12] The SNM constitution also gave clan elders an important role as grassroots decision makers; a role which would later be elevated to a much larger scale.

---

9 For more on technical details about the statebuilding process, see, in particular, M. Bradbury, *Becoming Somaliland* (Oxford: James Currey, 2008); Somaliland Academy for Peace and Development (APD), *Rebuilding Somaliland: Issues and Possibilities* (Lawrenceville, NJ: The Red Sea Press, 2005); I.M. Lewis, *A Modern History of the Somali* (Oxford: James Currey, 2002).

10 Dr Abdirahman Yusuf Artan, Member of House of Representatives (Kulmiye). Interview with Author (Hargeisa, August 2006).

11 M. Bradbury, 'Somaliland Country Report', CIIR Country Report (1997), p. 4; I.M. Lewis and A. Farah, 'Somalia: The Roots of Reconciliation: Peace Making Endeavours of Contemporary Lineage Leaders in "Somaliland"', Report for ActionAid (1993).

12 I.M. Lewis, *A Modern History*, op. cit., p. 215.

With this recognition of the centrality and importance of the clan, the SNM proposed combining 'the advantages of Somali democracy and egalitarianism with the benefits of modern national government';[13] by elevating the concept of *xeer* to the national level and utilising traditional practices in conjunction with modern democratic principles and practices the SNM anticipated effective, fair and peaceful governance in Somalia. This amalgamation of modern democracy and traditional Somali clan governance was also seen as the ideal way to address the issue of 'destructive clannism', a recurring problem in post-colonial Somalia and one that was a significant factor in the establishment of Barre's draconian anti-clan policies. By incorporating the clan rather than removing it or outlawing it, the SNM envisioned a disaggregated federal system with regional clan-based administrations responsible for the delivery of most public and political goods. As Drysdale notes, by placing primacy in the clan as a useful, necessary and stabilising element in a new government rather than as a divisive political factor, the SNM was successful in reversing attitudes against clannism that had been prevalent under Barre.[14] The proposal of decentralised rule throughout Somalia reflected the reality of clan dominance in geographic regions within Somalia, and also expressed both fears of oppression and nationalist desires existent amongst some clans, including the Isaaq. Devolution of power to the regional governments would place the majority of Somaliland under Isaaq rule and the majority of Isaaq under Somaliland rule.[15] By using the clan structures as a part of a federal democratic government, the leadership of the pre-1991 SNM envisioned the creation of a stable, and safe, political system in Somalia.

The Isaaq-dominated SNM also fully utilised the clan system and clan loyalties within the structure of the movement itself. Although the Isaaq clan is sub-divided into powerful sub-clan groupings, the concept of clan balance determined leadership within the movement, with the senior positions in the SNM rotated amongst the various sub-clans to ensure Isaaq solidarity and cooperation. In the broader movement, individuals were of lesser importance than the group; a practice that was demonstrated by the exclusion of certain SNM supporters from the minority Gadabuursi and Darood clans as they were unable to 'carry their clans with them' in support of the movement. Clan distribution was also used to determine the collection of funds for the movement; operating funds for the SNM were collected in a similar manner to that of *diya* payments.[16] From the beginning the SNM depended on the support of the clan groups for its continued operation and later, for its success. First almost entirely dependent on the Isaaq, the SNM eventually became more inclusive of all of the Somaliland clans.

---

13   SNM press release as cited in Ibid., p. 199.

14   J. Drysdale, op. cit., p. 160.

15   I.M. Lewis, *Blood and Bone: The Call of Kinship in Somali Society* (Lawrenceville, NJ: The Red Sea Press, 1994), p. 200.

16   Ibid., p. 202.

Whilst some viewed the Isaaq exclusivity of the SNM as tribalism or extreme Isaaq nationalism, an explanation based upon the practicalities of clan exclusivity is more likely than any extremist agenda. Barre's oppression against the Isaaq clan was seen by many as justification for action against the regime, and increased totalitarian measures experienced in the northwest fuelled Isaaq support for the SNM prior to the start of the war. As Somali clans act collectively when threatened, even with sub-clan divisions and competition within the Isaaq clan itself, a unified position was possible because of Barre's policy against the Isaaq as a whole. Because of this, gathering needed logistical support from the Isaaq was less complex than it would have been if other clans and their specific considerations or grievances had been included. Also, an element of trust played into the Isaaq exclusivity. When members of the Hawiye clan, which comprised the majority of the United Somali Congress (USC) in Somalia, approached the SNM asking to take part in the SNM Congress in London, they were refused participation as it was suspected that the Hawiye were complicit with the Barre regime and inclusion of the Hawiye would introduce the risk of internal SNM policies and actions being passed on to the dictator. Although elements of Isaaq nationalism cannot be entirely discounted, the functioning of the Somali clan system creates a situation in which depending on a single clan is more practical than being all inclusive.

During its time in London, the involvement of clan leadership in the SNM had been important for negotiating support within the UK and other areas with large Isaaq populations. Following its move to Ethiopia clan elders were tasked with a more active role, thus became entrenched in the operations of the movement. Because of its difficult history with the Somali population in the Ogaden, the Ethiopian government viewed all Somalis as being problematic and treated them as such. The Ogaden War also made the Ethiopian government wary of the intention of liberation movements, particularly those based within the Somali population. As a result, the Ethiopian government forcefully acted against the SNM in an attempt to quash any potential conflicts within Ethiopia itself. For the SNM leadership, 'that was a headache … we found out Barre had a fifth column in Ethiopia [fighting us]'.[17] As a way of convincing the Ethiopian government of the validity of the SNM presence in the country, and that the SNM was not targeting the Ethiopian government but rather the Barre regime, the first SNM council of elders (*guurti*)[18] was convened by the movement's political leadership.

---

17 Hassan Issa, Former Vice President of Somaliland. Interview with Author (Hargeisa, September 2006). Hassan Issa was a leading figure in the formation of the SNM in London, and also served as Vice Chairman of the SNM political wing as well as the first Vice President of Somaliland during the two-year SNM administration.

18 As previously, *Guurti* will be used to identify the modern utilisation of the traditional body, specifically the use of the council of elders by the SNM as well as within the government. As before, *guurti* will signify the non-central, traditional notion of the council of elders.

The *guurti* has long been integral to the Somali clan governance system. As the most respected council in the Somali-inhabited territories, the traditionally ad hoc body is responsible for resolving differences within or between the clans or to unite the clans in times of crisis or war and is therefore a vital component of clan governance. The SNM first utilised this traditional body in 1982 to reconcile between the SNM and the Ethiopian government, thereby elevating the *guurti* to a quasi-diplomatic position between a liberation movement and a foreign state government. As Hassan Issa, the man in charge of convening this first SNM *Guurti*, recalls, the predominantly Isaaq elders were 'rounded up' from the clans in Ethiopia and 'taken in the back of a pick-up truck' to Addis Ababa where they met with Ethiopian authorities to 'educate' them about the SNM.[19] When asked why the elders were tasked with this rather than a political or military figure, Issa simply replied, '[i]t's Africa'.[20] The SNM leadership felt that the elders, including two sultans, would garner more respect from the Ethiopian authorities than an official from the liberation movement as traditional figures would be more trusted than a political or military representative. The utilisation of the elders in this regard was for a very specific purpose: to invoke respect from the Ethiopian authorities in order to garner Ethiopian support for the SNM. According to Issa, the G*uurti* 'did a fantastic job' and the clan body therefore became a tool for the SNM.[21] As such, the body assumed its traditional role and became a mediation and reconciliation body for the movement. With the first SNM *Guurti*, however, how the clan was used changed as this new form of *guurti*, albeit a body tasked with reconciliation and mediation within the Somali population, also took on the added role of convincing and campaigning actors outside the Somali population on behalf of the SNM. Through this, the clan became a tool of the movement and the utilisation of the *guurti* by the SNM made the traditional institution a part of the movement's apparatus.

This quasi-political incarnation of the *Guurti* thus emerged as a created institution, acting first as a mediator between the SNM and the Ethiopian government and later between the SNM and the Somali population. When the SNM was expelled from Ethiopia, the movement was forced to look elsewhere for the resources needed to maintain its campaign. This changed situation brought about the re-emergence of the formal SNM *Guurti*. The second incarnation worked in the same manner as the previous body, but this time the elders were co-opted to garner the support of Ethiopian Somalis as well as the large Somaliland refugee population that had crossed the border following attacks by the Somalia military. Under the SNM clan elders were brought together to serve a specific purpose: to further the cause of the liberation movement. The eventual permanency of the SNM *Guurti* as an institution moved it away from its traditional ad hoc and decentralised nature. Instead of the elders convening and exercising power and

---

19 Hassan Issa. Interview with author, op. cit.
20 Ibid.
21 Ibid.

control outside the purview of the state or central political body in response to a specific situation as traditional *guurti* had done, the created *Guurti* became a body that was dispatched on behalf of the SNM. The ad hoc council was thus transformed into a mobile political body that became a valuable component of the SNM leadership.

Even though the targets of Barre's attacks in the north were primarily the Isaaq, all the northern clans were affected by the violence. Because many of the attacks were in retaliation for SNM actions and raids into Somaliland, though, support for the SNM within both in Somaliland and Ethiopia faced uncertainty as suffering increased. In targeting the Isaaq, Barre was not only fighting against those he viewed as rebellious, but also outwardly identifying the Isaaq and the SNM as the root cause of the suffering of the non-Isaaq population. Barre's divide-and-rule tactic threatened the survival of the SNM, as in continuing their actions the liberation movement was creating a situation in which it could have been defeated by the people it was trying to liberate. Because of this, the SNM was forced to move away from its Isaaq exclusivity in order to incorporate the other clans into the movement's operations and garner the support of the Somaliland population as a whole. Once again, the SNM utilised the clan elders, dispatching the *Guurti* to reconcile with the non-Isaaq clans and to bring them into the support base of the SNM. The *Guurti* was therefore tasked with linking the active SNM struggle to the new cross-clan refugee population as well as those remaining in the cities, and as the war continued so did the *Guurti* in negotiating with the clans and widening the support base for the SNM in northern Somalia.[22] The SNM *Guurti* continued this role when the SNM moved its base into Somaliland in 1988, and by 1990 the SNM and the *Guurti* had expanded to include all Somaliland clans.[23] By April 1990 the *Guurti* was formally institutionalised into the SNM governing structure as a separate branch of the leadership, making the traditional structure a permanent institution and giving it a leading role in the liberation movement.[24]

The *Guurti* is widely credited with obtaining logistical, financial and military support necessary for the SNM to move into Somalia, allowing it to directly confront Barre's troops. According to Dr Aden Abokor:

> [t]he only institution supporting the SNM was the institution of the clan. Everything was a contribution from the clan. Guns came from the clan. People came from the clan. Food came from the clan. Everything came from the clan.[25]

---

22 Ibid.
23 Dr Aden Abokor. Interview with author, op. cit.; I.M. Lewis, *Blood and Bone*, op. cit., p. 215.
24 Bobe Duale Yusuf, former member of SNM Central Committee and Programme Coordinator for Academy for Peace and Development. Interviews with Author (Hargeisa, August-September 2006).
25 Dr Aden Abokor. Interview with author, op. cit.

However, despite the new cross-clan base, '[a]s the scope of military operations widened and intensified the clan basis of units became, if anything, more sharply delineated'.[26] During the period of all-out war against Barre (1988–1990), the SNM had five 'regular' regiments comprised of the major Isaaq sub-clans, and other clans were encouraged to create their own fighting factions instead of joining one of the Isaaq regiments.[27] As a result, SNM military units were formed along strict clan and sub-clan lines with each unit fighting primarily within their own territory. To avoid clashes and misunderstandings between sub-clans, the SNM *Guurti* strove to ensure balance and cooperation between the clan units fighting for the movement.[28]

During the liberation struggle 'the $6 million question was how to involve the masses'.[29] The solution reached by the SNM was the utilisation of clan loyalties and governance. The elders were a key element in this, acting as a driving force by 'spreading the word of revolt and win[ning] support' of the Somaliland population both within Somalia and in Ethiopia.[30] Because of the relationship between the *Guurti* and society, and therefore the SNM and the people, the elders continually acted as a point of reassurance for the people during the conflict. Following the devastation of the civil war and the collapse of the government in Mogadishu, the people of Somaliland turned to the familiar and trusted clans and the ostensibly apolitical elders for provision and security. The *Guurti* therefore 'came into their own, empowered by civil war and devastation'.[31] Taking on the vital role of reconciliation in a war-torn society, the body once again became an agent of reassurance, mediation and leadership in post-war Somaliland.

The National Conferences: Traditional Peacemaking and Modern State-Making

During the war the SNM 'was able to not feed war against Barrism with Isaaqism' and eventually became a movement for all of the north.[32] Lewis notes that the SNM was successful in gaining the support of the population because it was a 'grassroots movement which sprang from the tribal structures of Somali society and not a movement based on the theoretical discourse of a few intellectuals or

---

26   I.M. Lewis, *Blood and Bone*, op. cit., p. 214.
27   Ibid.
28   G. Prunier, 'Somaliland: Birth of a New Country?' in C. Gurdon (ed.), *The Horn of Africa* (London: UCL Press Limited, 1994), pp. 61–75: p. 65.
29   Hassan Issa. Interview with author, op. cit.
30   Ibid.; Bobe Duale Yusuf. Interview with author, op. cit.
31   Mohammed Said Mohammed Gees, former SNM and government minister and current Executive Director of APD. Interview with author (Hargeisa, September 2006). Mohammed Said Gees is a leading scholar and member of civil society in Somaliland, and was a long-serving governmental minister under Egal.
32   F. Battera, 'State and Democracy Building in Sub-Saharan Africa: The Case of Somaliland- A Comparative Perspective', *Global Jurist Frontiers* 4.1 (2004), pp. 1–21: p. 8.

the blind determination of a few hotheads'.[33] The democratic nature of the SNM, together with its multifaceted decentralised leadership, are counted among the more valued legacies inherited from the movement by post-war Somaliland.[34] A component of this leadership, the institutionalisation of traditional leadership, is also an invaluable legacy that contributed greatly to the establishment and maintenance of stability in the territory following the end of Barre's rule.

Although the SNM had incorporated all of the Somaliland clans in some capacity by the end of the war, it was still seen by many as 'an armed expression of the Isaaq people'.[35] As such, tensions between the Isaaq and those clans that had largely supported of Barre – the Gadabuursi and Ise (Dir sub-clans), and the Dhulbahante and the Warsangeli (Darood sub-clans)[36] – threatened a continuation of the civil war in the north. Because of this potential, following the end of the conflict with Barre the SNM and the *Guurti* took steps towards the regional reconciliation they deemed necessary for the successful implementation of a federal Somalia government. As Hassan Issa acknowledges, the SNM and its supporters 'wanted something greater than revenge'.[37] Despite the continued opposition, 'given the role played by the marginal clans in the anti-SNM campaign, the SNM's behaviour in the very first few days of the takeover had a great importance for the possibility of northern cohesion'.[38] In areas where pro-Barre and anti-SNM elements were strong, the first point of concern was limiting retributive between the various clan groupings; many involved in this process recall the SNM's desire for forgiveness rather than retribution against those who had opposed them and, in some instances, their victory. The SNM leadership discerned that continued fighting or forceful domination would only hinder achieving the end goal of democratic government in Somalia; before the needs for democracy could be addressed the fractures within society needed to first be closed. According to Ali Farah, the clans 'needed reconciliation between them rather than the democratic process. They needed the *Guurti*'s help for this ... [they] changed confrontation into negotiation'.[39] One vital component of the clan system is negotiation and compromise leading to co-existence of competing familial groups; peaceful or cooperative inter- and intra-clan relations are balanced upon carefully negotiated agreements reached by the 'peacemaker' clan elders, often within a *guurti*.[40] The

---

33   I.M. Lewis, *Blood and Bone*, op. cit., p. 192.

34   APD, op. cit., p. 60.

35   G. Prunier, op. cit., p. 62.

36   M. Höhne, 'Traditional Authorities in Northern Somalia: Transformation of Positions and Power', Max Planck Institute for Social Anthropology Working Paper 82 (Halle: Max Planck Institute for Social Anthropology, 2006), p. 14.

37   Hassan Issa. Interview with author, op. cit.

38   G. Prunier, op. cit., p. 62.

39   Abdirahman Aw Ali Farah, former SNM Commander and former Vice President of Somaliland. Interview with author (Hargeisa, September 2006).

40   R. Richards, op. cit., p. 155

SNM heavily depended upon these elders as a vital reconciliation and mediation body in the process of reconciling and reconstructing a war-torn society and in creating a state. Reconciliation was the leading priority, and through a succession of national clan conferences the elders, as both a traditional *guurti* as well as an institution of the SNM, were again utilised to bring the clans together to support the larger project. Even though the SNM and the *Guurti* did not gain the full support of all the clans – opposition to the boundaries of Somaliland and the existence of the government continues today, primarily in the eastern provinces of Sanaag and Sool – the actions of the SNM and the *Guurti* are credited with success in reducing violence in the territory and establishing peaceful foundations upon which to build the bigger political project.

Somali society is characterised by confrontation, and military strength is the final sanction in any relationship. Therefore as the victors of war it was the responsibility and the right of the SNM to take the lead in the post-war north; the SNM was empowered from within. As Samatar articulates, however, 'I can recall no other example of a liberation movement which won power through the barrel of the gun and which was simultaneously so uninterested in ruling with its gun'.[41] Because of its position of power as the victor the SNM was 'able to sue for peace from a position of strength' rather than demanding compliance through force.[42] Minorities did not have much choice other than comply with the actions of the militarily superior SNM, as 'they had been given peace on a silver platter'.[43] Although the initiative for reconciliation in post-war Somaliland came from the SNM, the leadership again relied heavily on clan elders to negotiate a settlement between the clans as well as between society and the liberation movement.[44] In post-conflict Somaliland, community meetings (*shir*) involving the clans and led by *guurti* became an important component of negotiating a peaceful settlement and creating stability throughout the territory.[45] These 'national' *shir*, in addition to being peacebuilding conferences, resulted in the creation of the structure, function and purpose of the Somaliland government. Importantly, these *shir* also firmly rooted the Somaliland state in grassroots governance mechanisms, establishing local ownership from the start and domestically legitimising the state not only through the process but also through the actors involved. The Somaliland state came from within.

---

41 I. Samatar, 'Light at the End of the Tunnel: Some Reflections on the Struggle of the Somali National Movement', in H. Adam and R. Ford (eds), *Mending the Rips in the Sky: Options for Somali Communities in the 21st Century* (Lawrenceville, NJ: The Red Sea Press, 1997), pp. 21–48: p. 31.

42 I.M. Lewis, *A Pastoral Democracy* (Oxford: Oxford University Press, 1961), pp. 242–3; M. Bradbury, 'Peace-Enforcement, Peace-Making and Peace-Building: Options for Resolving the Somali Conflict', Exploratory Report for Oxfam (1993), p. 79.

43 Dr Aden Abokor. Interview with author, op. cit.

44 Abdirahman Aw Ali Farah, Interview with author, op. cit.

45 For more on the nature of these community meetings, see Chapter 4.

The Berbera Conference, 1991

It is important to note that national *shir* were rare occurrences in northern Somalia, with the last one prior to 1991 being held in 1954 in response to the British ceding a portion of Somaliland grazing area to Ethiopia.[46] With the need for inter and intra-clan reconciliation, however, a national meeting was the optimal prospect. The first of these was the Brotherhood Conference of the Northern Clans held in Berbera in February 1991. At what *Guurti* member Haji Abdi Hussein refers to as 'the Declaration of Peace Conference', the SNM leadership, various Isaaq clan elders and representatives of the minority clans came together to begin the reconciliation process.[47] In addition to the SNM *Guurti*, local *guurti* and individual clan elders were also part of the peace process, and at Berbera they were charged with the important task of negotiating and maintaining peace locally. Although convened by the SNM leadership, the Berbera conference was composed of and managed by clan elders, and it was this conference that 'demonstrated the skilfulness of the traditional elders in peacemaking and conflict management, a sign that confirms the richness of the peace making culture of Somaliland communities'.[48]

The objective of the Berbera Conference was to restore trust and confidence between the Isaaq and the non-Isaaq clans, and the start of this reconciliation process was the most obvious outcome of the *shir*. This conference achieved what one observer described as 'the SNM's conciliatory policy of peaceful co-existence between all the clans',[49] and at Berbera a 'surprising degree of peace [was] secured, largely through the efforts of the traditional clan elders'.[50] Holding a national conference to address post-war issues and possibilities set a precedent for post-war Somaliland. Although this first conference differed from those which followed in that it was convened and led by the SNM not the clans, it nevertheless laid the groundwork for larger conferences that would take place between April 1991 and February 1997. Instead of exhibiting authority through force, the SNM leadership consented to a peaceful community and clan-led process through these conferences, thereby invoking clan elders as those responsible for peace and reconciliation in post-war Somaliland.[51] Through this, they would also become an important actor in the statebuilding process.

---

46 M. Bradbury, 'Somaliland', op. cit., p. 19.

47 G. Prunier, op. cit., p. 62; APD, op. cit., pp. 60, 64; Haji Abdi Hussein, Member of the House of Elders. Interview with author (Hargeisa, September 2006).

48 J. Sweden, 'Somaliland's Quest for Recognition: A Challenge for the International Community', in H. Adam, et al. (eds), *War Destroys, Peace Nurtures: Somali Reconciliation and Development* (Lawrenceville, NJ: The Red Sea Press, 2004), pp. 169–78: p. 176.

49 APD, op. cit., p. 60.

50 I.M. Lewis, *Blood and Bone*, op. cit., p. 229.

51 J. Sweden, op. cit., p. 176; M. Bradbury, *Becoming Somaliland*, op. cit., p. 79.

The Burco Conference, 1991

The first conference following Berbera was the Grand Conference of Northern Clans held in Burco in April and May 1991. Convened and run by clan elders, it was at this conference that they exhibited the powerful position they had within the territory.[52] At Burco the former SNM *Guurti* asserted itself as an autonomous force and firmly established its role as an institution in the leadership of the territory. As Höhne notes, the Burco conference was the starting point for the new political powers that the *Guurti* has gained since 1991.[53]

The leaders and decision makers at Burco were clan elders, but other sectors of Somaliland society also took part. The purpose of the conference was to finalise and formalise the peace agreements that had been reached at the Berbera Conference and to continue discussion of Somaliland's place in the unified state of Somalia. However, the conference agenda was altered in May when Somaliland's independence was declared and creating a state became a primary concern. At Burco the elders tasked the SNM leadership with heading a new transitional government, not only appointing the membership but also in effect transferring sovereign power to the transitional government. The *Guurti* became an integral component of this new government, with the elders who were delegates at the Burco Conference filling the membership of the interim upper house of parliament. As both a legislative body and an advisory council the *Guurti* existed as both a traditional body and an institution within the government. This duality made the body concurrently both internal and external to the new government, sitting both within and above the institutions and the process.

In the early years of the emerging state the most important role for the *Guurti* was that of peacemaking and peacekeeping, and a significant accomplishment of the *Guurti* was grassroots reconciliation. Haji Abdi Hussein notes that the *Guurti* knew that a government could not be initiated with hostility remaining in the community, particularly if that government was to exercise power-sharing between the clans. Therefore, in the capacity of reconciliation the *Guurti* was a 'stepping stool for independence'.[54] During the two-year rule of the SNM the *Guurti* continued to expand its place within the new state and to entrench its position as a governing institution, undertaking or participating in major peace and security building initiatives such as demobilising militias and assisting local *guurti* in quelling outbreaks of violence. Twenty local peace and reconciliation conferences took place between the Burco Conference and the next national *shir* in 1993, including the Sheikh Conference in October 1992 at which the government gained control of the port of Berbera.[55] Whilst these were not national conferences,

---

52   APD, op. cit., pp. 15–16; G. Prunier, op. cit., p. 64.
53   M. Höhne, op. cit., p. 14.
54   Haji Abdi Hussein. Interview with author, op. cit.
55   APD, op. cit., p. 64. For detailed accounts of local level initiatives, see I.M. Lewis and A. Farah, 'Somalia: Roots of Reconciliation', op. cit. Agreements reached at the Sheikh

the new Somaliland *Guurti* was involved in most, sending delegates to the local negotiations. As an active presence in both local and national governance structures and initiatives, the *Guurti*'s influence extended far beyond that of the troubled transitional Tuur administration. During this period 'the *Guurti* was more interactive and productive than the government' and the body grew in importance and power as it was through the clan institution that continuity of the government was maintained.[56] Through the institutional representation of the traditional clan structure, the body was able to include the communities and clans not only in the government but also in creating the foundations for the state and the state apparatus through the utilisation of traditional governance practices.

The Borama Conference, 1993

In 1993 Somaliland held its next national conference in Borama, the 'capital' of the Gadabuursi clan. The decision to hold the conference amongst the Gadabuursi was a way to show that the state being created was not an Isaaq one.[57] The clan elders took further steps in removing the association with Isaaq dominance when they transferred rule in the territory from the Isaaq-associated SNM to a civilian administration. The peaceful transfer to civilian rule marked the start of the process of creating a democratic state in Somaliland. One hundred and fifty voting members from all the Somaliland clans took part in the clan controlled five-month long Borama Conference in what Prunier identifies as a showcase of the Somali decision making process.[58] As much a healing process as a political meeting, the Borama Conference became an arena in which the balance between the clans was of prime importance. As Prunier notes, 'electing the new president became almost a side issue ... the political and cultural display of social dynamics became essential'.[59] As the first national meeting since the declaration of independence, grievances about the direction of Somaliland were aired and dynamic negotiations continued.

At Borama the *Guurti* again proved its dual internal-external capacity and importance by not only continuing as a legislative component of the new government, but also in its advisory capacity by creating the institutions of the state and determining their membership. Just as it had been for the interim government, the civilian government's authority originated from the clan elders. As Abdikadir Mohammed Hassan 'Indho' states '[a]fter we settled things, we

---

Conference put an end to fighting over Berbera port, the largest threat of instability in post-conflict Somaliland.

56 Bobe Duale Yusuf. Interview with author, op. cit.

57 G. Prunier, op. cit., p. 66. The Gadabuursi had been a main actor in the fight over control of Berbera port, a conflict that was settled at the Sheikh Conference in 1992.

58 Dr Aden Abokor. Interview with author, op. cit.; G. Prunier, op. cit.; G. Prunier, 'Somaliland Goes it Alone', *Current History* 97.619 (1998), pp. 225–8.

59 G. Prunier, 'Somaliland: Birth?' op. cit., p. 6.

called the government to come to us'.[60] At the Borama Conference the *Guurti* assumed the powers of the SNM administration after the liberation movement relinquished control of the government, and therefore assumed the power of governing the territory. For a brief period in April and May 1993, the *Guurti* was the government.[61] Although rule by the *Guurti* was only for the duration of transition from military to civilian rule, it was during this time that the trust and respect of the elders became palpable; the elders holding onto power and not continuing the transition to a civilian rule was not a consideration by those involved. Following the 1991 Burco Conference, the *Guurti* and other clan elders had emerged with a reputation of being selfless, wise, courageous and peaceful because of the manner in which they had managed the conference and the successful reconciliation efforts. As Dr Abdirahman Yusuf Artan recalls, the elders 'really got their name and reputation there'.[62] The delegates at Borama carried this reputation with them, and their voluntary participation in the conference and the administrative transition exhibited their commitment to a peaceful and stable future for the territory. With the *Guurti* viewed as the neutral body that could be entrusted with handing the government back to the people, it was the elders at the Borama Conference that chose, appointed and empowered the new civilian administration headed by Egal.[63] Because of this role, the *Guurti* is often considered to be the 'father' of Somaliland and its success.[64] Mohammed Said Gees acknowledges the institution's foundational importance in identifying the *Guurti* as 'the seed' of the Somaliland government. Gees takes this further, though, in recognising not only the *Guurti*'s capacity to anoint the civilian administration with governing power, but also the position of the elders as the metaphorical rock of the Somaliland state: 'because of them, there is rule of law, order, a social system, etc. [They were] absolutely necessary for state-building'.[65] In addition to the body's role in appointing the government, the *Guurti* also acted in an advisory, almost parental capacity to the new government to ensure that the statebuilding process stayed on track. The *Guurti* was the backbone supporting the new state.

The role of a central and permanent *Guurti* developed significantly during and after the Borama Conference. Whereas under the transitional *Guurti* had been sanctioned as the peacemakers and the keepers of traditional, religious and cultural values, it was at Borama that the current role of the *Guurti* was constitutionally

---

60 Abdikadir Mohammed Hassan 'Indho', Member of Somaliland House of Elders. Interview with author (Hargeisa, September 2006).
61 Bobe Duale Yusuf. Interview with author, op. cit.
62 Dr Abdirahman Yusuf Artan. Interview with author, op. cit.
63 Abdirahman Aw Ali Farah. Interview with author, op. cit.; Dr Aden Abokor Interview with author, op. cit.
64 Awil Hussein Ahmed, Member of Somaliland House of Elders. Interview with author (Hargeisa, September 2006); Dini Abdullahi Hande, Member of Somaliland House of Elders. Interview with author (Hargeisa, September 2006).
65 Mohammed Said Mohammed Gees. Interview with author, op. cit.

codified within the National Charter as a body with both legislative and traditional or cultural responsibilities within the hybrid government.[66] This new role inarguably again changed the nature of the clan body by placing it firmly within the political structure of the state. Although it maintained its stabilising influence, following Borama the *Guurti* went from being a primarily reconciliatory body to becoming part of the political machinery of Somaliland.

The Hargeisa Conference, 1996–1997

One final major national conference was held in Hargeisa in 1996–1997. Partly in response to a renewal of violence in Somaliland, and partly as a means of ending deadlock between Egal and the Parliament over the drafting of a permanent constitution, the Hargeisa conference was a means of bringing together a fragmented population as well as a divided government. Whilst previous conferences were clan-based conferences with the onus being on the *Guurti* for reconciliation and beginning the creation of a state, the Hargeisa Conference was a political conference that was labelled a 'national conference' rather than a 'clan conference'. Although the Hargeisa Conference was announced by the House of Elders, it was convened and financed by Egal's government rather than the people and the Diaspora as past conferences had been. Petitions to establish a neutral *guurti* and preparatory committee were rejected by the government and the nearly 300 participants were hand-picked by the president.[67] With Egal controlling so much of the process, many maintain that the Hargeisa Conference was more an exercise of Egal's control over the peace process and the state, including the *Guurti*, than a *shir* in the way that Berbera, Burco and Borama had been.[68] Even though the *Guurti* was instrumental in reaching a peace agreement that ended the renewed violence, the body's internal-external position was changing as the *Guurti* became more entrenched in Egal's government; the dual positioning of the *Guurti* became an important resource for the president. The strong rule of Egal overshadowed the role of the *Guurti*, and as Bradbury notes, 'Egal's influence over the conference damaged the credibility of a national *shir* as a mechanism for political change in the future'.[69] These changing power relationships, leading to and part of the alteration and arguable politicisation of the *Guurti*, have had a significant impact on the present-day government, posing challenges and raising questions about the future role of the clan institution in the central government.

After nearly five months of negotiations, the Hargeisa Conference resulted in significant changes for Somaliland. A peace agreement was signed, bringing an end to the fighting, and Egal was re-selected as president. More noteworthy, however,

---

66   APD, op. cit.; M. Bradbury, 'Somaliland', op. cit., p. 22.
67   M. Bradbury, *Becoming Somaliland*, op. cit., pp. 124–5.
68   Mohammed Said Mohammed Gees. Interview with author, op. cit.; Bobe Yusuf Duale. Interview with author, op. cit.; Dr Aden Abokor. Interview with author, op. cit.
69   M. Bradbury, *Becoming Somaliland*, op. cit., p. 126.

the conference resulted in the start of a transition from the community or clan based (*beel*) government system that had thus far characterised the government to a multi-party democratic system.[70] An interim constitution reflecting this was established and the process of creating a permanent constitution was began. It was under this constitution, ratified in 2001, that the current position, powers and responsibilities of the *Guurti* were established. It is this constitutional placement and the symbolic role of the traditional structure within a democratising government that is the focus of the next section.

Table 6.1   Key Somaliland National Conferences

Conference (Location)	Dates	Purpose	Participants	Outcome
Brotherhood Conference of Northern Clans (Berbera)	15–27 Feb. 1991	End of conflict; reconciliation. *National clan conference*	Clan representatives from all the Somaliland clans; SNM leadership. *Financed by communities and Diaspora.*	Start of reconciliation between clans; end to Somalia civil war in Somaliland
The Grand Conference of Northern Clans (Burco)	27 Apr.–18 May 1991	Establish role of Somaliland in post-Barre Somalia. *National clan conference.*	150 voting delegates (clan elders); community and business leaders. *Financed by communities and Diaspora.*	Declaration of Independence; beginning of SNM administration of Somaliland.
Tawfiq Conference (Sheikh)	28 Oct.–8 Nov. 1992	Peace conference. End conflict over Berbera. *Clan conference*	40 elders from Gadabuursi, Dhulbahante and Isaaq clans; religious leaders. *Financed by communities and Diaspora.*	Ceasefire and political settlement; established Berbera and all public facilities and state properties as public assets; regularised the role of elder participation in governance (collective efforts of *Guurti* and *guurti*); formalisation of security arrangements (police, militias, army).

continued ...

---

70   APD, op. cit., p. 16.

Conference (Location)	Dates	Purpose	Participants	Outcome
Borama Peace and Reconciliation National Conference (Borama)	24 Jan.–May 1993	Establish Somaliland state apparatus. *National clan conference*	Clan elders; community and business leaders. Financed by communities and Diaspora.	Transition to civilian government; National and Peace Charters; election of Egal as president.
Hargeisa National Conference	15 Oct.1996– Feb. 1997	End return to violence; resolve dispute over creation of constitution. *National conference*	300 voting delegates (150 from Parliament, 150 newly selected clan representatives); 100 observers (including women). Financed mostly by the government.	Formal cessation of hostilities; renewed national consensus; re-election of Egal; increased representation of the opposition and minorities in Parliament; adoption of interim constitution – formally established state institutions.

Note: Table compiled by author using Somaliland Academy for Peace and Development Records; Somaliland *Guurti* archives; I.M. Lewis, *A Modern History*, op. cit.; M. Bradbury, *Becoming Somaliland*, op. cit.

The Constitutional Guurti

Although the shape and function of the *Guurti* has been developing since its inception in 1982, the 2001 Constitution officially codifies its role in Somaliland's multi-party democratic government. Articles 57 to 79 of the Somaliland Constitution specify both legislative and traditional duties of the house. Constitutionally, members of the House of Elders must be at least forty-five years old and must be male. In contrast to the House of Representatives, there are no formal education requirements other than a 'good knowledge of the religion [Islam]' and being 'versed in the traditions'.[71] There is also no stipulation for the member to hold a titled position. In terms of clan composition, following the Hargeisa Conference the membership of the House was amended to be more inclusive of all the clans of Somaliland so as to widen participation and representation. As a result, the membership is currently 'selected according to a consociational rule which divides posts according to a delicate balance respectful of clan weight and the right of minorities',[72] with the Isaaq sub-clans holding the majority of seats. The constitutional term of office for the House

---

71 Somaliland Government, 'Somaliland Constitution (2001)', Article 59. According to Article 41, members of the House of Representatives must be educated to a secondary school level or equivalent. Copies of English translation obtained from Somaliland House of Elders and Somaliland Ministry of Information, Hargeisa.

72 F. Battera, op. cit., p. 7, footnote 14.

of Elders is six years, although constitutional ambiguity over how the membership will be chosen in the future has yet to be resolved, leading to significant debate and, as will be examined in Chapter 7, a re-examination of the placement of the traditional body in the central government.

The current membership of the *Guurti* was nominated and selected by their sub-clan and their appointments were confirmed by the president. There are currently no specifications on how the members are chosen by their sub-clans. In terms of accountability, although many members claim to represent all of Somaliland, whether they represent their sub-clan or all the people is debated. Many in the House of Representatives, however, argue that as they are not checked by the population through elections, the *Guurti* members are accountable only to themselves and the president. Accusations also surface regarding the urban-rural distribution of seats, with claims that the majority of *Guurti* seats are held by sub-clan members from the major cities, resulting in the nomadic population and those in the rural areas being under-represented in the upper house.[73] Some within the government and civil society in Somaliland also argue that as a traditional body, the *Guurti* reached its pinnacle at the Borama Conference, after which it was co-opted by Egal as a political tool. Others, however, maintain that the traditional nature of the *Guurti* has not been eroded and is in fact the strongest facet of the Somaliland government.[74] Regardless of the criticisms, the inclusion of the *Guurti* is significant not only in the context of stability in peacebuilding and statebuilding, but also because of its perceived deviance. Three key roles of the *Guurti* in the government and the statebuilding process are widely identified: as a legislative organ; as the representation of the clan system and Somali traditions; and as the mediation and advisory body.

The Modern: The Legislative Body

The legislative role of the House of Elders is the most defined of its roles, with duties pertaining to legislation clearly specified in the constitution. As a component of the institutional state apparatus, constitutionally the House of Elders has sole purview over matters relating to religion, culture, traditions and security, thereby granting the upper house total power in issues pertaining to those areas. Its primary purpose in this regard is to ensure that proposed bills do not contradict cultural or religious laws and stipulations. Although constitutionally there is limited provision for the body or individual members to originate legislation pertaining to other areas, in practice this is often overlooked.[75] In its legislative capacity, the house also acts

---

73 Interviews with author (Hargeisa, August-September 2006).
74 Interviews with author (Hargeisa, August-September 2006).
75 Abdullahi Habane, General Secretary for Somaliland House of Elders. Interviews with author (Hargeisa, August-September 2006); Shi Ahmed Muse Obsiye, Security and Defence Committee Chairman of the House of Elders. Interview with author (Hargeisa, August 2006).

in an advisory capacity, exercising powers of review and revision over legislation passed by the lower house; a responsibility which is both its most important and its most contested legislative power. When asked, members of the upper house respond that the legislative function of the *Guurti* is an important component of the Somaliland government, just as the Senate is important in the United States and the House of Lords in Britain.[76] Indeed, members of the *Guurti* often compare the body's legislative capacity to those Western legislative institutions. However, in Somaliland the utilisation of the unelected body as a presidential tool, especially under Egal, as well as lack of resolution over the selection of members, creates concern over the power of the House in its legislative advisory capacity, a concern that will be discussed in the following chapter. Whilst the legislative role of the *Guurti* is subject to debate, in terms of the statebuilding process it is secondary to the body's other roles. Resolving questions about the institutionalised legislative role of the house is a component of the ongoing statebuilding process, but the remaining two roles are more significant for the early stages of building the Somaliland state. Its role as a legislative body gave the clan governance mechanism a place within the formal institutions of the government, but it also formalised the role of the clan within the governance structures of the modern state.

The Traditional: Representing the Clan System

Due to the structure and functions of the Somali clan system, sustained cooperation between the clans and sometimes sub-clans through institutions is difficult. Because of this, inter-clan governing structures in Somali society were historically ad hoc as they were adapted well to the needs of the nomadic Somali population as well as to the self-sufficiency of the clan system.[77] A permanent clan council was unparalleled in Somali society prior to the establishment of the *Guurti*. During the transition from the Barre regime to a Somaliland government, however, the lasting presence of the traditional body became vital to the success and survival of the nascent state. Because of this, the nature of the inclusion of the *Guurti* in the governing of Somaliland was 'based on the idea, the understanding, that in Somali culture elders always had a unique role'.[78]

Whilst the *Guurti*'s legislative purpose is clearly laid out in the constitution, another significant role of the body is more symbolic in nature: representing the clan system. Although the protection of tradition and culture is a mandated responsibility for the *Guurti*, its role in this regard goes beyond the legislative capacity articulated in the constitution. Whilst the House of Elders is a component of the modern institutional structure, the *Guurti* is also the inclusion of the clan

---

76 Interviews with author. (Hargeisa, August-September 2006).

77 S. Shivakumar, 'The Place of Indigenous Institutions in Constitutional Order', *Constitutional Political Economy* 14.1 (2003), pp. 3–21: p. 15; Mohammed Hassan Ibrahim 'Gani', Lead Researcher for APD. Interview with author (Hargeisa, August 2006).

78 Hassan Issa. Interview with author, op. cit.

that the SNM deemed necessary for the success of the state and democracy in Somaliland. Thus, the House of Elders, as both a legislative organ and the institutionalisation of the traditional governing structures, is a permanent representation of the Somaliland clans in the government. As one member of the upper house states, including the clan through the council of elders ensures that the government in Somaliland 'matches [Somaliland] culture'.[79] In this capacity, the House of Elders plays the vital role of not only linking the government to the people, but also ensuring that the functions and benefits of the clan system are not lost in the modern government. In this role, the inclusion of the post-war era clan body – a trusted body of leadership and governance – is not only a point of continuity and reassurance within the forming government and state, but it is also a domestically legitimising actor.

In this role the *Guurti* also acts as a safety net. As Mohammed Hassan 'Gani' observes, when the state is weak, absent or violent the clan fills the gaps of social, economic, political and security provision typically managed by the state.[80] In the former British Protectorate, clan structures were largely maintained out of necessity throughout the first Somalia government and Barre's regime as provision and security came primarily from the clan rather than the state. Once the state collapsed and 'peace and reconciliation were the most immediate need', traditional and religious leaders once again 'organised themselves to fill the vacuum of no central authority'.[81] Hassan Issa notes that in the nomadic society the only authority was the clan, so it is 'natural' for those authorities to re-emerge outside the purview of the state in times of crisis or state weakness.[82] Therefore, during the creation of the state in Somaliland, because the state was 'weak' the '*Guurti* [was] everything'.[83]

In post-war Somaliland, however, the clan authority did not re-emerge uncontested as the sole authority, nor is it being empowered external to the state apparatus. In creating the government, Somaliland's leaders '*ex post facto* accepted and partly legalised existing power-positions that had developed during the times of civil war, state-collapse and state reconstruction', drawing upon the powerful position that clan elders held during these times of crisis as a component of the foundations for the state.[84] In post-Barre Somaliland the state is empowering the continuation of this powerful position through the institutionalisation of the clan, and as a result the authority of the clan is emerging within the state apparatus. At the same time, however, the clan authority is also affording legitimacy to the government domestically. The traditional authority that rose up during times of crisis and helped establish the foundations for the new state has not faded into the

---

79 Abdikadir Mohammed Hassan 'Indho'. Interview with author, op. cit.
80 Interview with author, op. cit.
81 J. Sweden, op. cit., p. 175.
82 Hassan Issa. Interview with author, op. cit.
83 Mohammed Hassan Ibrahim 'Gani'. Interview with author, op. cit.
84 M. Höhne, op. cit., p. 17.

background upon the arrival of the government, but instead exists both within and alongside the central governing structure, creating a centralised and permanent amalgamation of state and clan.

Höhne notes that the Latin roots of the word 'tradition' (*tradere*) mean 'pass something' or 'hand something over', observing that '[t]his points to the active, process-oriented aspect of tradition, which connects the present with the past in a dynamic way'.[85] In other words, traditional leaders often 'mediate the link between the past, present and future'[86] with indigenous institutions 'often represent[ing] ways of doing things that have been handed down through successive generations'. As such, 'they are usually well-recognised and long accepted, and often carry the force of legitimacy'.[87] As traditional authorities have roles that are 'perceived as having a link to the past', a positive association with the familiar governance structure grants then legitimacy from their followers.[88] One member of the Somaliland House of Elders exemplifies these observations and associations in stating '[o]ur culture gives us the power'.[89] As a former vice president of Somaliland also acknowledges, there must be an element of clan governance in the government in order to gain the confidence of the people.[90] The people's trust in the government is deeply entwined with the legitimacy held, and given, by the traditional authority.

In Somaliland, the *Guurti* is inextricably linked to both the state and the people through the common denominator of the pervasive clan. Because of this, the government institution has been in a position where it is both a part of the state and the society, as well as a bridge between the two, linking the state to society and society to the state and 'hold[ing] together the government, society and culture'.[91] With the introduction of a democratic government, the traditional authority in the government became a point of reassurance for a population that had very little, if any, experience of democracy. In this 'Somaliland democracy', the inclusion of the clan elders was a vital component as 'culture makes the system stable';[92] in a time of upheaval and transition, the inclusion of the *Guurti* was an association to the familiar clan governance in an otherwise unfamiliar system. Whereas in many parts of the south the clan was a point of contention, in the north the leaders were able to utilise the clan to bridge the gap between the government project and the

---

85   Ibid., p. 3.

86   R. van Dijk and A. van Rouveroy van Nieuwaal, 'The Domestication of Chieftaincy in Africa: From the Imposed to the Imagined', in R. van Dijk and A. van Rouveroy van Nieuwaal (eds), *African Chieftaincy in a New Socio-Political Landscape* (Hamburg: LIT-Verlag, 1999), pp 1–20: p. 4.

87   S. Shivakumar, op. cit., p. 4.

88   M. Höhne, op. cit., p. 3.

89   Abdikadir Mohammed Hassan 'Indho'. Interview with author, op. cit.

90   Ahmed Yusuf Yassin, Vice President of Somaliland. Interview with Author (Hargeisa, August 2006).

91   Awil Hussein Ahmed. Interview with author, op. cit.

92   Abdikadir Mohammed Hassan 'Indho'. Interview with author, op. cit.

population. In its internal-external capacity, the *Guurti* became a chain linking the familiar forms of governance with the new; a tempering link that eased the creation of a central government in a territory that was understandably wary of centralised rule. Because of the 'turbulent times' and the recent history of Somaliland, it was not possible to 'get rid of the old ways quickly', thereby reinforcing the importance of the old in the new government. As a part of both the modern and the traditional, the upper house helped ease tensions in the transitions and transformations taking place in Somaliland. With the inclusion of the *Guurti* and by negotiating Somaliland culture and traditions with democracy and the modern state, the creators of the government and those that followed established a point of resilience that was invaluable in the socio-political upheaval that is statebuilding.

Because of the expressed legislative role of the body, many in the government argue that the inclusion of the traditional is merely symbolic, acting more as a point of reference and reassurance for the population than as a traditional body in practice. Few would dispute the importance of *Guurti* in this role, however, recognising that the transition period would have been more difficult without the presence of the 'old' clan governance in the 'new' government. Just as it did during the SNM campaign and the immediate post-war reconciliation period, the *Guurti*'s place in reconciling the old and the new and mediating between the traditional and the modern, even if only as a symbolic presence, created stability and lent legitimacy to the government, making this a vital role of the body.

The Bridge: Mediator and Advisor

The role of the *Guurti* as a bridge extends beyond the symbolic representation of the clan system in a democratic government. This role also extends into another more practical function of the body: the mediation capacity of the council of elders. The constitution grants the upper house the power to advise and oversee the government as well as alert the House of Representatives of any 'shortcomings of the administration of the Government'.[93] These constitutional responsibilities have been broadly interpreted by the government and the body itself during the formation of the government, with considerable latitude conceded, resulting in the *Guurti*'s intended role as the mediating influence in Somaliland politics and the state formation process.[94] As part of this, the upper house has been handed the responsibility to reconcile between branches of the government and more controversially, the power to extend the mandates of the branches of government if the need arises.

Whereas in its more symbolic role the House of Elders connects the people to the government through the institution of the clan, here the *Guurti* acts in a quasi-judicial manner that is similar to the historic role of the ad hoc clan councils as the *Guurti* becomes the mediator within the government itself. In this mediation role,

---

93 Somaliland Constitution (2001), Article 61.
94 Mohammed Said Mohammed Gees. Interview with author, op. cit.

the *Guurti* not only upholds its responsibility to ensure that the government actions do not contradict culture and tradition, but also ensures that contention within the government is resolved. One value of indigenous institutions is that they 'reflect fundamental understandings among affected individuals, who must deal with each other within the context of a particular problem area on how to overcome dilemmas of collective action'.[95] Whilst there is a broad range of situations in which this is applicable, including conflict resolution and development, it is also appropriate when discussing the *Guurti*'s role in intra-governmental reconciliation. During the process of statebuilding in Somaliland, the *Guurti*, as the representation of clan governance and also because of this, has repeatedly provided fora in which problems can be addressed and resolved, as well as in some instances acting as the referee in those fora. Even though the body's role in the statebuilding process changed following the Hargeisa Conference as it became more closely and openly aligned with the Egal administration, the advisory capacity of the *Guurti* continued, ensuring its placement as a body both within and suspended outside the government. As one member of the House of Elders remarks, the continuing and complex internal-external placement of the *Guurti* has made the body 'a bridge between the Government [president] and the parliament', even though it itself is a component of that parliament.[96] As well as acting as a bridge, and sometimes a buffer, the upper house has also acted as a political seismograph, cautioning when the actions or inactions of the government pose a threat to stability in the state as a whole. Although this role has weakened in recent times, it was an important component of the early stages of statebuilding. Indeed, part of the upper house's capacity in this role is to fill in where the government is weak, again reverting to clan governance as a fall-back when it is needed for continuity and stability. Both the mediation and the advisory roles that have emerged derive from the *Guurti*'s traditional association, but with the upper house mediating and advising within a government of which it is a part it has been granted immeasurable power in determining the future course of the government and therefore itself.

The *Guurti* has regularly exerted its role as mediator and advisor, most notably when changes in the composite membership of the government has threatened stability or presented challenges to the state. Following the 2003 presidential election in which an 80 vote margin separated the winner and the runner-up, the *Guurti* negotiated the concession of the runner-up candidate; this intervention was viewed by many as a politically neutral action carried out in the interest of maintaining stability in the first major test of democratic elections in the territory. The result was a peaceful outcome, a continuation of the integrity of the government and the electoral process, and a smooth transition from an appointed to an elected presidency. The *Guurti* also exercised its role as mediator following the 2005 House of Representatives election. When the newly elected lower house held its first session, contention between the political parties over

---

95 S. Shivakumar, op. cit., p. 3.
96 Abdullahi Dini Hande. Interview with autor, op. cit.

leadership of the house ensued. The resulting stalemate threatened to destabilise the government and undermine the election process. The *Guurti* intervened, negotiating an agreement between all three parties that gave control of the house to a coalition of the opposition parties.[97] The *Guurti* is often looked to when an intra-governmental problem arises, and this quasi-judicial role has been invaluable in maintaining governmental stability during the process of statebuilding. In many ways, the upper house has ensured that political positions and relationships within the Somaliland government remain balanced, cooling hotspots before they can develop into serious threats to the continuation of the statebuilding and democratisation processes. Changing attitudes towards the upper house and significant actions undertaken by the house itself, however, threaten this role. The members of the body are increasingly viewed as politicians rather than traditional elders, and the legitimacy stemming from the traditional nature of the body has been compromised.[98] However, the changing nature of the body does not negate the role it has played to date in the statebuilding process.

In its advisory capacity the *Guurti* also acts as an overseer of the government, testing the state of affairs of both the government and the territory and advising on what is needed for continued stability. Whilst this responsibility could fall under the house's security responsibilities, in practice this has extended beyond that outlined in the constitution and instead reflects the role of the *Guurti* established in the 1993 Peace Charter. This is most evidently expressed in the house's ability to extend the mandates of the branches of government in times when it is determined that elections or other membership changes would be impossible, impractical or destabilising. This power allows for the *Guurti* alone to extend the term of office of the members of government and also allows for the body to propose the postponement of elections. Whilst the *Guurti* itself cannot officially cancel or reschedule the electoral process, by extending the mandate of a governmental body or institution the house is effectively doing just that. Prior to the first presidential election in 2003 the *Guurti* exercised the power of extension in order to ensure that elections took place only when stability and logistical capacity were assured. The mandate of the lower house was also extended in 2005 to allow more time to prepare for elections. More controversially, in 2006, the *Guurti* extended its own mandate, citing election fatigue and uncertainty over the procedures for determining membership of the house as the reasons for postponement. This power was again exercised with the postponement of the 2008 local and presidential elections as security concerns in the eastern provinces of Sanaag and Sool were deemed prohibitive to conducting national elections. The presidential election was postponed a further three times due a myriad of considerations, including problems with the voter registration process, infighting between the political parties over

---

97 M. Bradbury, *Becoming Somaliland*, op. cit., pp. 226–9.
98 L. Moe, 'Somaliland Report: Addressing legitimacy issues in fragile post-conflict situations to advance conflict transformation and peace-building', Berghof Foundation/ University of Queensland (2013).

when the elections would be held and deep mistrust and suspicion within and between political actors within Somaliland, including the *Guurti*.[99] Presidential elections were ultimately held in 2010, and the result was a peaceful process and a prompt and peaceful transition of power between political parties. However, the crisis over the elections, a crisis which had begun with the *Guurti*'s 2006 self-extension, posed a severe and significant threat to not only democracy but also political stability in Somaliland. The *Guurti*'s power of extension has proved itself problematic, and because of the declined impartiality and increased politicisation of the body the power of extension must be curtailed for the sake of future stability and continued political development in Somaliland (see Chapter 7). Indeed, the 2006 and 2010 crises effectively ended the *Guurti*'s role in this capacity, and it is questionable as to whether the body maintains the trust needed to act in its role as government advisor. However, during the early stages of creating and strengthening the state and modern democratic practices, the *Guurti*'s advisory and mediation role within the government was invaluable in ensuring continuity of and trust in the democratisation process and to maintain stability in the territory.

Whilst all the roles of the *Guurti* define its capacity as an integral component of both the government and society, the *Guurti* membership widely maintains that their most important contributions are keeping the peace, both within the territory and within the government. Interestingly, however, the body views itself as a legislative body first and a reconciliation or mediation body second.[100] In its self-written public presentation of purpose, the *Guurti* portrays itself as a modern governmental institution, with its legislative capacity of primary importance.[101] In speaking with numerous members of the house, they indicate that maintaining the legislative position is a means of ensuring a future role for the body; by positioning the body as legislative rather than reconciliatory, there is justification for the house within a modern democratic government. Some members also discuss the legislative position in relation to the British House of Lords or the American Senate, removing the connotation of the clan and positing the institution as a legislative body akin to those in Western states. In doing this, however, those members may be looking to the future, but they are also omitting the vital advisory, mediation and reconciliation roles that have been exercised by the *Guurti* and were definitive of its position within the government. As a legislative body the *Guurti* is an institution of modern government, but its duality as a body both within and external to the government provided the guidance and bridges without which the successes in Somaliland would not be as marked.

---

99 APD/Interpeace, 'A Vote for Peace II: A Report on the 2010 Somaliland Presidential Election Process', (APD/Interpeace, 2012); M. Walls, 'The Emergence of a Somali State: Building peace from civil war in Somaliland', *African Affairs* 108.432 (2009), pp. 371–89.

100 Interviews with author with members of the *Guurti*, August-September 2006.

101 Somaliland House of Elders, 'Somaliland Guurti: About Us', Report compiled by Somaliland *Guurti* (Date Unknown).

Conclusions

Although the traditional *guurti* has been altered by circumstance and political actions to fit its contemporary institutionalised role, the trusted clan association has contributed to the upper house's success, not only in the area of security but also in obtaining popular support for the government and the introduction of democratic concepts and practices. As Lewis identifies:

> [i]n comparison with the heavy-handed and largely unsuccessful UN and other international efforts to impose peace from the top in southern Somalia, this [peace and statebuilding in Somaliland] was an impressive testimony to the effectiveness of traditional grass-roots Somali diplomacy.[102]

Leaders in the north were able to utilise the clan – both practically and symbolically – to facilitate the introduction of a central democratic government and also to ensure continued stability throughout the statebuilding process. Potentially an area of competing legitimacy in post-war Somaliland,[103] the legitimising power of the clan was accounted for through its inclusion in the government and the state. This inclusion was a benefit to the process. Indeed, through negotiation, mediation and facilitation, clan elders, through countless local *shir* and *guurti*, have contributed to the maintenance of peace, stability and co-existence within a potentially volatile and often politically fragile society.[104] With the introduction of democratic government, the traditional authority in the government, tasked with guidance as well as restraint, became a point of reassurance for a population that had very little, if any, experience of democracy and had very violent experiences with centralised rule. According to Abdirahman Aw Ali Farah, those responsible for the creation of Somaliland had observed that they could not 'jump from the lowest part of the ladder to the top; we needed the *Guurti*, and we needed them to make the clans share something. This was preferable to imposing democracy that no one knew'.[105] With the inclusion of the *Guurti* and by negotiating Somaliland culture and traditions with democracy and the modern state, the creators of the government and those that followed founded a system of governance that works for Somaliland. Even though the role of the clan in the government may be largely symbolic, nonetheless it has been an important component of the governing of Somaliland.

Positing the traditional body within the government, however, further altered the traditional notion of the body and changed the nature of the council of elders

---

102 I.M. Lewis, *Blood and Bone*, op. cit., p. 216.
103 See S. Closson','What Do Unrecognised States Tell Us About Sovereignty?' in N. Caspersen and G. Stansfield (eds) *Unrecognised States in the International System* (London: Routledge, 2011), pp. 58–70.
104 M. Walls, op. cit.
105 Abdirahman Aw Ali Farah, op. cit.

as the historically apolitical body became a legislative institution in a multi-party democratic government structure. Although the *Guurti* does in many ways resemble the traditional body that negotiated agreements and established customary law, it is also now directly implicated in the political practice of creating legislation and functioning as a government institution, making political neutrality difficult if not impossible. Further, the *Guurti* is entrenched in the political realm as the advisor and referee of the government; even if the body does maintain impartiality, its involvement in this capacity makes it an intrinsic actor in the political process. Just as Mohammed Said Gees sees the Somali people as existing in both the Somali and the Western worlds, so does the *Guurti*, existing in both the old and new ways of governing in Somaliland.

Many in the Somaliland government claim that the both the SNM *Guurti* and the multifaceted House of Elders is why peace has been sustained in Somaliland but not Somalia. The inclusion of clan governance did contribute to the stability of the territory and the political process, but one must be careful as to not place all the credit with the *Guurti* as other significant factors contributing to Somaliland's success were also present. Certainly the benign neglect of the British colonisers and isolation in the unified state allowed for the continuation of clan practices and the emergence of a sense of solidarity in the face of neglect and violence. In addition, the dominance of the Isaaq in the territory and the SNM, and the SNM's status of victor over Barre, helped ease the post-conflict transition to independent statehood and stability. The non-interference of the international community must also not be overlooked. Without the presence of foreign peacekeepers or statebuilders, Somaliland was able to foster peace and to domestically create a government, making it a Somaliland project rather than an international project as is seen in the south. Finally, as an internal-external actor the Diaspora, through funding and political guidance, has had an incalculable impact. The inclusion of these other factors in the consideration of accomplishments in the north, however, does not minimise the role of the clan and of the grassroots process. Although the *Guurti* may have had more favourable conditions in which to work than it would have had in the south, this does not exclude the value of its presence in not only peace and reconciliation but also the creation of a government and a state. Somaliland was able to achieve what has been accomplished without the interference of the international community; and because the external influences were minimal, Somaliland was able to create a state in a way that was seen as best for Somaliland. Rather than the traditional authority acting as a backwards or unpredictable actor in the state, the inclusion of the clan, dependence on the clan and, when needed, primacy of the clan has been vital in the creation of a stable territory and a stable government in Somaliland. For Somaliland, the institutionalised traditional authority is not a sacrifice of acceptable statehood, but rather a necessity for acceptable statehood to be achieved in the emerging state.

Many within the government are apt to emphasise that the inclusion of the traditional sets the aspiring state apart from established Western states, but they also recognise that for Somaliland this deviation was essential for the introduction of the modern government. Influenced by external global discourses, those creating the Somaliland government incorporated normative ideals for success whilst at the same time tailoring these in order to prevent a repeat of past problems and failures of government. In Somaliland, history, culture and tradition were incorporated into the statebuilding process in order to foster stability; the state came from within Somaliland rather than as part of a package from the outside. Although the path has not been entirely smooth, the creation of a hybrid government in Somaliland has allowed for the statebuilding process to take place. However, as the government in Somaliland continues to stabilise and grow, and as democratic governance and practices in Somaliland continue to take hold, the necessity of the body in its traditionally associated capacities is being questioned. The question now facing the territory is how long can the hybrid survive? The relationship between old and new is changing and evolving as political space in Somaliland stabilises and develops. The changing relationships in Somaliland show that the statebuilding process is ongoing, and with that they bring to the fore important considerations for the future. Somaliland presents the case that statebuilding does not stop with the establishment of institutions. More significantly, though, Somaliland also raises questions pertaining to the linearity of statebuilding. The inclusion of the clan may have been vital to the establishment and early stages of the statebuilding process in Somaliland, but is it still necessary for the continuation of the process? It is very likely that the future structure of the state in Somaliland will not include the clan. However, the flexibility in the structure and the process that allows for this evolution and change, at least in Somaliland, was certainly afforded to it by the clan.

Chapter 7

Somaliland at the Crossroads?

In Somaliland, the utilisation of the clan elders for the establishment of peace and stability enabled the creation of a foundation upon which to create a state as well as creating a necessary link between 'old' Somali governance and the desired 'new' democracy. As with any political process or governing system, though, change is inevitable and flexibility is necessary. Somaliland is certainly not immune from this. The utilisation and inclusion of the clan in Somaliland's statebuilding process from the beginning has been vital not only for stability, but also for legitimacy. The *Guurti*'s legitimacy, whilst rooted in its role in the fight against Barre, its role in post-conflict peacebuilding, and its role in 'upholding customary principles of consensus and inclusion to counterbalance the competitive nature of multi-party politics',[1] also stems from trust and familiarity. As the representation the clan, and through that society, in the turbulent political process and system, it was central to rooting society in the statebuilding process and arguably in rooting the state in society, thereby serving to shrink the legitimacy gap often encountered in externally-led statebuilding. As Gees notes, 'many people are nostalgic about the *Guurti* because in troubled times when we needed them the *Guurti* was there'.[2] Certainly, the *Guurti* worked hard throughout the fight against Barre and through the early stages of statebuilding. However, without its traditional association the body would have been little more than another political actor; the *Guurti* has been an agent of legitimisation not merely because of its work but also because of its connotation. As the state develops and as the 'new' becomes more familiar, though, the role of the 'old' *Guurti* has changed. No longer with its importance derived primarily through clan association, the *Guurti* is finding itself a target of the socio-political change that it had been so instrumental in leading and mediating. The *Guurti*, once viewed as invaluable to stability, is now the subject of an uncertain future within Somaliland. But that uncertainty should not be taken as a negative. Rather, it is a sign of a developing political system.

With the introduction of democratic practices in the territory, the position of the now politicised but still unelected traditional authority is the government is being called into question. Because statebuilding is a process, as Somaliland – both as

---

1 L. Moe, 'Somaliland Report: Addressing legitimacy issues in fragile post-conflict situations to advance conflict transformation and peace-building', Berghof Foundation/ University of Queensland (2013).

2 Mohammed Said Mohammed Gees, former leading member of the SNM Central Committee, former government minister and current Executive Director of APD. Interview with author (Hargeisa, September 2006).

a state and as an idea – grows, change is inevitable. The inclusion of the clan and the nature of that inclusion is one such area where change is possible. Somaliland has evolved, and as it has the necessity of the clan inclusion is being questioned. In line with common perceptions of traditional or indigenous authorities, many in Somaliland and the influential Somaliland Diaspora view the centralised clan and modern democracy as being incompatible. Many of the concerns surrounding the position of the *Guurti* stem from the extraordinary amount of power the body possesses within the government; constitutional ambiguity once vital to providing the flexibility necessary for the creation of the government is now seen as problematic as the government consolidates and the democratisation process moves forward. Indeed, fear of this came to a head with the series of postponements of the presidential elections starting in 2008, with accusations that the *Guurti* had been corrupted and co-opted by the president as a means to ensure his continuation in power, resulting in a disruption of the democratic process.[3] With unquestioned influence over society acquired from its traditional association and with seemingly unchecked power within the government, many fear a *Guurti* run amuck. As is common in Somali society, this is best summarised through the use of a proverb. As former Vice President Abdirahman Aw Ali Farah explains, 'there are small camels and big camels. If you see the small camels here and then destroying this and this, it is nothing. But if you see the she camel, the big she camel doing the same thing that's terrible'.[4] If problems arise with the responsible actor – the she camel – who is to guide the rest? Put differently, and using another proverb, who heals the doctor when the doctor is sick?[5]

Whilst heightened during the presidential election crisis, questions over the future of the *Guurti* reached a pinnacle in 2006, and it is this point that best exemplifies not only questions pertaining to the future of the clan in the government, but also the continuation of the statebuilding process in Somaliland. With the term of the House of Elders set to expire in October 2006 and with no officially recognised law filling a constitutional gap concerning the method through which to determine new membership, the position of the body in the government and its assumed powers came under scrutiny. A string of events leading to extreme contention within the government raised serious questions about the future of not only the House of Elders, but also the developing government, and the future of the hybrid nature of the government became the centre of debate. The issue to be addressed, therefore, is the future of the traditional authority in Somaliland's democratising government. The purpose of this chapter is to examine this firstly

---

3 See M. Höhne, 'Limits of hybrid political orders: the case of Somaliland', *Journal of Eastern African Studies* 7.2 (2013), pp. 199–217.

4 Abdirahman Aw Ali Farah, former Vice president of Somaliland. Interview with author. (Hargeisa, September 2006).

5 Abdirahman Aw Ali Farah. Interview with author, op. cit.; Mohammed Hassan Ibrahim 'Gani', Lead Researcher for APD. Conversation with author (Hargeisa, September 2006).

by explaining the incendiary point for this debate: Law 19 and the *Guurti*'s extension of its own mandated term in office. Following this, three positions in the debate emanating from this crisis will be presented, leading to an examination of the question of the future for the *Guurti* and the hybridity of the Somaliland state. Finally, a conclusion on the evolving position of the traditional authority in the growing Somaliland government will be offered. The purpose here is not to demonstrate that all is lost in Somaliland, but rather to identify the current debates over the future of the *Guurti* and the clan in the government. It is to look at the process in Somaliland as just that: a process rather than a project. As the process continues and as the state, domestic expectations of the state and, indeed, the nation evolve, is the clan – such a vital actor at the state – still needed or desired?

Law 19 and the Controversial Self-Extension

As is common in the Somaliland constitution, provisions for flexibility and growth were included in many articles, including those pertaining to the upper house. When the framework needed to be translated into practice, however, problems and concerns arose. The ambiguous language of the Somaliland Constitution has proven beneficial throughout the statebuilding process, providing the flexibility necessary for fostering and creating a state structure and practices that are well suited to the needs of the territory. As the state develops, however, these ambiguities are becoming evident and, in some instances, problematic for the state apparatus. The lack of clarity over determining the membership of the House of Elders is one such instance.

The crisis over the *Guurti* can be traced to constitutional wording concerning determining the membership of the upper house. Actions by all branches of the Somaliland government in attempting to resolve this ambiguity created a constitutional crisis that opened debate on the hybrid nature of the government.[6] As Article 58 of the Somaliland Constitution stipulates:

1. The members of the House of Elders shall be elected in a manner to be determined by law.

---

6 Somaliland Government, 'Somaliland Constitution (2001)', emphasis added. To avoid concerns over mistranslation of these articles into English, the Somali language version of the constitution must be cited. In the Somali version the word *doorasho* appears in Article 57, whilst *xulashadiisa* is used in Article 62. Whilst both can be directly translated into 'choice', the former carries the primary connotation of election; indeed, the plural form of *doorasho* directly translates as 'elections' rather than 'choices'. *Xulashadiisa*, on the other hand, carries the primary meaning of selecting. Translation and explanation provided by Mohammed Hassan Ibrahim 'Gani' (Hargeisa, September 2006). Also, *Ifiye Somali-English Dictionary* (Nairobi: Somali Partner Academicians, 2000).

2. The period of office of the House of Elders is six (6) years beginning from the date of its first meeting.

Article 62 of the Somaliland Constitution then reads:

> [t]he inaugural meeting of the House of Elders shall take place within 30 (thirty) days of the date when their *selection* is completed.[7]

Ambiguity in language used in the clauses pertaining to whether the upper house is elected (*doorasho*) or selected (*xulashadiisa*) proved problematic in terms of procedures leading to the end of the term of the first constitutional *Guurti*. In addition, the phrase 'to be determined by law', whilst a common phrase within the Somaliland Constitution and a point of flexibility, mandates that clarification on specific procedures to take place, presumably before the end of the first *Guurti*'s term.[8] It is also important to note that no mention of popular elections is made in reference to the upper house, again falling under the auspices of the 'to be determined by law' provision. Whilst the SNM *Guurti* and the first civilian House of Elders were selected, the vague and unclear constitutional wording raised the question of whether the house is to be 'elected' and therefore subject to democratisation, or whether the constitutional wording mandates continued selection by the clans.

As explained in Chapter 6, the House of Elders has the power to extend the mandated terms of the elected government bodies. Whilst this power has proved valuable in the creation of the government, allowing for stability to be established before the first round of democratic elections as well as providing a constitutional safety net for the introduction of democratic practices, the power of extension is unclear when it comes to the mandate of the *Guurti* itself. Unlike for those branches of government specifically intended to be subject to democratic elections, the constitution does not specify what is to take place in the event that no law has been passed closing the gap concerning the procedure for determining the membership of the *Guurti*. With the end of the upper house's term imminent, in May 2006 the *Guurti* extended its own mandate, sparking governmental infighting between the

---

7 Somaliland Government, 'Somaliland Constitution (2001)', emphasis added. Copies of English translation obtained from Somaliland House of Elders and Somaliland Ministry of Information, Hargeisa.

8 To avoid concerns over mistranslation of these articles into English, the Somali language version of the constitution must be cited. In the Somali version the word *doorasho* appears in Article 57, whilst *xulashadiisa* is used in Article 62. Whilst both can be directly translated into 'choice', the former carries the primary connotation of election; indeed, the plural form of *doorasho* directly translates as 'elections' rather than 'choices'. *Xulashadiisa*, on the other hand, carries the primary meaning of selecting. Translation and explanation provided by Mohammed Hassan Ibrahim 'Gani', September 2006. Also, *Ifiye Somali-English Dictionary* (Nairobi: Somali Partner Academicians, 2000).

House of Elders, House of Representatives, President and Supreme Court. The resulting struggles for and exertions of power threatened to bring the legislative process to a halt and deadlock the government. As a result, debate on the political implications of the *Guurti*'s self-extension and the body's future placement within the government began. At the centre of the debate over the self-extension are two actions: a disputed 2003 law; and a 2006 collaborative act by the President, the Supreme Court and the *Guurti* itself.

In 2003, the House of Representatives took a step towards closing the constitutional gap pertaining to determining the membership of the House of Elders by passing a bill that has come to be known as Law 19. In this law it was stated:

> in case that the *Guurti* nomination cannot be held because of circumstances beyond control or because of technical problems, the president can propose to the House of Representatives for the House to review the justified proposal and to decide on an appropriate time frame required to overcome the obstacles.[9]

Originally part of a larger now-abandoned bill proposing procedures for the indirect election of the *Guurti*, Law 19 was introduced as a separate piece of legislation and passed by the House of Representatives on 25 March 2003. After reportedly also being passed through the House of Elders, the bill was supposedly signed by then President Dahir Rayale Kahin. Law 19 grants the power of extension for the upper house to the House of Representatives upon the request of the president, ensuring not only the continued integrity of the *Guurti* in a situation where an extension of its term was necessary, but also removing the possibility of the body indefinitely securing its position by unilaterally extending its own mandate. Placing this responsibility with the House of Representatives and the president created a legal check on the power of the *Guurti* and on the other branches of government; placing this power within two separate branches reduced the possibility of either the House of Representatives or the president co-opting the upper house. Law 19 effectively began the process of reigning in the potentially very powerful *Guurti*.

However, in May 2006, as the expiration for the term of the *Guurti* drew near, the body extended its own mandate for an additional four years following a direct presidential request for the action.[10] The President's proposal, drawn up following a pre-emptive consultation with the Supreme Court, identifies constitutional articles that loosely interpreted establish a constitutional basis for the self-extension. The justification derived from this interpretation was simple: means through which to

---

9 Somaliland House of Representatives, 'Go'aanka Ansixinta Qodobka 19aad Ee Mashruuc-Sharciga Doorashada Dadban Ee Golaha Guurtida & Hakinta Intiisa Kale, (Bill for Indirect Election of The House of Elders)', 25 March 2003. Translated by Mohammed Hassan Ibrahim 'Gani'.

10 Interviews by author with members of the Executive and the *Guurti* (Hargeisa, August-September 2006).

determine the membership of the *Guurti* had not yet been established; the *Guurti* is the only body in the government with the constitutionally determined power to extend any term of office; therefore the *Guurti* could and should extend its own term in order to maintain the legal and practical integrity of the body.[11] Citing the recent democratising moves made with the parliamentary and presidential elections, the president stemmed calls for the immediate election of the body by making the case for the extension rather than immediate elections. He maintained that firstly the uncertainty over whether the body would be elected or selected had yet to be resolved. Rayale also explained that an extension of the mandate was preferred over immediately re-determining the membership as the recent national elections for the president and the House of Representatives had caused voter fatigue. He continued in arguing that the territory did not have the resources or the logistical capabilities to stage another round of elections so soon after the September 2005 elections for the lower house. In addition, it was claimed, the lack of a national census and voter registration procedures would make electing the membership determined by clan representation rather than geographical location a logistical 'nightmare'.[12] Therefore, the president proposed a four-year extension of the *Guurti*'s mandate in order to allow for the establishment of acceptable procedures for determining the future membership of the house. Rayale sought advice from the Supreme Court prior to the self-extension, thus compiling a constitutional argument for the action.[13] The court determined that the *Guurti*'s role maintained importance in Somaliland and therefore could not be compromised by insecurity surrounding its membership. The justices also deemed that because of internal and regional factors such as confrontation within the eastern provinces and the rise of the Union of Islamic Courts in the south, as well as economic insecurity, Somaliland was in a 'delicate situation [and they] don't know when it [could] explode'.[14] Because of this, and because there was no constitutional provision for the extension of the *Guurti*'s mandate, it was concluded that the president had the power to ask the *Guurti* to extend its own mandate. As the leading justice on the court at the time stated, '[w]e give our advice constitutionally. As a constitutional court we have the

---

11 President Dahir Rayale Kahin, 'Letter to Somaliland *Guurti*', 24 April 2006.

12 Mohamoud Garad Mohammed, Commissioner Somaliland National Electoral Commission (NEC). Interview with author (Hargeisa, September 2006); Mustafa Rashad, Consultant with Somaliland NEC. Interview with author (Hargeisa, September 2006); Ahmed Yusuf Yassin, Vice President of Somaliland. Interview with author. (Hargeisa, September 2006).

13 Somaliland Supreme Court, 'Soo jeedin Tallo-bixin Sharci (Response to President's Request for Legal Advice)', 24 April 2006; Dahir Rayale Kahin, 'Degreeto Madaxweyne No. 117/052006: Soo jeedinta kordhinta muddada Golaha Guurtida (President's Request to the House of Elders)', 2 May 2006; Somaliland House of Elders, 'Ujeeddo: Go'aanka Korodhsiimada Mudada ilka Golaha Guurtida JSL (House of Elder's Extension of House of Elders)', 6 May 2006. All translated by Mohammed Hassan Ibrahim 'Gani'.

14 Mohamoud Hirsi Farah. Interview with author, op. cit.

right to arbitrate disputes. We gave the green light to the president to extend the term of the *Guurti*. That's all we did'.[15]

The action taken by the president, however, was immediately met with extreme opposition from members of parliament, members of civil society, and even some clan elders themselves. This opposition was not directed as much at Rayale's refutation of elections but rather focused on the manner in which this transpired and the disregarding of Law 19. Indeed, the president and his administration, as well as many members of the *Guurti*, denied the existence of Law 19, maintaining that the bill was never signed by the president and therefore has no legal foundation.[16] The Supreme Court went as far as stating that Law 19, if it existed, would be unconstitutional as the court had determined that only the *Guurti* has the power to extend mandates.[17] The President consulting the Supreme Court *before* making this recommendation rather than allowing the court to make a post-facto interpretation has led many to believe that the president used the court to bypass Law 19, effectively nullifying this legislation and subverting the democratically elected house. Many of those in opposition to Rayale's actions speculated that by using the court to legally justify the *Guurti*'s self-extension, thereby securing the position of the membership for another four years, the president was co-opting the upper house in order to counter the actions of the newly elected and opposition-controlled House of Representatives. Some, such as Dr Aden Abokor, go as far as indicating that Rayale may have 'scratched the back' of the *Guurti* in order to ensure an extension of his own position following the end of his term of office in May 2008.[18] As predicted by Dr Abokor, in April 2008, citing security concerns, the *Guurti* extended the term of the president by one year. Subsequent postponements of the election followed until the elections were finally held in June 2010. What may have been a decision justifiably based on maintaining peace and security in the territory was not received as such, but rather was seen as manipulation of the upper house by the president as a means of securing the political positions of all involved. There had long been a fear in Somaliland that the *Guurti* had been corrupted into a political tool under the presidency of Egal. Following the self-extension crisis, this fear translated into vocal and public suspicions about the nature of the clan body in the government. Trust in the body that had derived

---

15   Ibid.

16   Copies of the bill produced for the researcher by the leadership of the House of Representatives show Rayale's signature, but the executive and the Supreme Court maintain that the bill was never signed by the president. They do not go as far as accusing forgery, but they insist that the bill and the signature are not legitimate. Interviews conducted by author (Hargeisa, August-September 2006).

17   Mohamoud Hirsi Farah, Justice of the Somaliland Supreme Court. Interview with author (Hargeisa, September 2006).

18   Interviews conducted by author (Hargeisa, August-September 2006); Dr Aden Abokor, Progressio Country Representative. Interview with author (Hargeisa, September 2006).

from the traditional association and respect for the elders and their work, and the stabilising legitimacy stemming from that was significantly undermined by this crisis. For many, the *Guurti* was no longer the traditional mechanism of government incorporated into the modern government, but instead was a powerful body comprised of self-interested politicians that could easily be bought.

Whilst some viewed the self-extension crisis as indicative of inevitable problems with the inclusion of the clan in the Somaliland government, others perceived a structural deficiency that had the potential to destabilise the new state. Still others viewed no problem, instead claiming that Somaliland was simply experiencing growing pains. Whilst there are strong claims on all sides, the root of this debate can be identified not as the *Guurti*'s self-extension and the president's actions, but rather the position and functions of the traditional authority in the hybrid state. The self-extension crisis tested the strength of the Somaliland government and raised concerns about the current balance between traditional Somali governance structures and modern democratic government. It is interesting to note that at the time of writing, the legal issues at the root of the crisis have yet to be resolved, and the composition and constitutional mandates for the clan body remain the same. However, that does not mean that the role or importance of the clan body in the central government has remained static; the self-extension crisis had a significant impact on not only the legitimacy of and given by the body, but also the balance between the old and the new in the government. Reconciling the new with the old in Somaliland was beneficial to the early stages of the statebuilding process, especially in establishing the foundations for the state and in introducing the externally-valued democratic component of the government, but what to do with the old when the new takes root? The proceeding section will address this, identifying problems arising from the changing power relationships within the hybrid government.

The President vs. The House vs. The House vs. The Supreme Court

One of the key concerns highlighted by the self-extension crisis is the changing power relationship resulting from the parliamentary elections. Whereas the membership of the pre-election House of Representatives had been nominated by the clans and approved by the president, the 2005 elections significantly altered the influence the president had over the membership of the lower house. This alteration, coupled with the change in party composition within the house, thereby transformed the relationship between the president and parliament. With the opposition parties winning the majority of seats in the lower house, for the first time in its brief history the Somaliland government in its entirety was not controlled by Egal's party (UDUB). Although meant to be apolitical, it is widely acknowledged that the majority of the members of the upper house have long belonged to the UDUB party, which was not a serious or outward concern whilst UDUB held a majority throughout the government. With the lower house being controlled by the opposition parties, however, the politically neutral stance of the upper house was called into question and the legislative division between the political parties unsurprisingly brought with it new problems.

The official reasoning for the *Guurti*'s self-extension was it was necessary for the stability of Somaliland and the government. However, there was much speculation within Somaliland's civil society that the president feared for the safety of his own political position and thus seized upon the impending expiration of the term of the House of Elders as a means through which to balance his own power against that of the newly elected House of Representatives. Much of the debate surrounding this action centred on this speculation. As the end of the *Guurti*'s mandate approached the lower house prepared to build upon the legal guidelines established by the disputed Law 19 by proposing a bill that would establish popular elections for the upper house, thereby making a statement of intent that potentially posed a threat to Rayale's future in the government.[19] The *Guurti* had developed a close working relationship with Egal during Somaliland's early years; both had been integral actors in the early statebuilding and Egal has capitalised on the power and influence that the *Guurti* had offered. As a member of Egal's UDUB party, Rayale enjoyed many benefits of that close relationship. In proposing to potentially open the body to control by the opposition parties, the president's position could be threatened if another close election like the one in 2003 were to take place. In addition to this, with a fully elected parliament and increased democratic accountability, the power of the presidency would be severely checked. Thus, the speculation emerged that by maintaining an appointed House of Elders the president was able to promise job security for the current membership as a way to maintain executive influence and power within the parliament; influence and power that could be significantly lessened with an elected body. In denying the existence of Law 19 and bypassing the lower house in the extension of the *Guurti*'s mandate, the president could ensure his continued influence. In return, the members of the House of Elders would be guaranteed an extension of their own positions. This alleged patronage would allow for the president to balance the power of an elected and very vocal opposition-led House of Representatives, a body which has shown its intent to act as a severe check on the otherwise unimpeded powers of the presidency. Backed by the Supreme Court, which was already known to be non-independent, this move gave the Somaliland executive immense power. Interestingly, if something similar had happened whilst Egal was president it likely would not have attracted the same level of negative attention. However, the Somaliland state had grown and developed significantly since the time of Egal. An Egal-style presidency, one characterised by significant political latitude, was no longer possible, and the self-extension crisis made that very apparent.

---

19   Abdirahman Osman Alin Shirwac, Member of Somaliland House of Representatives (UCID) and Chair of the House Judiciary Committee. Interviews with author (Hargeisa, September 2006).

Regardless of the actual reasoning behind the action, however, in extending the *Guurti*'s mandate the president and the *Guurti* have not only alienated the House of Representatives, but have also unintentionally empowered the body. In what is seen as an indicator of the commitment being made to the process of democratisation, the House of Representatives refused to step aside for what was widely perceived to be corruption on the part of the president and the ruling party and instead made their displeasure known both verbally and in action. Immediately following the *Guurti*'s self-extension, the House of Representatives refused to address bills proposed by the president or the *Guurti*, arguing that the legislative process had been compromised by the actions of the executive, the court and the upper house. In turn, the *Guurti* and the President also refused to compromise on legislation coming from the House of Representatives, effectively bringing the legislative process to a standstill. Although this initially appeared as a major obstacle and destabilising incident, negotiations to resolve the impasse soon began. Although the public representation of the crisis is centred on the self-extension, the crux of the resulting debate over the House of Elders is not the inclusion of the clan or even the extension of the *Guurti*'s mandate but rather the placement and functions of the institution within the evolving government. As a result, the balance in the relationships in government, particularly between the traditional and the modern, are being re-examined and reconsidered by the government and other political and civil society elites in the territory in order to determine the best way forward for Somaliland.

Lines Drawn in the Sand

The *Guurti*'s self-extension and the ensuing stalemate created a crisis in the government which many feared would derail the successes in Somaliland's continuing statebuilding process. The crisis also put the neutrality and reputation of the *Guurti* in 'disrepute', thereby damaging the tradition-based mediating role of the house.[20] Although the seemingly related dispute emanating from the later extension of the president's mandate was resolved and elections were held, the future for determining the membership of the *Guurti* remains uncertain.[21] The self-extension set a precedent granting immeasurable power both to the executive as well as the upper house of parliament, but conversely it also created an opportunity in which discussion over the future nature and composition of the government could take place. The circumstances surrounding the extension of the *Guurti*'s mandate sparked open debate on how to determine the membership of the upper house, but more fundamentally it introduced discussion on the place of traditional

---

20 Somaliland Times, 'Somaliland Elections to be Held in December 2008 and March 2009', *Somaliland Times* Issue 331 (24 May 2008).
21 Mohammed Hassan Ibrahim 'Gani'. Email correspondence with author (June 2008).

authority and the relationship between old and new in Somaliland's growing and evolving government.

Whilst the crisis resulting from the self-extension of the *Guurti* is just one of many obstacles facing Somaliland's government, it was the first significant test of the marriage between traditional Somali governance and modern democratic government. The stable hybridity of the Somaliland government approached a crossroads with the self-extension of the *Guurti*: the governance system evolving with the introduction of democratic practices could either successfully overcome this obstacle or it could grind to a halt, thereby raising doubts about the future of the government. The self-extension was a divisive as well as decisive moment. If the changing power relationship instigated by the 2005 parliamentary elections kindled a situation in which checks and balances within the government were functionally nullified, what was the purpose of continuing with the project of democracy? More fundamentally, with a perceived link within the government and in society between democracy and recognition, what would be the purpose of continuing with the process of self-led statebuilding? With accusations rampant between the various branches of government, the possibility of a breakdown in the growing state in Somaliland became a threat. With the governmental body specifically tasked with reconciliation between branches of government firmly entrenched in the middle of the crisis, the question being asked was, what is the future for Somaliland's continuing project of creating a state?

In September 2006, and in reaction to the self-extension crisis, the House of Representatives pushed through legislation establishing electoral law for the *Guurti*.[22] Although the legislation was quickly defeated by the upper house, it was the first concrete attempt at formally and legally altering the nature of the House of Elders from a traditional body to a modern political and democratically elected one. This attempted change was highly significant for the territory. The formation of the government in Somaliland was built on the recognition that incorporating the clan was necessary as modern democracy could not be introduced or succeed without mediation between traditional Somali governance structures and modern political parties and democratic government. The creation and inclusion of the *Guurti* was the agent of this, even if the reconciling role undertaken by the body was more symbolic than functional. By formally transforming this traditional body into an elected body invariably open to party politics, the nature of the body would also change, effectively disconnecting the previously essential traditional element of the government. Within Somaliland debate over this issue is on-going. Opinion is divided as to whether or not the government, or the people, are ready to remove the traditional body, and therefore the symbolic clan association, from the institutions of the state. Within the government and amongst political and civic leaders, three sides to the debate maintain three different yet significant

---

22 With the *Guurti* mandate set to expire in October 2006, the House of Representatives passed the bill on 16 September 2006. It went before the House of Elders on 17 September 2006 where it failed to pass the house's vote.

contributions on the future of the hybrid Somaliland government. There are those who believe that the formal inclusion of the clan elders as elders must remain a vital component in the Somaliland government; those who believe that the inclusion of the traditional is retarding the modernisation process undertaken with the introduction of democratic practices; and those who bridge the divide in advocating that although the role of the elders will change in time, the territory is not yet ready to lose the stabilising impact of the traditional body.[23] For all three sides, the method through which the membership of the upper house is chosen, and the impact of those methods on the balance within government and between government and society, is the centre of discussion. For that reason, discussion here must address these three positions on determining the membership of the upper house in order to offer analysis on the evolving relationship between the old and the new in Somaliland's government and statebuilding process. Whilst the membership in these 'camps' is not static and exclusive, each is dominated by a sector of the elites guiding and driving the statebuilding process in Somaliland.

Maintaining the Status Quo

The first of the positions within the debate is best described as the 'UDUB camp' as it is primarily composed of most of the *Guurti* membership and leading UDUB party members, including members of previous administrations, the Supreme Court, and UDUB members in the House of Representatives. Identified by many as the instigators of the crisis because of the actions that enabled the self-extension, this side of the debate argues that the *Guurti* continues to be a 'necessary and vital pillar' that cannot be left out of the government.[24] This belief is furthered by *Guurti* member Abdikadir Mohammed Hassan 'Indho', who claims that the members of the elected House of Representatives may know democracy they 'learned elsewhere', but they are 'still young and do not know what [they] are doing'.[25] Because of the continued importance of the clan in maintaining stability, the *Guurti* remains a vital component in ensuring that the democracy known by the members of the lower house matches the needs of Somaliland. There is also a firm belief within this camp that the *Guurti* will be necessary until Somaliland is recognised by the international community, as the *Guurti* is filling the gap of recognition by ensuring there is peace in the territory as well as ensuring that there

---

23 The assessment of this debate is based on interviews conducted with members of the government, political leaders and civic leaders, as well as observation of government meetings and sessions, participation in community meetings, and informal conversations with political and civic leaders in Hargeisa.

24 Wording from Dini Abdillahi Hande, Member of Somaliland House of Elders. Interview with author (Hargeisa, September 2006).

25 Abdikadir Mohammed Hassan 'Indho', Member of the House of Elders and Chairman of Human Rights and Social Affairs Committee. Interview with author (Hargeisa, August 2006).

is more guiding the state than the young men in the House of Representatives, many of whom are Diaspora returnees and did not take part in the early stages of statebuilding.[26] In its many roles the *Guurti* often acted as a court of last resort, ensuring that stability in the territory and the government was maintained and that the statebuilding project was not derailed.[27] As such, the *Guurti* has been necessary to alleviate tension within society as well as within the balance between the modern and the traditional, a role that those in this camp maintain is still necessary. This argument is summarised best by former foreign minister Abdullahi Duale who recognises that in the statebuilding process 'there are sometimes gray areas', and the *Guurti* helps prevent serious mistakes that Duale claims 'we can ill-afford'. In its numerous roles the upper house has acted as a Somaliland 'think tank', providing much needed guidance and advice when a 'win-win situation' is needed.[28] In other words, the *Guurti* acts as the 'head of them [all]' in order to temper the potential repercussions of marrying the old and the new and the internal and the external.[29] Because of this, this camp maintains, the manner of the clan inclusion in the government must not be altered. Those holding this position in the debate view the *Guurti* not as a problematic traditional institution, but as an essential pillar of the government.

This position also maintains that the House of Elders is primarily a legislative body. Despite this, however, the leaders of the *Guurti* project self-importance, stating that the clan-based institution continues to act as a bridge and is thus the enabling factor for stability and democracy to succeed in the territory. In essence, the members of the house often perceive of themselves as the 'effective link between all parties, all people' that is necessary for the continuation of the government.[30] This placement as both a part of and at the same time external to the legislature not only reflects the *Guurti*'s internal-external capacity, but also contributes to a sweeping confusion concerning the present and future role of the body. This ill-defined dual-faceted nature of the upper house, both internal-external and legislative-reconciliatory (quasi-judicial), creates an uneasy functional relationship between the roles within the house. With the legislative role viewed as a more secure position for the future, the membership portrays this as the primary function of the body. At the same time, however, the *Guurti* and the rest of the UDUB camp argue against electing the members of the upper house, stating that the body must maintain its clan base in order to remain distinct from and, more

---

26 Ahmed Yusuf Yassin. Interview with author, op. cit.
27 Ibid.
28 Abdullahi Mohammed Duale, Minister of Foreign Affairs. Interview with author (Hargeisa, September 2006).
29 Abdikadir Mohammed Hassan 'Indho', Member of House of Elders and Chairman of the Human Rights and Social Affairs Committee. Interviews with author (Hargeisa, August and September 2006).
30 Haji Abdi Hussein, Member House of Elders and Chairman of the Standing Committee. Interview with author (Hargeisa, August 2006).

importantly, elevated above the lower house and party politics. This position claims that introducing elections to the upper house would forever eradicate the function of traditional structures in the government, which is something they argue Somaliland simply cannot do.[31] As such, as this position upholds, any changes in the nature or functions of the body that have taken place are predominantly rhetorical and maintaining the status quo in regards to the *Guurti* is the optimal option for continued stability in the government.

Elect the Guurti

The second position in the debate is situated at the other end of the spectrum and is propelled by members of the Kulmiye and UCID parties, particularly those members in the House of Representatives. Within this strand of the argument there is a strong push for a more modern Somaliland government. Many feel that by maintaining even the notion of the traditional in the government democracy's potential can never be fulfilled. The unelected legislative body is seen as a hindrance to the democratic ideal and is therefore preventing Somaliland from becoming a successful and acceptable modern state. As MP Abdirahman Osman Alin Shirwac notes, '[Somaliland] cannot change society, modernise society in the future with the institution of the traditional holding it back. We are stuck in one place and that is very dangerous'.[32] The belief that society and the government must modernise in order for Somaliland to be a state capable of earning international recognition is commonly expressed by those positioning themselves within this camp.

Those maintaining this position widely believe that modernisation will take place primarily through democratisation, and thus the once integral inclusion of the traditional is no longer needed and could become a destabilising factor. This is best summarised by MP Ibrahim Jama Ali 'Reyte':

> [p]eople go on about the hybrid state, that the state should be indigenous. It should be based on local cultures, peculiarities, etc. Every state should reflect that. It should be decided from within and designed to serve the interests of society. But the state needs to be controlled by the people. The only way to do this is through democratisation ... The state is not hybrid, it is natural. We have finally settled on one form. We should stick to it. Somaliland cannot invent something new. None of this hybrid nonsense.[33]

---

31   Much of this argument was also expressed or articulated at a special session of the *Guurti* held in part to discuss legislation pertaining to the selection procedure for the upper house that had been proposed in the lower house. Proceedings of *Guurti* Special Session (Hargeisa, 30 August 2006). Translated by Mohammed Ali Kahin.

32   Abdirahman Osman Alin Shirwac. Interview with author, op. cit.

33   Ibrahim Jama Ali 'Reyte', Member of Somaliland House of Representatives (Kulmiye). Interview with author (Hargeisa, September 2006).

As indicated by the attempts at mandating popular elections for the upper house, the lower house has pushed for democratisation of the Somaliland government to also include the *Guurti*. The argument presented as justification for this is a lengthy one. It is maintained that the self-extension of the *Guurti* is indicative of the increasing politicisation of the upper house, as well as fears that the House of Elders could be dangerously co-opted by a branch of government to balance against another. Because of this, as long as the upper house continues to exercise legislative powers that can check, and in some instances halt, the actions of the elected lower house or to advise the president, the unelected *Guurti* is an obstacle to successful modern democratic government in the territory. Those within this camp maintain that a bicameral parliament continues to be important, but not with its current unelected and 'easily manipulated' body.[34] As the Speaker of the House of Representatives remarks, '[it is] only UDUB in the House of Elders. They are unelected ... There is no fair debate'.[35] In addition, and reminiscent of the World Bank report by Hashi, within this camp it is argued that in maintaining the high position of the clan in the political system the *Guurti* is holding the territory back, preventing modernisation and leaving an opening for clan confrontation to re-emerge within the government. Therefore, according to this position, the current form of the *Guurti* is posing a threat to the future stability and success of the government.[36]

Whilst distrust of the close ties with the UDUB party heavily factors into this position, attitudes of superiority based on education within this group are also important. The requirements for membership of the upper house do not contain educational qualifications aside from knowledge of religion and culture. Constitutionally, members of the lower house must have at least a secondary education. In practice, many members of the lower house are Diaspora returnees and were therefore many were educated in Europe. Many also come from professions such as medicine, education and law. Summarised in an analogy provided by Bashe Mohammed Farah, having an uneducated legislative body with veto power is akin to having a five-year old proofreading a piece of academic writing. Many within the lower house find it insulting that the 'old men' have a powerful veto over the more educated and 'democratically experienced' lower house's legislative endeavours. Farah continues with the argument in maintaining that if the system of checks and

---

34 Advocates of this position widely argue that the upper house is easily manipulated by the executive.

35 Ibrahim Jama Ali 'Reyte'. Interview with author, op. cit. This attitude was also expressed in numerous interviews and discussions undertaken in Hargeisa.

36 Abdulrahman Mohammed Abdullah, Speaker of the House, Somaliland House of Representatives (UCID). Interviews with author (Hargeisa, August and September 2006). The significance of the number of Diaspora returnees can be identified by acknowledging where the majority of the members returned from: the United States, the United Kingdom, Denmark and the Netherlands. Arguably, these men and women bring with them experience of Western democracies and, increasingly, become involved in politics, business and civil society in Somaliland.

balances in the government is to be effective, the membership of both houses needs to be equally qualified and knowledgeable to ensure that the parliament is in a better position to balance the powerful executive.[37] Whilst some members of the lower house find it troublesome or even insulting that their knowledge and experience can be overridden by the elders, it is within the latter part of that argument where the primary concern of many of those maintaining this position lies. Many believe the membership of the *Guurti* to be 'uneducated old men' who are 'not capable of reading and writing'.[38] Because of this an element of insecurity exists for those within the House of Elders; in the small Somaliland economy there is shrinking opportunity, particularly for those with little or no education. As such, it is claimed that the men in the upper house can be easily 'bought' in exchange for job security. As Ali Farah relates, Egal granted the upper house 'unnecessary legislative power to secure his position', and that since then the members of the *Guurti* have been nothing more than people who serve the president in order to secure their own positions.[39] According to this stance, this mutually beneficial relationship for the president and the elders thus undermines the system of checks and balances and threatens the progression of democratisation within Somaliland, regardless of the political affiliation of the president.

Unease over the ability of the president to co-opt the House of Elders has led many to express concerns over the unelected status of the House of Elders. The firmly held belief is the constitution stipulates that parliament is elected and therefore the government cannot fulfil its democratic promise unless both houses are elected.[40] As Reyte conveys, the identified problem is not with the institution itself, but the people in it and how they have come to hold their positions: '[i]t is not a *guurti*, it is a House of Parliament, it is legislative ... How can we call it legitimate with one person nominating someone and that person becomes a legislator?'[41] The fear within this side of the debate is that if this open door for increased executive power is not closed, and if the body remains unelected, the government 'will develop into a monster that [Somaliland] cannot remedy'.[42]

Although within this strand there is dissatisfaction with the current position of the *Guurti*, the aim is not to abolish the House of Elders but rather to alter it. Those proposing change feel that the traditional body that was instrumental in bringing and maintaining peace and security in the territory has outlived its purpose in the now stable territory; it is time to move beyond the clan and replace the redundant old with the new democratic ideals. Therefore, two possible futures for the *Guurti*

---

37 Bashe Mohammed Farah, Deputy Speaker of Somaliland House of Representatives (Kulmiye). Interview with author (Hargeisa, September 2006).
38 Ibrahim Jama Ali 'Reyte'. Interview with author, op. cit.; Abdulrahman Mohammed Abdullah. Interview with author, op. cit.
39 Abdirahman Aw Ali Farah. Interview with author, op. cit.
40 Ibid.
41 Ibrahim Jama Ali 'Reyte'. Interview with author, op. cit.
42 Abdirahman Aw Ali Farah. Interview with author, op. cit.

have been proposed: to be an elected body, thereby eliminating the old form of Somali governance; or to be an appointed tradition-based body with no legislative powers. Here a unicameral legislature is preferable to a bicameral body that is not fully elected by the people. For this camp, if the *Guurti* is to remain unelected its political and legislative capacity must be removed.

Modify in the Future

The third and final position, held primarily by political and social actors external to the government, contains components of both arguments already presented. Removed from the political infighting and positioning taking place in the government, this group presents what is perhaps the least personally motivated assessment. Within this position it is recognised that the current structure of the government is not perfect, particularly in regards to constitutional functions and ambiguities for the president and the *Guurti*. They recognise that the flexibility of the constitution was initially beneficial, but that fissures that are now becoming apparent can be destabilising as evidenced by the self-extension crisis. However, this position maintains that these obstacles and potential crises are merely growing pains that must be and will be addressed and resolved. It is acknowledged that in the future the nature and functions of government institutions may change, but it is also recognised that this is part of the statebuilding process. As a result, this side of the debate asserts a more wait-and-see approach: change is inevitable, but change must come through the traditional practices of negotiation, compromise and consensus rather than as the result of quick-fix solutions. This wait-and-see approach does not, however, exclude discussion on the future of the state.

It is maintained that the traditional house is still necessary for the stability of the government and the security of the territory, but that a new balance must be found between the old and the new as democratic practices become more familiar to the government and the people. Mohammed Said Gees summarises a belief held by many in stating that as the government gets stronger the *Guurti* is marginalised as it is no longer the crutch on which Somaliland rests. Because the *Guurti* does not 'speak the language of democracy that is at the national level' the fear is that the house will independently begin to seek a new role for itself as a means of strengthening its position, thereby creating the possibility for manipulation by powerful actors. As democratisation takes Somaliland into the next phase of the statebuilding process, a new role for the *Guurti* must be agreed upon by the government and the people so that the body can correspond with the evolving state. Gees offers the epitome of this position: 'I am not a fan of the *Guurti*, but I feel they are useful for Somaliland at present. They are doing a good job. But on the other hand, it [creating a state] is a process'.[43] Whilst not proposing the removal of the *Guurti* from the government, this statement reflects the recognition that the body's position in the government will change and the influence of the

---

43 Mohammed Said Mohammed Gees. Interview with author, op. cit.

elders will diminish as the state continues to grow. Whilst change in the future is foreseen, what shape that will take is uncertain.

What is believed, though, is that the *Guurti* alone cannot shape its future. Alterations in the executive and lower house were constitutionally mandated through the introduction of democratic elections. Whilst the modern was expected to grow and evolve, a reactionary change in the traditional was not accounted for. As Bobe Duale Yusuf offers:

> [a]s times have changed, no one has revised the role of the *Guurti*. From time to time we must re-examine their role. We must ask how can we use the *Guurti* in the democratisation process? What type of *Guurti* is suited to the democratisation process? ... The *Guurti* is not living on an island. They are living within society. As society transforms, the *Guurti* transforms.[44]

At the same time, however, this position maintains that the time has not yet come for large-scale modification of the body's position and function within the government. Rather, Somaliland must finish the reconciliation process, particularly concerning the eastern provinces of Sanaag and Sool, and until it does so it continues to need a 'watchdog' to be 'looking upon the performance of the government ... the *Guurti* is needed to oversee all this'.[45] This presents a precarious position within which the body must continue to operate; the centrality of the *Guurti* in the self-extension crisis rendered it incapable of effectively carrying out its oversight or mediation roles and severely damaged its ability to carry out those roles in the future. Therefore, without resolving the crisis regarding determining the membership of the body the upper house and, importantly, its various roles remain in a state of uncertainty. Consequently, according to this position, the future of the *Guurti* must be carefully negotiated as it is essential to balance the need for change with the need for a continuation of the tradition-associated mediating and reconciling roles in the ongoing building of the Somaliland state.

Although this position maintains that Somaliland is not yet ready to make any drastic changes to the composition or structure of the government, particularly in terms of severing the link between the old and the new, they also uphold that the upper house cannot remain an unelected legislative body indefinitely. As the democratisation process continues, the *Guurti* will be forced to change. Many believe that the future of the *Guurti* is as a purely legislative body, meaning that elections will take place and the association with the traditional will eventually be removed. Even so, it is believed that electing the *Guurti* at the end of their

---

44 Bobe Yusuf Duale, former SNM commander and current Programme Director for APD. Interview with author (Hargeisa, September 2006).

45 Ibid. Duale was referring to the president's actions regarding the self-extension, but in particular he cites disagreement and instability in the eastern regions of Sanaag and Sool which are long-term concerns of Somaliland. He also includes constitutional ambiguity, institutional immaturity and financial weakness as areas where reconciliation continues.

original term would have been disastrous. Firstly, it is generally agreed that the territory would not have been ready for another national election, either financially or logistically, and therefore an extension of the house's mandate was preferable to immediate elections.[46] Secondly, many assert that the 'new' in Somaliland is not yet established enough to function as the democracy envisioned by those pushing for a more modern government. It is feared that without the mediating old, the new will not be able to maintain the stability necessary for the continued development of the government. As such, the presence of the old in the government is still needed as a point of reference and reassurance to maintain stability whilst the modern component of the state strengthens. Thus, although the role of the *Guurti* will inevitably change, according to this camp, Somaliland is not yet strong enough to relinquish its link to the traditional.

In relation to the self-extension crisis, criticism from much of Somaliland's civil society is similar to that of the opposition members of the lower house: it centres not on the extension of the house's term, but rather on the manner in which this extension was carried out as well as the role the body is playing in the current government. There is a strong desire to protect the House of Elders as it is 'an innovation, an invention, a Somaliland product'.[47] It is argued that as long as the clan remains the basis of Somali life, a representation of that must be included in the government. There is also a strong aversion to creating two similar elected houses of parliament, a consideration that is at odds with the proposition to make the upper house a purely legislative and political body. As Hassan Issa states:

> the second chamber should not be the same as the first. They must be different for checks and balances. The second is needed to soften edges, to ameliorate the imperfections of the first. It is needed to soften the dictatorship of the majority.[48]

According to this position, the best option for Somaliland, therefore, is to ensure that the *Guurti* remains distinctive in its traditional association whilst at the same time finding a way for the body to evolve as the state modernises. The need for a new role for the house is apparent. However, finding a way to maintain the traditional whilst at the same time responding to the demands of modernisation will pose unique problems for Somaliland; problems which are not unanticipated by those within this side of the debate. Even though how this balance is achieved is as of yet uncertain, for this side of the debate the solution to these problems and uncertainties can and must be found through traditional Somali politics: negotiation and compromise to resolve and move beyond the impasse. Without a resolution achieved through consensus, these issues can never fully be resolved.

---

46   Mohamoud Garad Mohammed. Interview with author, op. cit.; Mustafa Rashad. Interview with author, op. cit.
47   Bobe Yusuf Duale. Interview with author, op. cit.
48   Hassan Issa, former Vice President of Somaliland. Interview with author (Hargeisa, September 2006).

Beyond the Crossroads?

Throughout the self-extension crisis, the *Guurti* continued to function as a mediation and consensus-seeking body, both at the local level and at the national level. Within the crisis, the traditional and symbolic practices of the clan in the central government have continued despite the damaged position of the *Guurti*, raising questions about the possibility of removing the formal clan body without removing clan governance, or the desirability of that. Although the responses to the *Guurti*'s self-extension varied, the identification of one key realisation is consistent throughout: obstacles stemming from the hybrid nature of the government will be encountered during the continued growth and evolution of the state. It is also consistently recognised that addressing and resolving these obstacles and crises that stem from them is a stage of the statebuilding process and part of creating a state that continues to work for Somaliland. As such, the parties involved in the debate have identified several specific concerns to be addressed. Amongst the highlighted issues are those relating to democratic selection and balancing relationships and power in the government.

The self-extension of the *Guurti* was viewed by many as an attack on the modern democratic component of the government; overpowering and bypassing the House of Representatives made the democratically elected lower house appear to be powerless and therefore meaningless. In addition, manipulating constitutional ambiguity threatened the ability of the document to act as a framework or guide for the government and led some to question parliament's ability to check and therefore constrain the executive. Outsider observation, however, largely viewed the crisis as one of many obstacles to overcome in the statebuilding, nation-building and democratisation processes. The crossroads reached in Somaliland meant that the project of introducing democracy either could have been ended with the president's assertion of power, or the process could be strengthened by the recognition of problems to overcome. Ongoing negotiations to address and resolve the problem indicate the latter.

The crisis emanating from the *Guurti*'s self-extension highlights a core issue for Somaliland's government: namely, what happens when the traditionally-based body cannot function in a way that it was originally meant to. Many claim that the disagreement and subsequent distrust between the House of Representatives and the House of Elders was orchestrated by then president Rayale as a means through which he could ensure his own political position. However, this accusation remains just that: an accusation. Whether his concern for the stability of the country or his own position was the rationale behind the actions leading to the legislative impasse is uncertain. Regardless of the reasoning, however, the parties' insistence on these accusations only serves to mask the underlying issue of the evolving position of clan governance in a government that is increasingly becoming 'newer'. With the upper house in a position that compromises its capacity to mediate and reconcile within the government, two key functions in the continuing stability of the government, concerns over this underlying issue intensify. With its impartiality in doubt, the *Guurti*'s tradition-based role has been undermined. With the encroachment of the new into the realm of the old, and with the traditional body becoming subject to both beneficial and destructive political practices and influences, the future role for the old and the hybrid are uncertain.

The crossroads reached has raised many important concerns, especially how long is the current state of the once vital hybrid construction beneficially viable to the government and territory? The deepening division is not only one created by actions leading up to the self-extension, but is also indicative of the tension between the old and new: the old Somali clan governance system and the new Western style of democracy introduced by the SNM and furthered largely by returning members of the Diaspora. These tensions may have been brought forth by the self-extension, but they have precipitated debate over the future of the House of Elders and, more fundamentally, the placement of the traditional in the democratic government. The basis of stability in the formation of the Somaliland state was the inclusion of both traditional structures of governance and modern democratic institutions and practices. However, the basis for the stability necessary to create the state could also be the basis for instability if the relationship between the traditional and modern becomes unbalanced.

Certainly, this debate narrows to the central focus of the integration of both the clans and modern practices and institutions in the government structure. If the clan inclusion continues as it is currently, one set of considerations must be addressed; and if the upper house is altered in the name of modernisation another set stemming from the further politicisation of the traditional body will have to be resolved. Despite the polarity of the arguments, one conclusion is consistent: the role of the upper house of parliament will change. Whether the body becomes a predominately legislative one upon the phasing out of the selected clan-based membership or whether it loses its legislative powers is yet to be seen. Although many argue that in order for Somaliland to become the ideal democratic state the clan should not have the position that it holds today, it is unlikely that it will disappear entirely within the government; even a lasting symbolic association with the clan would preserve its place and, arguably, be necessary. Resolving the disagreement over the *Guurti*, however, will inevitably alter the nature of the body and will set the stage for the future role of the traditional authority. Even if only through establishing new rules for membership selection procedures, change is certain for the upper house of parliament.

Conclusions

There is no doubt that the *Guurti*'s self-extension heightened awareness of obstacles encountered in the continuing process of statebuilding in Somaliland. Political infighting, constitutional weakness and tensions between the old way of governing and the new democratic system, as well as between domestic necessities and external pressures, are all testing the Somaliland people and the hybrid government. With the role of the body charged with mediating conflicts and ameliorating difficulties being called into question, these tests have become much more acute. The *Guurti* has served as a mediating factor not only for the government institutions and other conflicting parties in the territory, but also for statebuilding process as a whole. The institutionalisation of the traditional has served to act as a link, albeit largely symbolically, between traditional Somali politics and the new democratic system of governing. Most people interviewed agree that the *Guurti* was the key to the success of forming a government, maintaining peace and introducing democracy in Somaliland. The obstacle to address now, however, is maintaining the link to the traditional and its stabilising influence during and after the continuing democratisation of the government. The *Guurti* was created as an apolitical body whose membership was composed of the men who strived to create peace and stability in the territory and the nascent government. Today's *Guurti*, however, is evidence of the increasingly political alterations of the body stemming from its position and power within the government. The self-extension appeared to many to be an action that is vastly different from the appearance of unselfish, community-serving men that the comprised the 1991 *Guurti*.[49] As part of the machinery of the state, the *Guurti* has become politicised, whether intentionally or not, and therefore the originally intended composition of the government has been altered: the *Guurti* has become more dictated to by the political process than originally intended. This alteration itself has raised significant questions for the future role of the body.

One consistent realisation in the debates surrounding the *Guurti* is the need for continued negotiation and re-negotiation between the old and the new – the internal and the external – in the Somaliland government. The hybridity of the government reflects Somaliland's complex social, political and economic circumstances and the centrality of the clan system, as well as reflecting desires for more economic and political engagement with the international community. This facilitates the success of not only maintaining a balance between society and government, but also a balance between the externally desired modern democratic statehood and the domestically valued clan traditions and governance structures. What is now being called into question is not the success of this creation, but rather its future as the old guard is being questioned by the new. Because of both increasing opportunity

---

[49] Amongst others, Mohammed Hassan Ibrahim 'Gani'. Conversations with author (Hargeisa, August and September 2006); Dr Aden Abokor. Interview with author, op. cit.; Dr Abdirahman Yusuf Artan, Member of Somaliland House of Representatives (Kulmiye). Interview with author (Hargeisa, September 2006); Dr Abdirahman Yusuf Artan. Conversations with author (Hargeisa, September 2006); Bobe Duale Yusuf. Interview with author, op. cit.; Ibrahim Jama Ali 'Reyte'. Interview with author, op. cit.; Mohammed Said Mohammed Gees. Conversations with author (Hargeisa, August and September 2006); Saeed Ahmed, Commissioner for NEC. Conversations with author (Hargeisa, September 2006); Saeed Ahmed. Interview with author (Hargeisa, September 2006); 'Somaliland Forum for Civic Dialogue', Participation by author (Hargeisa, September 2006).

and a return of Somalilanders from the Diaspora, the number of new elites in Somaliland is growing and the constant tension between the old and new ways of doing things is becoming apparent. As the new members of this group push to realise the idealised modern democratic statehood, however, the danger is that they will push too far, thereby unbalancing the negotiation between the Western and the Somali. On the other hand, if nothing changes the democratic project, and with that the stability of the state and hopes for recognition, will undoubtedly be threatened. With this comes the possibility that the stabilising distinctiveness of the Somaliland government that has proven to be successful thus far will become a destabilising point of contention. For the institution that was included in the government in part to help bring about the dream of acceptable modern statehood, little consideration was given for if the dream started to become reality. Therefore, with growth comes the realisation for the need to re-negotiate the hybrid nature of the government in order to restore the reconciliation and the balance. The changing juxtaposition of these two governing structures is best viewed as a continuation of the negotiation of the state and a rebalancing of the demands: what was needed at the beginning of the process might not be a component that survives the process in its original form.

Regardless of the problems or obstacles encountered in the continuing statebuilding process in Somaliland, one thing is important to highlight and to bear in mind: the people of Somaliland and their political leaders continue to recognise the need for growth and change and, more importantly, they are addressing these in their own way. Indeed, the hybridisation here is more than just the institutionalisation of the *Guurti*; amongst other things it is also evidenced in the reliance on traditional practices of negotiation and consensus. The hybrid nature is the utilisation, integration and dependence on traditional practices in addition to the institution. It is part of the foundations of the state and part of the statebuilding process itself. The institutionalisation makes it a formal inclusion, but in both practical and symbolic capacities the hybrid goes much deeper. In many ways, the practices of the traditional *guurti* underpin the statebuilding practice, even in areas where clan elders are not involved or where the central *Guurti* has been compromised. Statebuilding in Somaliland originally took place through a series of formally held *shir*, and it continues through informal *shir*-like negotiations when obstacles arise or when problems loom. As Deputy Speaker of the House of Representatives Bashe Mohammed Farah, a proponent of modernising the *Guurti*, confidently asserts, the key to continued stability is 'go[ing] back to traditions. We will solve problems by the traditional way. And we must and we will have the patience to wait'.[50] In Somaliland, the state has, and continues to be, negotiated rather than imposed.

It is impossible to ascertain whether or not Somaliland would have witnessed the stability it has if it had followed a statebuilding blueprint established or imposed by international actors. If the lack of progress in southern Somalia is

---

50 Bashe Mohammed Farah. Interview with author, op. cit.

any indication, though, the road could have been much bumpier if Somaliland would have been engaged in an internationally led project. It is often easy to forget that Somaliland has created as state virtually on its own, yet the isolation of the territory has been a benefit to what has been created. The scarcity of international involvement in Somaliland's state formation has allowed for the process to reflect Somaliland society and to respond to issues best handled by those who understand Somaliland society and Somali political and societal relations. The emerging state in Somaliland reflects the needs and the desires of the population, and it reflects the political processes of society. The quest for recognition and the desire to be 'Somaliland' is a strong component of nation-building in the territory and undoubtedly contributes to the success of the statebuilding process. However, part of the narrative within Somaliland is that without the institutions of state, the dream of recognition cannot be realised; the statebuilding process and the nation-building process are mutually constitutive. The institutions in Somaliland, both tangible bodies and institutions of practice, are not institutions 'from a box': they do not come from a template but rather reflect the state that is being built. They reflect the intersection of politics and the population, and they reflect the underlying social structures that shape and determine the relationship between the people and the state. The legitimacy gap indicative of many statebuilding projects is narrow in Somaliland: Society is embedded in the state and the project, and the state is embedded in society.

As needs, desires and demands of society change, as the relationship between the political processes and society changes, and as political culture changes, the state and institutions reflecting those will change. The flexibility to adapt and make those changes is a strength of the Somaliland statebuilding process; a characteristic that is often absent from externally-led statebuilding projects. Even though the growth of the Somaliland state has brought with it delayed concerns, the inclusion of the traditional authority in the government was indeed a benefit to the process from the beginning as it allowed for the foundations on which to build a state. There may still be kinks in the system, and obstacles will continue to appear, but the statebuilding process in Somaliland is ongoing. The debate over the role of the clan is evidence of that. In being a Somaliland project, though, future adjustments to the government are likely to reflect what is desired and needed in Somaliland at that time. The key to future success, therefore, is to continue to negotiate, to continue to compromise, and to continue the process of creating a Somaliland state the Somaliland way.

Chapter 8
Conclusions

In today's increasingly interconnected world, states cannot function in isolation. Even those states or entities not in direct contact with international institutions or developmental organisations are still subject to being externally influenced by normative standards and policy precedents. Domestically-led statebuilding and indigenous development programmes are not exempt from this; international norms of what it means to be an acceptable or successful state dictate domestic policy within developing states and, in particular, unrecognised states. For the latter, conforming to acceptable standards of statehood is perceived to be vital to attracting and maximising investment and developmental assistance that can only be obtained following recognition of sovereignty. For some, therefore, the style and functions of the state becomes a tool for economic and political survival. Like many unrecognised states, Somaliland's government outwardly exhibits compliance with many international norms of acceptable statehood. The reflection of the demands of acceptable statehood, coupled with statements made by political leaders and the government's active and aggressive promotion of statehood, indicate that for Somaliland the style and structure of the state can be seen as a strategic tool in that they are key to attracting recognition of sovereignty. Whilst the steps taken to attract international recognition can be rationalised as such, the creation and evolution of functioning political structures, practices and societal investment are more entrenched than just an extraversionary strategy for the purposes of recognition.[1] The state presented by Somaliland is not a facade or a pretence: the creation of an acceptable state and the continuing development of that state indicate a more subtle yet also more involved process; what may have been a strategy has become a tangible reality. In an international environment focused on an ideal style of statehood and demanding acceptable governance and government, with continuation of the statebuilding process dependent upon continuing support from the domestic population, and with the desired end result being increasing external political relationships, political structures and government actions become a vital component of a more deeply invested form of political extraversion. In the case of Somaliland, the lasting impacts on the social and political relationships resulting from this must also be recognised.

Pegg and King note that many de facto states benefit from the support of a strong patron state: Northern Cyprus is supported by Turkey, many Eastern European de

---

1 See J-F. Bayart, 'Africa in the World: A History of Extraversion', *African Affairs* 99.395 (2000), pp. 217–67; J-F. Bayart, *The State in Africa: Politics of the Belly* (London: Longman, 1993).

facto states are backed by Russia, and Taiwan has friendly relations with the West.[2] Somaliland, however, does not have this level of backing. Even though Ethiopia and Djibouti have fostered diplomatic ties with Somaliland, neither acts as a patron state for the territory. Whereas others are propped up by external support, for Somaliland support and legitimacy for the state must come from within if the project is to succeed. The need for the establishment of a modern acceptable state and the quest for recognition are therefore directing the relationship between Somaliland society and the forming state; a relationship that is being cultivated through a negotiated co-existence and co-dependence between the modern and traditional structures. What is emerging in response to both domestic demands and international desires is more ensconced than a superficial strategy for recognition. Rather, it is a form of political extraversion in which the strategies for international inclusion and interaction, together with domestic acceptance and support, encompass the political practices and structures of the territory. In many ways, this is where the external and the internal in Somaliland are most entwined; they cannot be separated as the external, through this strategy, has been woven into the internal. Institutions reflect primarily external demands, governance attends largely to internal necessities, and the narrative holding it together – the narrative feeding the Somaliland identity – propels the continuation of the balancing act between the two.

For more than two decades the process of statebuilding in Somaliland has been underpinned by the quest for recognition of sovereign statehood. It is such a central component of the Somaliland narrative that it has also become part of the Somaliland identity. The Somaliland process has in large part been able to continue as it has because there is societal investment in it,[3] and that societal investment comes largely from the idea of this is necessary to achieve what we want, and we're all in it together. The 'want' here is not necessarily a state that conforms to the external liberal model, but rather recognition of sovereignty that will bring tangible benefits such as increased trade and travel. This is perhaps best epitomised by a market trader in Hargeisa who, when asked what he wanted the state to be, stated that it should provide him with a passport. While modern democratic structures and practices are certainly becoming more of the 'want' for many Somalilanders, the expectation of recognition arguably continues to be predominant in the territory, and societal investment is rooted in that. The narrative of recognition is so entrenched in the Somaliland process that it has become part of Somaliland's identity, both the externally portrayed and the internally adopted.

---

2   S. Pegg, *International Society and De Facto States* (Aldershot: Ashgate, 1998); C. King, 'The Benefits of Ethnic War: Understanding Eurasia's Unrecognized States', *World Politics* 53.4 (2001), pp. 524–52. See also, D. Lynch, *Engaging Eurasia's Separatist States* (Washington DC: United States Institute of Peace Press, 2004).

3   See Somaliland Academy for Peace and Development (ADP) and WSP-International (2003) 'Facilitating Somaliland's Democratic Transition'. Nairobi/Hargeisa: Dialogue for Peace Somali Programme Report, p. 4.

The Somaliland identity is not necessarily centred on people saying 'I am a Somalilander'. Instead, it is the identity of the political entity itself. From the beginning the Somaliland identity has highlighted its separateness from the south. It has invoked the brutality of the Barre regime and the genocidal campaign he waged in the north. Somalilanders have also been described as more refined than other Somalis based on the British colonial experience as opposed to the Italian experience in the south. This distinction of separateness helped define the Somaliland population. As the statebuilding process continued, the Somaliland identity evolved and strengthened. From the beginning, the people of Somaliland were 'sold' the idea that a democratic government was necessary for recognition of sovereignty, and much of what could be seen as acceptance by the population was the idea that the drastic changes taking place were necessary for recognition. The power of this identity rests with its legitimising capacity; it serves to justify the state both inside and out. Externally, Somaliland is presented as a stable democratic state worthy of recognition. Internally, it is not a desire for recognition, but rather an expectation of recognition; an expectation that facilitates societal investment in political action deemed necessary to fulfilling that expectation. In the narrative and the identity of Somaliland, these two cannot be separated. In many ways, the external has become inextricably engrained in the internal, a factor that may place strain on the Somaliland process. However, although Somaliland is not a recognised state entity, the internal component of the narrative acts as a strong force reinforcing the bond between the people and the state; a bond which continues to serve in a legitimising capacity. 'Somaliland' is not just an unrecognised state contently existing within the confines of Somalia. 'Somaliland' is a political project built on and actively seeking recognition of sovereign statehood, and within that 'Somaliland' is a modern democracy rooted in the clan system and with significant societal investment in doing what is necessary – maintaining peace and continuing with democratisation – to achieve that desired recognition. Meeting expectations of external legitimacy while at the same time maintaining vital internal legitimacy is central to not only continuing the process, but also to the Somaliland identity.

This is not to claim that all Somalilanders are fully invested in this identity and this process. There are regions in the territory that reject their inclusion in the Somaliland project, and there is dissatisfaction, largely amongst the minority clans. Certainly there are also Somalilanders who are apathetic to the process. Also, more than twenty years after its declaration of independence Somaliland's unrecognised status may put strain on this identity. How long can the political leaders continue to justify their actions based on the promise of recognition? How long can the state be held together on the basis that peace and political change are necessary for the ultimate goal? Conversely, as the institutions and modern practices grow and ideas about the state change, one must ask whether that once vital cohesive and unifying force is still necessary. Are the new way of governing, the peace, the stability and the growth that have been experienced in the past two decades rooted enough in the territory that the 'state' can exist without the enticement of recognition?

A 'Model' of Statebuilding?

Throughout the literature on Somaliland it is common to see reference to the territory as being a model for state development in Africa.[4] Indeed, the project in Somaliland has been able to foster what many other development or statebuilding projects in Africa have not been able to achieve: peace, stability and growth. By all appearances Somaliland is a functioning modern democratic state that conforms to expectations of successful statehood and is separate from the rest of Somalia. However, the Somaliland state deviates from the normative blueprint as Somaliland is meeting the demands of modern statehood in its own way that bolsters domestic support and legitimacy for the unfamiliar modern practices. Somaliland, in the absence of direct international interference or involvement, created a government structure that reflects the best of both worlds that many Somalilanders, and the Somaliland state, live in.[5]

Mohammed Said Gees contends that the 'lack of recognition and the absence of international involvement and support have given the people an opportunity and freedom to craft an indigenous form of social and political organization with a democratic framework'. The freedom experienced by Somaliland in creating its state allowed for the hybrid creation that Gees claims is the only form of state that could survive within the 'dominant Somali clan culture'.[6] Despite the success in Somaliland, however, Gees also maintains that Somaliland is not a model of statehood; a sentiment shared by many. Indeed, the 'imperfection of the Somaliland state' and the unfinished statebuilding process are evidence that putting Somaliland on a pedestal would be a mistake.[7] Much of what has held Somaliland together thus far and this long has not been a strong central state apparatus exerting its power and control throughout the

---

4 See, for example, M. Bradbury, A. Abokor and H. Yusuf, 'Somaliland: Choosing Politics Over Violence', *Review of African Political Economy* 30.97 (2003), pp. 455–78; M. Bryden, 'State-Within-a-Failed State: Somaliland and the Challenge of International Recognition', In P. Kingston and I. Spears (eds), *States-Within-States: Incipient Political Entities in the Post-Cold War Era* (Basingstoke: Palgrave Macmillan, 2004), pp. 167–88; K. Evans, 'A Somali Journey', *The Courier* 162 (March-April 1997), pp. 55–7; S. Horner, 'Somalia: Can the Jigsaw be Pieced Together?' *The Courier* 162 (March–April 1997), pp. 46–53; J. Drysdale, *Stoics Without Pillows: A Way Forward for the Somalilands* (London: HAAN Associates, 2000); Somaliland Government, 'Somaliland: Demand for International Recognition', Policy Document for the Government of Somaliland (Hargeisa: Somaliland Ministry of Information, 2001); M. Gees, 'Is Somaliland a Model?' Unpublished manuscript (2006); T. Othieno, 'A New Donor Approach to Fragile Societies: The Case of Somaliland', ODI Opinion 103 (2008).

5 This is referencing Bobe Duale Yusuf's observation that Somaliland exists in two worlds: the Western and the Somali. Bobe Duale Yusuf, former SNM commander and current Programme Director for APD. Interview with author (Hargeisa, September 2006).

6 M. Gees, 'Is Somaliland a Model?' op. cit.

7 Conversations with Mohammed Said Mohammed Gees and Mohammed Hassan Ibrahim 'Gani' (Hargeisa, August-September 2006); M. Gees, 'Is Somaliland a Model?' op. cit.

territory. Indeed, the opposite is more accurate of the central government – although growing in strength, it is relatively weak and has little authoritative control over the population. Much of the day-to-day governance in Somaliland continues to derive from the clan system, with traditional codes of practice and traditional law and justice mechanisms more prevalent than codified 'Western' law and action. As the state continues to grow and develop, however, the hybridity of this system of governance as it currently stands is being tested on numerous fronts. With internal pressure for further modernisation of the government increasing, tensions between the old Somali style of governance and the new democratic institutions in the government are becoming more apparent. However, creating a state is a lengthy and tumultuous process and encountering some obstacles must be expected as the process continues. Still, much can be gleaned from Somaliland's statebuilding process. In spite of the hurdles, important lessons can be taken from the case of Somaliland in regards to the process of building a state as well as what a successful state can look like. Rather than debating whether or not Somaliland is a model, perhaps the more appropriate question to ask is what kind of model can Somaliland be?

Claiming that the Somaliland state can be a model for statebuilding is at the same time imprudent and meritorious. It is erroneous to say that the process Somaliland is going through in creating its state can be dissected and the resulting components and practices can be applied elsewhere. The Somaliland state cannot be a new blueprint for statebuilding; the state in Somaliland is tailored specifically to Somaliland's society and the specific circumstances of the territory during its statebuilding process and therefore cannot be transposed onto another situation. What has worked in Somaliland, namely the inclusion of traditional authority in the central government and the utilisation of clan governance, may not be appropriate for a territory with a contentious relationship with traditional governance or for a territory with an ethnically divided population. Somaliland's existence as an unrecognised state seeking sovereign recognition also certainly factors into Somaliland's success, as does a very active and financially supporting Diaspora community.[8] Conversely, however, the experiences of Somaliland, particularly the deviance in the state, can offer valuable lessons. Specifically, Somaliland shows that the creation or development of a state can reflect the unique history, society, traditions, cultures and practices within the territory; a practice that is not a primary component of current externally-led policy. For some such as Ghani and Lockhart, statebuilding is about 'closing the sovereignty gap' between the juridical and the empirical, and the way to best do that is for external actors to 'fix' empirical weaknesses identified as inhibiting success.[9] Although they also maintain that within local capabilities and resources

---

8 See I. Ahmed, Remittances and their Economic Impact in Post-War Somaliland. *Disasters* 24.4 (2000): 380–89; A. Lindley, *Somalia Country Study*. Commissioned for a report on Informal Remittance Systems in African, Caribbean and Pacific Countries. Compas (Oxford: DFID, EC, Deloitte and Touche, 2005).

9 A. Ghani and C. Lockhart, 'Closing the Sovereignty Gap: An Approach to Statebuilding', Overseas Development Institute Working Paper 253 (London: ODI, 2005).

'[b]ackwardness can actually offer some advantages', theirs is a technocratic guide offering a framework that does not venture beyond technical components of the state such as economic capacity or physical infrastructure.[10] Indeed, what they offer is reflective of what Bendana's 'top down, externally guided, supply-driven, elitist and interventionist' characterisation of peacebuilding.[11] This type of 'fixing' a state, however, does not guarantee the gap between the empirical and the juridical will be bridged. Reflective of much of the stance of those engaged in statebuilding literature and practice, Ghani and Lockhart do not acknowledge that valuable local capabilities and resources may also include indigenous or traditional systems of governance that will challenge the dominant accepted framework of modern government, but may also be key to creating stable governing structures within non-Western states. However, as a form of collective memory, tradition involves organising the past in relation to the present: '[t]radition represents not only what "is" done in a society but what "should be" done'.[12] The prominent placement of a 'backwards' traditional institution or structure, as Somaliland shows, can be a crucial piece of statebuilding or state strengthening projects. Away from the tradition-centric nature of this case, Somaliland also shows the value in those institutions and actors that may have been rejected by the international community. The state in Somaliland can be seen as progressing through the stages of legitimisation, with the end result being the externally sought after Weberian bureaucratic authority. In many ways, Somaliland is following the 'Weberian path', something that is not characteristic of externally-led projects. Indeed, the Somaliland case raises important questions; amongst them are those about the role of locally valued and trusted actors in the success of statebuilding.

Within Ghani and Lockhart's discussion on externally-led projects and closing the sovereignty gap, as is often the case in reform, statebuilding and development literature, there is another key omission: their offering does not take into account the sovereignty exercised by external actors and the power relationships that come with that. The involvement of international actors in a statebuilding project creates an element of competition over power and resources, with rewards going to those chosen by the external actors at the expense of others. Often the domestic winners are those who need to be quelled and brought on board a project, resulting in fragmentation and often further violence as competition increases. This can be identified in numerous projects, including those in Somaliland's regional neighbours. This competition breeding violence has been identified in interventions in Ethiopia

---

10 A. Ghani and C. Lockhart, *Fixing Failed States: A Framework for Rebuilding a Fractured World* (Oxford: Oxford University Press, 2008), pp. 225, 226.

11 A. Bendana, 'What Kind of Peace is Being Built? Critical Assessments from the South', International Development Research Centre Discussion Paper (Ottawa, Canada, January 2003), p. 4.

12 U. Beck, A. Giddens and S. Lash, *Reflexive Modernization: Politics, Tradition, and Aesthetics in the Modern Social Order* (Palo Alto: Stanford University Press, 1994), pp. 63, 65.

during the conflict with Eritrea,[13] as well as in projects in Somalia and Sudan. In the former, both the empowerment and exclusion of warlords within statebuilding attempts have resulted in increased violence and fragmentation within the state.[14] In Darfur, as Young notes, a flawed and narrow approach to intervention resulted in the concentration of power in the hands of 'belligerents' who did not discount continuing violence.[15] In externally-led projects, inclusion occurs on the terms of the external actors involved and as such creates the potential for continuing instability once those external actors exit. Both Sudan and Somalia show how damaging this can be as political problems at the root of a conflict are often not addressed or resolved.[16] Domestically led statebuilding projects, on the other hand, benefit from not being directly subjected to this complex and often damaging 'external factor', and local ownership is a component of the statebuilding process rather than a desired end result. Although exclusion from direct international intervention can create difficulties, removing the complexities of an agenda-driven international actor operating under set guidelines or expectations can prove highly beneficial for an emerging or rebuilding state. Somaliland is such a case.

D.I.Y. Statebuilding

Certainly, statebuilding in Somaliland has not been problem free, and the vision of how the state will function in relation to both domestic and international concerns has been altered from its original form to reflect the changing circumstances in and around Somaliland. Whilst democratic government has always been the stated

---

13   C. Kahn, 'Conflict, Arms, and Militarization: The Dynamics of Darfur's IDP Camps', Report No. 15 (Geneva: Small Arms Survey, 2008). Kahn argues that competition introduced by the presence of the international community in the Darfur conflict fragments the various rebel movements involved. See also, M. Duffield and J. Prendergast, *Without Troops and Tanks: Humanitarian Intervention in Eritrea and Ethiopia* (Trenton, NJ: Red Sea Press/Africa World Press, Inc., 1994).

14   S. Hansen, 'Warlords and Peace Strategies: The Case of Somalia', *The Journal of Conflict Studies* (Fall 2003), pp. 57–78: pp. 63–8. Hansen notes that the inclusion of warlords in the government often resulted in the fragmentation of warlord groups as other powerful actors within those groups broke away in attempts to earn a seat at the table.

15   J. Young, 'Sudan: A Flawed Peace Process Leading to a Flawed Peace', *Review of African Political Economy* 32.103 (2005), pp. 99–113: p. 100.

16   R. Smith, *The Utility of Force: The Art of War in the Modern World* (London: Penguin, 2007). In his analysis of the use of force, Smith claims that the interventionist means of addressing instability and conflict never address the complex underlying political and social problems and therefore will never result in a conclusive end to a conflict. Although discussing the use of force in peacekeeping or other forceful interventions, the conclusion made can also be applied to non-forceful interventions: going through a standard operating procedure without addressing the underlying problems fuelling a conflict or a 'dysfunctional' state only result in a continuation of the instability.

goal of the leadership in the territory, the internal dynamics impacting upon how the democratic component can and will function have changed. The advantage of the Somaliland state, however, is that it can account for the flexibility needed to incorporate these necessary changes in a way that would not be assured if the statebuilding process had been externally guided or imposed. The Somaliland state has a significant amount of latitude in the exercise of sovereignty stemming not only from the indigenous and locally owned and invested process, but also from the presence of the traditional authority in the government. This inclusion creates a level of central governance that not only resides within the government but also exists despite it, ensuring that during periods of transition or in the event of a political crisis the government, or the powers of governance, could continue to exist through the traditional institution. In its place both within and above the government, sovereignty exercised by the traditional authority is extensible, creating a situation in which the *Guurti* is able to fill the gaps when the government is weak, absent or vulnerable. That sovereignty is also rooted in Somaliland rather than with an external actor. The inclusion of the clan institution also serves to ease fears about centralised rule; including the powerful and familiar clan elders in the government created a body tasked with guidance as well as restraint on potentially power hungry individuals. By including this Somali component of governance alongside modern institutions in the central government, the founders of Somaliland created a safeguard for the post-conflict forming state in which past experiences had made the population wary of strong centralised rule. By institutionalising the traditional, the founders of the new Somaliland state created an internal safety net not only for central governance within the territory, but also for the continuum of government during the introduction of a democratic state. For Somaliland, the utilisation of traditional authority was the best, and possibly only, option for the stabilisation of a contentious and potentially volatile society during a period of extreme transition such as statebuilding. The vital role of this 'deviant' and 'backwards' inclusion on the path to today's state must not be overlooked.

Somaliland was able to achieve its remarkable successes largely because it was able to create a government structure and practices that reflect Somaliland's particular circumstances and demands. However, hesitancy surrounding the utilisation of tribal or clan systems in a central government, particularly within Somalia, would have ensured that the institutionalisation of the stabilising traditional would have been difficult, if not impossible, if the international community had taken command over the creation of the state. Shil reflects Weber's characterisation of traditional legitimacy as the 'eternal yesterday' in noting that discourse and practice have long been at unease with empowering such structures as the dominant emphasis is on moving forward and improvement – modernising – rather than existing in the past with tradition.[17] Ironically, what is perceived of to be an unpredictable, uncontrollable or non-modern factor was a key to the stability of the modern in Somaliland. Whilst

---

17 E. Shils, *Tradition* (Chicago: University of Chicago Press, 2006). See also, E. Shils, 'Nation, Nationality, Nationalism and Civil Society', *Nations and Nationalism* 1.1

those in the government are adamant that the presence of the central *Guurti* is not hindering its campaign for recognition, they are equally certain that the inclusion of the body would not have been a reality if the UN had taken control of rebuilding Somaliland. Indeed, many in Somaliland view the numerous failed attempts at statebuilding in the south as evidence that international involvement would have been devastating for the north.[18] One of the most advantageous decisions made by the founders of the Somaliland state, therefore, was the rejection of UN assistance offered through the UNOSOM missions.

A remarkable facet of the Somaliland state is that its founders created a relatively stable democratic government virtually on their own. Undoubtedly, there are consequential detriments to the lack of foreign involvement, such as a lack of monetary investment and, according to some, a lack of guidance in introducing democracy. However, Somaliland was not entirely without those, as the Diaspora community provided much of the financial and ideological support that would otherwise have come from the international community. Sitting both within Somaliland society and external to it, the Diaspora also operates in an internal-external capacity; it is a pipeline of sorts. In this case, however, the Diaspora itself is invested in the outcome in a way that international interveners could not be. The Diaspora could not provide to the scale that the international community could, but here the benefits far outweigh the costs: both political and traditional leaders in Somaliland were able to create what works for the territory and society and were able to undertake the process of introducing the new in their own way, at their own pace and without the conditionality that external involvement in the process of creating a state would entail.[19] This is not to say

---

(1995), pp. 93–118; M. Weber, 'Politics as Vocation (1948)', in H.H. Gerth and C. Wright Mills (eds), *From Max Weber: Essays in Sociology* (London: Routledge, 1967), pp. 77–128.

18 On 16 November 2008, the president of Somalia, Abdullahi Yusuf warned that the Somalia's government was again on the verge of collapse. The weak and highly detested internationally created government has only operated within Somalia since February 2006 when it moved to the city of Baidoa and made it the provisional seat of government. Prior to this, the government was in exile in Kenya. IRIN News, 'Somalia: TFG on Brink of Collapse', IRIN News Online (16 November 2008).

19 It is important to note that there has been a minimal, predominantly non-invasive international presence or involvement in Somaliland since its declaration of independence, but this presence is almost exclusively through wider Somalia projects rather than Somaliland specific endeavours and they rarely involve the process of creating an independent state. One example of this is that approximately 70 per cent of the costs for the 2005 parliamentary elections were covered by the European Union. The EU funding for the parliamentary elections was under the guise of promoting democracy in Somalia rather than specifically Somaliland. Also, the UN and many international NGOs operate within Somaliland. However, this involvement, as with most involvement in Somaliland, has not included direct involvement in the state formation process. That is to say, those involved in Somaliland have had minimal, if any, involvement in directing the state formation process in Somaliland, instead focusing more on physical infrastructure or social concerns.

that the Somaliland state was created in an environment of isolation; the indirect influence of international norms of statehood certainly impacted upon the process and the decisions made in regards to the shape and functions of the government, and it was perceived of as vital to comply with these norms if Somaliland were to be taken seriously as a 'state'. Rather than having this directly imposed on them through an externally led statebuilding project, though, Somaliland's leaders were able to adapt these influences to suit the needs of the people and the territory and to work in conjunction with Somaliland's traditional governance structures. In deviating from the pre-established path determined by the international community and implemented through statebuilding projects, the Somaliland state certainly challenges the people to accept a new way of governing, but it also challenges the dominant modern conception of what it takes to be an 'acceptable' or 'successful' state and the means through which to achieve that.

Non-intervention in the statebuilding process in Somaliland not only allows for the state to reflect the unique history, society and circumstances of the territory, but the successes of this process permit comment to be made on the dominant practices of statebuilding and conditional governance reform within developing states. Without direct interference, leaders in Somaliland have created, or have made great strides in creating, a desirable end result and have managed to avoid the catastrophic attempts at imposing an externally created government that have characterised interactions with post-1991 Somalia. Although Somaliland does have the significant political and economic motivation of recognition of sovereignty impacting upon the process, that does not negate the willingness demonstrated by not only the leaders of Somaliland but also the people to engage with the international community's terms and yet still maintain autonomy over the process of creating a state. It cannot be said that all states or territories would show the same success if similarly left alone, but the case of Somaliland does warrant a reconsideration of dominant conceptions of what it takes to be successful and how to get there. The dominance of an ideal type of state and a framework for how to achieve this state, with numerous checklists indicating stipulations and conditions to be met, is prevalent within literature and practice. Historically and globally, however, this 'ideal' state does not exist in practice; it exists only as a tool of liberal interventionism, creating a situation in which it is questionable as to whether or not the 'ideal' can actually be achieved. Statebuilding practice is wrought with failure and reform policies targeting the creation of an idealised acceptable state show varied and restricted success. With these limitations considered, the issue of what it means and takes to be acceptable deserves to be re-addressed.

Learning from Somaliland

Somaliland's fate if it had accepted the UN's initial offer of international assistance cannot be known. It can be assumed, however, that the territory would not now be lauded for its accomplishments or stability. In grounding the state in society and by utilising its governing structure, those involved in the creation of Somaliland found their key to success. The lack of resources available to Somaliland ensured that political and traditional leaders would have to depend on domestic capabilities and support in order to create the state, and internalising the statebuilding process entrenched the state in society and society in the state. Because of a lack of funds for security, traditional methods of reconciliation were used to demobilise the militias and prevent the fighting that raged through the south. Invoking the common memory of isolation and brutality created a sense of Somaliland identity around which the people could rally and which would create a link between the project and the people. As with any statebuilding process, elites alone cannot carry the state, and in Somaliland they do not. Finally, including the pervasive clans in the forming government ensured continuity and trust throughout the process. Lack of international involvement placed the statebuilding process in the hands of the people and leaders, meaning that not only could the state reflect Somaliland but also that the society was invested in the outcome. The fine balance in Somaliland was not achieved without sacrifice, but the stability and security in Somaliland throughout the process proves that the balance reached has been effective. The Somaliland state truly belongs to Somaliland.

Despite the centrality of the clan system in the formation of Somaliland, there is no guarantee that Somaliland will never eliminate or alter the place of the traditional within the government. Whilst the loss of the clan institution in the central government would mean losing what has been an integral component thus far and what characterises the Somaliland project, it could also be determined by the leaders in Somaliland that the clan institution was a part of the process of statebuilding but not the resulting state. The path to democracy in Somaliland was dependent upon the Somaliland clans. Now that democracy is taking root, however, the government in Somaliland must decide what the future role for the clans is. It would be a worrying loss if the *Guurti* was ousted because of internal pressure stemming by interpretations of what is desired to become a modern state, as premature removal of a pivotal component of the balance could prove disastrous for the state. However, it is possible that leaders in Somaliland will determine that the stabilising influence of the clan is no longer needed. Whatever the future, one thing Somaliland has shown thus far is that no decision will be made without lengthy debate and consensus from within the state. The future of the traditional institution may be under debate, but the lessons to be taken are immense. Even if the *Guurti* is removed or altered from its present form, the inclusion of and dependence on the traditional institution throughout the statebuilding process in Somaliland shows the value of this local dynamic and the vital role it played in creating a state.

Using the terminology of Finnemore, Somaliland is both 'learning' and being 'taught' statehood. At the same time, however, Somaliland is also contributing to the practice of 'teaching' statehood.[20] In her comparative examination of Western

---

20 M. Finnemore, *National Interests in International Society* (Ithaca: Cornell University Press, 1996).

and non-Western approaches to the study of international relations, Bilgin argues that there is an unwarranted distinction between 'Western' and 'non-Western' approaches as they are 'almost the same but not quite' and often produce similar outcomes.[21] Whilst Bilgin is discussing analytical and theoretical approaches to the study of IR, the notion of 'almost the same but not quite' raises interesting considerations for practice, particularly in relation to statebuilding. As the case of Somaliland shows, the 'almost the same but not quite' state can produce similar functions and outcomes to those desired by the international community. Bilgin's conclusion can be identified more broadly, however, particularly in her identification of a suffused or increasingly symbiotic relationship between the Western and non-Western. It has been argued that western demands dominate policy leading to the exclusion of the unknown or unfamiliar. At the same time, however, seemingly non-Western approaches have been incorporated into practice, albeit in a very limited capacity. Recent trends include the inclusion and utilisation of traditional structures in local governance building and localised development projects.[22] This acknowledgment of the benefits afforded by indigenous structures and practices shows a willingness to engage with these structures, although only on a level that is supportive of the agreed normative consensus of the acceptable modern state. The utilisation of both Western and indigenous structures and practices, however, can be beneficial not only to local development projects, but also to both internationally and domestically led statebuilding projects.

Cramer and Goodhand argue that the state apparatus and functions cannot be treated in isolation to local and regional contexts and considerations. In reference to statebuilding policies in Afghanistan they note the exclusion of more localised considerations; an exclusion that they argue has significantly contributed to difficulties in the statebuilding project.[23] Although this critique identifies a problem with the limited scope of current policy, it has also been noted that much of the widespread deficiencies, particularly in regards to statebuilding, are due to the 'state of knowledge and practice regarding the establishment and/or reconstitution of effective governance in post-conflict and war-torn societies is still in its infancy'. As such, '[statebuilding] templates, particularly when they

---

21 Bilgin quoting Bhabha. P. Bilgin, 'Thinking Past "Western" IR?' *Third World Quarterly* 29.1 (2008), pp. 5–23: p. 6.

22 See for example, M. Duffield, *Development, Security and Unending War: Governing the World of Peoples* (Cambridge: Polity, 2007); United Nations Economic Commission for Africa, 'Relevance of African Traditional Institutions of Governance', UNECA Report (2007); United Nations Economic Commission for Africa, 'ADF IV Traditional Governance Focus Group Issues Paper', Africa Development Forum, Addis Ababa, 11–15 October 2004; G. Lutz and W. Linder, 'Traditional Structures in Local Governance for Local Development', World Bank Institute Desk Study (Berne: University of Berne, 2004).

23 C. Cramer and J. Goodhand, 'Try Again, Fail Again, Fail Better? War, the State, and the "Post-Conflict" Challenge in Afghanistan', *Development and Change* 33.5 (2002), pp. 885–909.

reflect particular ideological biases, risk oversimplification and conflation and tend to discount the impact of the situational and historical factors'.[24] Governance reform in relatively stable states is an established practice that is promoted for continuing stability and economic growth and has shown a degree of success for the international community. Statebuilding, on the other hand, has a failing record. As Ottaway notes, this is largely due to overambitious policy, creating a situation in which an acceptable result becomes unattainable as the necessary resources are unavailable.[25] In responses to state failure, collapse, weakness or fragility, as well as poor or weak governance, current international policy is often plagued by tunnel vision in regards to the best approach to the situation.[26] There is an ardent focus on what is perceived to be necessary as guided by the conception of success and how to achieve or control this, thereby overlooking, disregarding or bypassing individual needs or desires. Overambitious, unattainable and sometimes damaging policies are implemented, pushed and maintained. Short time frames, external agendas, lack of local ownership and failure to legitimise the process and the state contribute to these failures. As such, within policy there is a need to reconsider not only global and regional political and security contexts, as Cramer and Goodhand as well as Ottaway and Mair argue, but also to intricately involve the complexities and domestic capabilities of individual cases when addressing statebuilding projects.[27] The current predominant guidance for creating governments in the ideal or the familiar conception of the modern state falls short of establishing an international environment conducive to accepting and integrating the distinctiveness of individual states and societies within practice; conditions that are necessary for legitimacy and ownership. This is a failure of policy, but that is secondary to failures stemming from the inflexibility of the liberal normative framework of statehood. Where some actors are viewed as acceptable and empowered in these projects, others are excluded in what can be described as a means of governance. With statebuilding practices bounded by comfort in the known and the familiar state reflecting normative ideals and practices, uncertainty in going beyond that can inhibit a more specialised approach to statebuilding or reform projects in contentious or turbulent territories; an approach that considers

---

24 D. Brinkerhoff, 'Rebuilding Governance in Failed States and Post-Conflict Societies: Core Concepts and Cross-Cutting Themes', *Public Administration and Development* 25.1 (2005), pp. 3–14: pp. 3, 13.

25 M. Ottaway, 'Promoting Democracy After Conflict: The Difficult Choices', *International Studies Perspectives* 4.3 (2003), pp. 314–22.

26 Coyne refers to this as the 'nirvana fallacy', claiming that the assumption that reconstruction efforts will always produce a positive outcome is a failure of current policy. C. Coyne, 'Reconstructing Weak and Failed States: Foreign Intervention and the Nirvana Fallacy', *Foreign Policy Analysis* 2.4 (2006), pp. 343–60.

27 M. Ottaway and S. Mair, 'States at Risk and Failed States: Putting Security First', Policy Outlook for the Carnegie Endowment for International Peace and the German Institute for International and Security Affairs Democracy and Rule of Law Project (September 2004).

not only regional factors, but also domestic circumstances, characteristics, structures societies, cultures and traditions.

Therefore, one of the key criticisms to be made to the current conception of acceptable statehood is its rigidity. But within that and in relation to policy there is also a lack of trust in actors, structures or practices that cannot be found in or that contravene what is perceived to be right for a state. However, these perceptions are based on what is known in the world that is imposing the norms. As such, those supposed backwards, unpredictable, uncontrollable or even powerless factors are often seen as posing a threat to the expected stability of what is perceived to be successful. Somaliland, though, has shown that the inclusion of one of these factors in a central government is not a weakness but rather a strength, and that autonomous compliance with normative values can occur in a government structure that is inclusive of a 'backwards' institution. The demonstration of trust in and of willingness to engage with international norms, however, has not been reciprocated by the international community. Even though the stability of Somaliland is broadly recognised, the value to be found in Somaliland's hybrid system has yet to be widely acknowledged. Instead, the clan's place within the government is often discussed in historical context or is avoided because of fears of romanticising or glorifying its role. This discounts political actors and processes within the statebuilding process, leading to an oversimplification or a misrepresentation of what has taken place. At this point, the quest for Somaliland's international engagement has gone beyond instrumentality and has moved into questions of trust and partnership. Until the international community is willing to look outside the narrow vision of what is acceptable, though, formal engagement is unlikely as there will be hesitancy to form a partnership with the uncertainty and the unknown that Somaliland's government presents. Somaliland's success, however, shows that the traditional is not something to instinctively reject, and more importantly it opens the possibility for an element of trust in local capabilities and capacities that does not exist within the current dominant framework.

Approaches to creating states would benefit from a less restricted approach that facilitates the ownership and legitimacy required for success, as well as allowing for a less rigid process rather than blueprinted project. Othieno argues as much, stating that donors need to address the needs and desires of society rather than becoming involved in a situation or crisis with the narrow focus of the 'traditional response to crisis'.[28] Whereas the international community should recognise that alternatives to the current model of acceptable statehood would increase stability in areas, such as many states in Africa where the Western model has not shown much success, the international community has yet to establish an environment in which alternative conceptions of successful statehood could be attained. Instead, the current perception of success continues to dominate policy, thereby sustaining a narrow conception of how a successful state can look

---

28 T. Othieno, 'A New Donor Approach to Fragile Societies: The Case of Somaliland', ODI Opinion 103 (London: ODI, July 2008).

and function. This narrowness leads to a lack of flexibility, a detriment not only to the resulting state, but also to the process as there is less room to negotiate, and indeed re-negotiate, the state throughout the process. There is reluctance on the part of international organisations and donors to relinquish control of internationally funded projects or to invest in what is perceived to be a risky or unknown situation; control of the process is a form of tutelage in the scheme of liberal intervention. But stepping outside these confines by incorporating regional or domestic factors and concerns into statebuilding is necessary if such projects are to be effective. This is not to suggest that the international community adopt a hands-off approach, as international security concerns and agendas ensure that this is unlikely and impractical. However, a reconsidered approach must not be dictated by a blueprint, a template or an idealised and unattainable model, but rather should reflect the individual desires, needs and demands of the state or territory in question. It must also be flexible so as to facilitate evolution and growth that takes place throughout the process. As evidenced by failed statebuilding projects, the supposedly modern state is not the curative it is expected to be and can instead prove to be dysfunctional or destructive. Ghani and Lockhart, as well as Brinkerhoff, are correct in arguing that there needs to be a re-examination of a statebuilding policy and that reconsideration should include local and regional considerations in addition to international desires and demands. They are also correct in identifying that there is no state without inclusion of the public or society and all that goes with it. Externally imposed statebuilding or reform projects in a contentious or post-conflict territory will always be prone to failure as long as they do not engage with or account for the local population, the local history and specific local circumstances.

However, these reconsiderations must go beyond the frequently espoused technocratic components of policy. In being more inclusive of those factors outside the scope of the acceptable framework, in reflecting society and in taking into account the specific context and history of the territory, statebuilding policies can begin to increase domestic investment in the project and therefore increase the chances of 'success'. Interventionist policies must move beyond the template and the established steps and restrictions in order to be conducive to policies that allow for a more open posture. They must be aware of their own power effects and try to minimise them in order to overcome the power-blind approach espoused by those such as Ghani and Lockhart. They must work to support an inclusive process and avoid rewarding violence, and like the elders in Somaliland, interveners must also work on establishing a consensual means to curb unrestricted power. Finally, international policies must be grounded in trust rather than looking for specific outcomes. Although these desires and demands admittedly are utopian in nature, they indicate a way in which international actors should consider their actions and policies. Perhaps the emphasis, therefore, should be less on statebuilding and more on state-formation, with the process being assisted by the international community but the state being created from within. Broadening the conception of what is acceptable for the state and how to obtain this will allow for an acceptance of the indigenous, local or traditional as an important component of fostering – not imposing – success. Statebuilding is a socio-political process, not a technocratic project, and it must be treated as such.

The Road Less Travelled

In Somaliland, governance came before formal institutions, reversing the established pattern of the technocratic state. The unrecognised state allows for, and in many ways demands, the development of ideas of governance prior to their attachment to institutions of government. This creates a space whereby an idea of state emerges; a model of what could be for the territory and a foundation for the creation of the state. This idea will ultimately have two audiences; an internal and an external. The internal audience needs to be convinced of the project for a new state as acceptance of the idea and the resulting state move to establish internal legitimacy. However, to move from unrecognised to recognised the state needs external legitimacy and this will shape how it presents itself to the outside world. The need for external recognition will create pressures to conform to certain international norms, but because this is done after governance has been established the state avoids some of the dangers of the Potemkin Village statehood. The structures of the state can better withstand challenges because it has internal legitimacy that brings with it support. The desire to be recognised will also create a cohesion that should counter against the evolution, or even potential fracturing, of the idea. Neither the idea of the state nor the technocratic state can exist in isolation: a relationship must exist between internal imaginings and external expectations. Closing the gap of expectations of legitimacy is a necessity not only for stability within unrecognised states, but also within statebuilding.

In discussions on statebuilding, focus is almost exclusively on how the demands of external legitimacy are met. But a state is not a state based purely on the legal recognition of territorial boundaries or on how well it complies with an empirical checklist. In unrecognised states there are remarkable cases of modern day state formation that re-politicise state making and allow for a recognition of 'notions of ... social contract-based state-society relations' that are most commonly linked with the evolution of modern Western states.[29] Yet unrecognised states are also faced with unprecedented external empirical demands. There must be a recognition that balancing these demands is particularly prevalent not only in entities seeking to become states, but also in those undergoing the statebuilding process.

When a researcher first arrives in Somaliland it is likely that they will not know what to expect. They will probably not expect the openness of political debate that is common not only in the government and civil society but also on

---

29 B. Bliesemann de Guevara, (2012) 'Statebuilding and State Formation', in B. Bliesemann de Guevara (ed.) *Statebuilding and State-Formation: The political sociology of intervention.* (London: Routledge, 2012), pp. 1–20: p. 3.

the streets. They may not expect the stability encountered. Knowing Somaliland's quest for recognition, they may expect to find a 'storefront' state – a state putting up the pretences of acceptable statehood as a component of a broader strategy of recognition. However, that is not what they will find. As a non-Somali in Somaliland, and certainly as a researcher, it is common to be frequently asked to comment on how Somaliland 'is doing'. A researcher attempting to maintain impartiality will refrain from a definitive assessment or comment. As a researcher in Somaliland during the self-extension crisis, I was asked this frequently. Every time, though, I could not help thinking that what I would say is how what was taking place was not the end of the road but merely a speed bump; that Somaliland is undergoing a self-led statebuilding process, and it is a remarkable thing to watch. And that is the best way to summarise overall what is taking place in Somaliland – it is not a perfect process but it is a process that continues even when obstacles are encountered. It is a form of statebuilding that one does not encounter every day.

The statebuilding process in Somaliland has not been perfect or problem free, but it is a process and it is one that belongs to the Somaliland actors. Power was not granted from the outside, but rather comes from within. For Somaliland, the internally driven statebuilding process has been successful and has created relative stability for the territory and its population. As the state grows, important decisions will have to be made concerning the future composition and function of the government, and this must be achieved without losing what works for the territory. For the international community, Somaliland has proven that a beneficial compromise can be reached between the known and the unknown: one does not have to be marginalised or excluded for the sake of the other. It has also proven the benefit of balancing the needs of those within with the expectations of those outside. Somaliland can be a model for statebuilding, but it cannot and should not be new blueprint or template. The created state is an indication of the realities of what is possible in statebuilding but is also both an anathema to and a reflection of the path to the frequently espoused yet unattainable ideal. It serves as an example that going off plan can work. Somaliland did not follow the prescribed path to success, but instead took an alternative but parallel route. As Mohammed Gees reflects, Somaliland could be a model, but it needs to keep moving forward. And only Somalilanders can do that.[30]

---

30   Mohammed Hassan Ibrahim 'Gani', Lead Researcher for APD. Interview with author (Hargeisa, August 2006).

Bibliography

Abdulkadir, F., 2004. Can Clan Representation Contribute to Rebuilding 21st Century Somalia? In: H. Adam, R. Ford and E. Adan Ismail (eds), *War Destroys, Peace Nurtures: Somali Reconciliation and Development*. Lawrenceville, NJ: The Red Sea Press, pp. 391–6.

Abokor, A., Kibble, S., Yusuf, H. and Barrett, G., 2006. Further Steps to Democracy: The Somaliland Parliamentary Elections, September 2005. London, Progressio Report.

Abrahamsen, R., 2001. Development Policy and the Democratic Peace in Sub-Saharan Africa. *Journal of Conflict, Security and Development*, 1(3), pp. 79–103.

Adam, H., 1995. Somalia: A Terrible Beauty Being Born? In: I.W. Zartman (ed.), *Collapsed States: The Disintegration and Restoration of Legitimate Authority*. London: Lynne Rienner, pp. 69–90.

Adam, H. and Ford, R., (eds), 1997. *Mending the Rips in the Sky: Options for Somali Communities in the 21st Century*. Lawrenceville, NJ: The Red Sea Press.

Adam, H., Ford, R. and Adan Ismail, E., (eds), 2004. *War Destroys, Peace Nurtures: Somali Reconciliation and Development*. Lawrenceville, NJ: The Red Sea Press.

Africa Watch., 1990. A Government at War With Its Own People. New York, Africa Watch Report.

Ahmed, I., 2000. Remittances and their Economic Impact in the Post-War Somaliland. *Disasters*, 24(4), pp. 380–89.

Ahmed, I., and Green, R., 1999. The Heritage of War and State Collapse in Somalia and Somaliland: Local-Level Effects, External Interventions and Reconstructions. *Third World Quarterly*, 20(1), pp. 113–27.

Aideed, A., 2006. Is Somaliland at the End of the Road? 13 May, *The Republican*. Hargeisa.

——, 2006. Why the Debate on Extension of the Life of the Guurti is a Blessing? 20 May, *The Republican*. Hargeisa.

Anderson, B., 1991. *Imagined Communities*. Revised edition. London: Verso Books.

Ayoob, M., 2001. State Making, State Breaking and State Failure. In: C. Crocker, F.O. Hampson and P. Aal (eds), *Turbulent Peace: The Challenges of Managing International Conflict*. Washington DC: United States Institute for Peace, pp. 127–42.

Barkey, K., 1994. *Bandits and Bureaucrats: The Ottoman Route to State Centralization*. Ithaca: Cornell University Press.

Barnett, M., 2006. Building a Republican Peace: Stabilizing States after War. *International Security*, 30(4), pp. 87–112.

Bates, R., 2001. *Prosperity and Violence: The Political Economy of Development*. New York: W.W. Norton.

Battera, F., 2004. State and Democracy Building in Sub-Saharan Africa: The Case of Somaliland: A Comparative Perspective. *Global Jurist Frontiers*, 4(1), pp. 1–21.

Bayart, J.-F., 1993. *The State in Africa: Politics of the Belly*. London: Longman.

——, 2000. Africa in the World: A History of Extraversion. *African Affairs*, 99(395), pp. 217–67.

Bayart, J.-F., Hibou, B. and Ellis, S., 1999. *The Criminalisation of the State in Africa*. Oxford: James Currey.

Beck, U., Giddens, A. and Lash, S., 1994. *Reflexive Modernization: Politics, Tradition, and Aesthetics in the Modern Social Order*. Palo Alto, CA: Stanford University Press.

Bendana, A., 2003. What Kind of Peace is Being Built? Critical Assessments from the South. Ottawa, International Development Research Centre Discussion Paper.

Berger, M., 2007. States of Nature and the Nature of States: The Fate of Nations, the Collapse of States and the Future of the World. *Third World Quarterly*, 28(6), pp. 1203–14.

Bilgin, P., 2008. Thinking Past 'Western' IR? *Third World Quarterly*, 29(1), pp. 5–23.

Bliesemann de Guevara, B. (ed.), 2012. *Statebuilding and State-Formation: The Political Sociolgy of Intervention*. London: Routledge

Bliesemann de Guevara, B., 2012. Statebuilding and State Formation. In: B. Bliesemann de Guevara (ed.), *Statebuilding and State-Formation: The Political Sociolgy of Intervention*. London: Routledge, pp. 1–20.

Bøås, M. and Jennings, K., 2005. Insecurity and Development: The Rhetoric of the 'Failed State'. *The European Journal of Development Research*, 17(3), pp. 385–95.

Bolton, J., 1994. Wrong Turn in Somalia. *Foreign Affairs*, 73(1), pp. 109–23.

Boutros-Ghali, B., 1992. *An Agenda for Peace: Preventive Diplomacy, Peacemaking and Peacekeeping*. New York: United Nations.

Bradbury, M., 1993. Peace-enforcement, Peace-making and Peace-building: Options for Resolving the Somali Conflict. London, Oxfam Exploratory Report.

——, 1993. The Case of the Yellow Settee: Experiences of Doing Development in Post-War Somaliland. London, ActionAid Report.

——, 1993. The Somali Conflict: Prospects for Peace. London, Oxfam Research Paper No 9.

——, 1997. Somaliland Country Report. London, Catholic Institute for International Relations Report.

——, 2002. An Undiscovered Option: A Way Forward for Somalia? Nairobi/Geneva, WSP International/Interpeace Report.
——, 2008. *Becoming Somaliland*. Oxford: Oxford University Press.
Bradbury, M. and Hansen, S., 2007. Somaliland: A New Democracy in the Horn of Africa? *Review of African Political Economy*, 34(113), pp. 461–76.
Bradbury, M., Abokor, A. and Yusuf, H., 2003. Somaliland: Choosing Politics Over Violence. *Review of African Political Economy*, 30(97), pp. 455–78.
Brinkerhoff, D., 2005. Rebuilding Governance in Failed States and Post-Conflict Societies: Core Concepts and Cross-Cutting Themes. *Public Administration and Development*, 25(1), pp. 3–14.
Brons, M., 2001. *Society, Security, Sovereignty and the State in Somalia*. Utrecht: International Books.
Brownlie, I., 1998. *Principles of Public International Law*, 5th edn. Oxford: Clarendon Press.
Bryden, M., 2003. The Banana Test: Is Somaliland ready for recognition? *Annales d'Éthiopie*, Volume 19, pp. 341–64.
——, 2004. Somalia and Somaliland: Envisioning a Dialogue on the Question of Somali Unity. *African Security Review*, 13(2), pp. 23–33.
——, 2004. State-Within-a-Failed-State: Somaliland and the Challenge of International Recognition. In: P. Kingston and I. Spears (eds), *States Within States: Incipient Political Entities in the Post-Cold War Era*. Basingstoke: Palgrave Macmillan, pp. 167–188.
Bush, G.H.W., 1990. *Address Before a Joint Session of the Congress on the Persian Gulf Crisis and the Federal Budget Deficit, 11 September*. Washington DC.
——, 1991. *Address Before a Joint Session of Congress on the Cessation of the Persian Gulf Conflict, 6 March*. Washington DC.
Buzan, B., 1993. *People, States and Fear: An Agenda for International Security Studies in the Post-Cold War Era*, 2nd edn. Hemel Hempstead: Harvester.
Call, C., 2008. Ending Wars, Building States. In: C. Call and V. Wyeth (eds), *Building States to Build Peace*. London: Lynne Rienner, pp. 1–22.
Call, C. and V. Wyeth (eds), 2008. *Building States to Build Peace*. London: Lynne Rienner.
Carment, D., 2003. Assessing State Failure: Implications for Theory and Policy. *Third World Quarterly*, 24(3), pp. 407–27.
Carothers, T., 2004. *Critical Mission: Essays on Democracy Promotion*. Washington DC: Carnegie Endowment for International Peace.
Carrel, P., 1960. *Ministry of Defence and External Affairs Internal Memo Hargeisa to London (3 March)*, London: Memo SD/EA/18/8/6.
Caspersen, N., 2006. *Unrecognised States: Shadow Economies, Democratisation and Hopes for Independence*. Lancaster, Lancaster University Seminar Series.
——, 2008. *Self-Determination vs. Democracy? Democratization in De Facto States*. San Francisco, 49th Annual International Studies Association Convention.
——, 2012. *Unreccognised States: The Struggle for Sovereignty in the Modern International System*. Cambridge: Polity.

Caspersen, N. and Stansfield, G. (eds), 2011. *Unrecognised States in the International System*. London: Routledge.
Catholic Institute for International Relations., 2005. Somaliland Elections to the House of Representatives, 29th September 2005. London, International Election Observation Team Interim Report.
Chabal, P. and Daloz, J.-P., 1999. *Africa Works: Disorder as Political Instrument*. Oxford: James Currey.
Chandler, D., 2005. Editor's Introduction: Peace Without Politics. *International Peacekeeping*, 12(3), pp. 307–21.
——, 2006. *Empire in Denial: The Politics of Statebuilding*. London: Pluto Press.
——, 2007. The Statebuilding Dilemma: Good governance or democratic government? In A. Hehir and N. Robinson (eds), *Statebuilding: Theory and Practice*. London: Routledge.
——, 2010. *International Statebuilding: The Rise of Post-Liberal Governance*. London: Routledge.
Chesterman, S., Ignatieff, M. and Thakur, R. 2005., Introduction: Making States Work. In: S. Chesterman, M. Ignatieff and R. Thakur (eds), *Making States Work: State Failure and the Crisis of Governance*. Washington DC: Brookings Institute Press, pp. 1–10.
Chopra, J., 2003. Building State Failure in East Timor. In: J. Milliken (ed.), *State Failure, Collapse and Reconstruction*. Oxford: Blackwell, pp. 223–44.
Clapham, C., 1996. *Africa and the International System: The Politics of State Survival*. Cambridge: Cambridge University Press.
——, 2003. The Challenge to the State in a Globalized World. In: J. Milliken (ed.), *State Failure, Collapse and Reconstruction*. Oxford: Blackwell, pp. 25–44.
——, 2004. The Global-Local Politics of State Decay. In: R. Rotberg (ed.), *When States Fail: Causes and Consequences*. Princeton, NJ: Princeton University Press, pp. 77–93.
Cliffe, L., 2005. Imperialism and African Social Formations. *Review of African Political Economy*, 32(103), pp. 5–7.
Cliffe, L. and Luckham, R., 1999. Complex Political Emergencies and the State: Failure and the Fate of the State. *Third World Quarterly*, 20(1), pp. 27–50.
Closson, S., 2011. What Do Unrecognised States Tell Us About Sovereignty? In: N. Caspersen and G. Stansfield (eds), *Unrecognised States in the International System*. London: Routledge, pp. 58–70.
Collier, P. 2000., Economic Causes of Civil Conflict and their Implications for Policy. Washington DC, World Bank Working Paper 28134.
Collier, P. and Hoeffler, A., 2004. Greed and Grievance in Civil War. Oxford, Oxford Economic Papers No. 56.
Collier, P., Hoeffler, A. and Rohner, D., 2006. Beyond Greed and Grievance: Feasibility and Civil War. Oxford, The Centre for the Study of African Economies Working Paper Series Paper 254.
Compagnon, D., 1991. The Somali Opposition Fronts: Some Comments and Questions. *Horn of Africa*, 13(1–2), pp. 29–54.

——, 1998. Somali Armed Movements: The Interplay of Political Entrepreneurship and Clan-Based Factions. In: C. Clapham (ed.), *African Guerrillas*. Oxford: James Currey, pp. 73–90.

Cooke, B., 2003. A New Continuity with Colonial Administration: Participation in Development Management. *Third World Quarterly*, 24(1), pp. 47–61.

Cotran, E., 1963. Legal Problems Arising out of the Formation of the Somali Republic. *The International and Comparative Law Quarterly*, 12(3), pp. 1010–26.

Cowen, M. and Shenton, R.W., 1996. *Doctrines of Development*. London: Routledge.

Cox, M., 2000. Wilsonian Resurgent? The Clinton Administration and the Promotion of Demoracy. In: M. Cox, G. Ikenberry and T. Inoguchi (eds), *American Democracy Promotion: Impulses, Strategies and Impacts*. Oxford: Oxford University Press.

Coyne, C., 2006. Reconstructing Weak and Failed States: Foreign Intervention and the Nirvana Fallacy. *Foreign Policy Analysis*, 2(4), pp. 343–60.

Cramer, C. and Goodhand, J., 2002. Try Again, Fail Again, Fail Better? War, the State, and the 'Post-Conflict' Challenge in Afghanistan. *Development and Change*, 33(5), pp. 885–909.

Davies, J., 1996. *Reunification of the Somali People*. Bochum, Germany: Institut für Entwicklungsforschung und Entwicklungspolitik of the Ruhr Universität.

Davis, G., 2004. A History of the Social Development Network in the World Bank, 1973–2002. Washington DC, World Bank Social Development Papers Number 56.

Debiel, T. 2005. Dealing with Fragile States: Entry Points and Approaches for Development Cooperation. University of Bonn, Centre for Development Research Discussion Paper No. 101.

DfID, 2001. Making Government Work for Poor People: Building State Capability. London, DfID Report.

——, 2005. Country Engagement Plan for Somalia. London, DfID Report.

——, 2005. Why We Need to Work More Effectively in Fragile States. London, DfID Report.

Diamond, L., 2005. *Squandered Victory: The American Occupation and the Bungled Effort to Bring Democracy to Iraq*. New York: Times Books.

——, 2006. What Went Wrong and Right in Iraq. In: F. Fukuyama (ed.), *Nation-Building: Beyond Afghanistan and Iraq*. Baltimore: The Johns Hopkins University Press, 173–95.

van Dijk, R. and van Rouveroy van Nieuwaal, A., 1999. The Domestication of Chieftaincy in Africa: From the Imposed to the Imagined. In: R. van Dijk and A. van Rouveroy van Nieuwaal (eds), *African Chieftancy in a New Socio-Political Landscape*. Hamburg: LIT-Verlag, pp. 1–20.

Dobbins, J., et al., 2003. *America's Role in Nation-Building from Germany to Iraq*. Santa Monica, CA: RAND Corporation.

——, 2005. *The UN's Role in Nation Building: From the Congo to Iraq*. Santa Monica, CA: RAND Corporation.

Donais, T., 2009. Empowerment or Imposition? Dilemmas of local ownership in post-conflict peacebuilding processes. *Peace and Change*, 34(1), pp. 3–26.

Dool, A., 2001. Good Governance: Self-Administering Regions within a Democratic Union. *Somalia*, Issue 4, pp. 5–36.

Doornbos, M., 2002. Somalia: Alternative Scenarios for Political Reconstruction. *African Affairs*, 101(402), pp. 93–107.

Doty, R., 1996. Sovereignty and the Nation: Constructing the Boundaries of National Identity. In: T. Biersteker and C. Weber (eds), *State Sovereignty as Social Construct*. Cambridge: Cambridge University Press, pp. 121–47.

Dowden, R., 2008. An Alien Inheritance. *Prospect*, September, pp. 42–5.

Drysdale, J., 1994. *Whatever Happened to Somalia: A Tale of Tragic Blunders*. London: HAAN Associates.

——, 2000. *Stoics Without Pillows: A Way Forward for the Somalilands*. London: HAAN Associates.

Duffield, M., 2001. *Global Governance and the New Wars*. London: Zed.

——, 2007. *Development, Security and Unending War*. Cambridge: Polity.

Duffield, M. and Prendergast, J., 1994. *Without Troops and Tanks: Humanitarian Intervention in Eritrea and Ethiopia*. Trenton, NJ: Red Sea Press/Africa World Press, Inc.

von Einsiedel, S. 2005. Policy Responses to State Failure. In: S. Chesterman, M. Ignatieff and R. Thakur (eds), *Making States Work: State Failure and the Crisis of Governance*. New York: United Nations University Press, pp. 13–35.

Englebert, P., 2002. Born-again Buganda or the Limits of Traditional Resurgence in Africa. *Journal of Modern African Studies*, 40(3), pp. 345–68.

Evans, K., 1997. A Somali Journey. *The Courier*, March-April, Issue 162, pp. 55–7.

Farah, A. and Lewis, I., 1993. Somalia: The Roots of Reconciliation: Peace Making Endeavours of Contemporary Lineage Leaders in 'Somaliland'. London, ActionAid Report.

Field of Dreams. 1989. [Film] Directed by P.A. Robinson. United States: Gordon Company.

Finnemore, M., 1996. *National Interests in International Society*. London: Cornell University Press.

Finnemore, M. and Sikkink, K., 1998. International Norm Dynamics and Political Change. *International Organization*, 52(4), pp. 887–917.

Freedom House, 2007. Somaliland Country Report. available at http://www.freedomhouse.org.

Fukuyama, F., 2004. *State-Building: Governance and World Order in the 21st Century*. Ithaca: Cornell University Press.

——, 2006. *Nation-Building: Beyond Afghanistan and Iraq*. Baltimore, MD: The Johns Hopkins University Press.

——, 2011. *The Origins of Political Order: From Prehuman Times to the French Revolution*. London: Profile Books.

Fund for Peace, 2013. 2013 Failed States Index Scores. available at http://fundforpeace.org/.

Gabose, D., 2006. Extension: An End to Democratization. 20 May, *The Republican*. Hargeisa.
Garrigue, N., 2004. Commented Review of the Desk Study Titled: 'Traditional Structures in Local Governance for Local Development'. Geneva, Report for the World Bank Institute's Community Empowerment and Social Inclusion Learning Program.
Gees, M., 2006. Is Somaliland a Model? Unpublised manuscript.
Ghani, A. and Lockhart, C., 2005. Closing the Sovereignty Gap: An Approach to State-Building. London, Overseas Development Institute Report.
——, 2008. *Fixing Failed states: A Framework for Rebuilding a Fractured World*. Oxford: Oxford University Press.
Ghani, A., Lockhart, C. and Carnahan, M., 2006. An Agenda for State-Building in the Twenty-First Century. *The Fletcher Forum of World Affairs*, 30(1), pp. 101–23.
Gilkes, P., 1994. Descent into Chaos: Somalia, January 1991–December 1992. In: C. Gurden (ed.), *The Horn of Africa*. London: UCL Press, pp. 47–60.
Giustozzi, A. and Ullah, N., 2006. 'Tribes' and Warlords in Southern Afghanistan, 1980–2005. London, LSE Crisis States Research Centre Working Paper No. 7.
Goldstone, J. and Ulfelder, J., 2004–2005. How to Construct Stable Democracies. *The Washington Quarterly*, 28(1), pp. 9–20.
Gourevitch, A., 2004. The Unfailing of the State. *Journal of International Affairs*, 58(1), pp. 255–60.
Gros, J., 1996. Towards a Taxonomy of Failed States in the New World Order: decaying Somalia, Liberia, Rwanda and Haiti. *Third World Quarterly*, 17(3), pp. 448–61.
Hall, D., 1960. Inward Telegram to the Secretary of State for the Colonies from Somaliland Protectorate (16–17 January). London, Foreign Office Telegram No. 34.
——, 1960. Inward Telegram to the Secretary of State for the Colonies from Somaliland Protectorate (25 January). London, Foreign Office Telegram No. 50.
Hansen, S., 2003. Warlords and Peace Strategies: The Case of Somalia. *The Journal of Conflict Studies*, 23(2), pp. 57–78.
Harrison, G., 2004. *The World Bank and Africa: The Construction of Governance States*. London: Routledge.
——, 2005. The World Bank, Governance and Theories of Political Action in Africa. *British Journal of Politics and International Relations*, 7(2), pp. 240–60.
Hashi, A., 2005. The Implication of Traditional Leadership, 'Guurti' and Other Non-State Actors in Local Governance in Somaliland. New York, Community Empowerment and Social Inclusion Program of the World Bank Institute.
Herbst, J., 1990. The Creation and Maintenance of National Boundaries in Africa. *International Organization*, 43, pp. 673–92.
——, 1996–1997. Responding to State Failure in Africa. *International Security*, 21(3), pp. 120–44.

——, 2000. *States and Power in Africa: Comparative Lessons in Authority and Control.* Princeton, NJ: Princeton University Press.

Herbst, J., 2004. In Africa, What Does It Take to Be a Country? 2 January, *Washington Post*, sec. A, p. 21.

Hibou, B. (ed.), 2004. *Privatising the State.* London: Hurst and Co.

Hill, J., 2005. Beyond the Other? A postcolonial critique of the failed state thesis. *African Identities*, 3(2), pp. 139–54.

Hindess, B., 2007. The Past is Another Culture. *International Political Sociology*, 1(4), pp. 325–38.

von Hippel, K., 1996. Seminar on Decentralised Political Structures for Somalia 20–22 June 1996. Nairobi, EU European Commission Somalia Unit.

——, 1996. Second Seminar on Decentralised Political Structures for Somalia 16–18 November 1996. Nairobi, EU European Commission Somalia Unit.

Hirsti 'Morgan', M., 1987. The Somali Democratic Republic Ministry of Defence Report ('The Morgan Report') (23 January). Mogadishu, Somalia Government Report.

Höhne, M., 2006. Traditional Authorities in Northern Somalia: Transformation of Positions and Power. Halle, Max Planck Institute for Social Anthropology Working Paper 82.

——, 2013. Limits of Hybrid Political Orders: The case of Somaliland. *Journal of Eastern African Studies*, 7:2, pp. 199–217.

Hollekim, R., Hansen, S. and Sorensen, G., 2006. Somaliland: Electons for the Lower House of Parliament September 2005. Oslo, Norwegian Resource Bank for Democracy and Human Rights.

Holsti, K., 1996. *The State, War and the State of War.* New York: Cambridge University Press.

Horner, S., 1997. Somalia: Can the Jigsaw be Pieced Together? *The Courier*, Issue 162, pp. 46–53.

Huliaras, A., 2002. The Viability of Somaliland: Internal Constraints and Regional Geopolitics. *Journal of Contemporary African Studies*, 20(2), pp. 157–82.

Hurd, I., 1999. Legitimacy and Authority in International Politics. *International Organization*, 53(2), pp. 379–408.

International Commission on Intervention and State Sovereignty, 2001. *The Responsibility to Protect*, Ottawa: International Development Research Centre.

International Conference of American States. 1933. *Convention on Rights and Duties of States.* Montevideo, Uruguay, Seventh International Conference of American States.

International Crisis Group, 2006. Somaliland: Time for African Union Leadership. Nairobi/Brussels, ICG Africa Report No. 110.

——, 2002. Salvaging Somalia's Chance for Peace. Nairobi/Brussels, ICG Africa Briefing No. 11.

——, 2003. Negotiating a Blueprint for Peace in Somalia. Nairobi/Brussels, ICG Africa Report No. 59.

——, 2003. Somaliland: Democratisation and its Discontents. Nairobi/Brussels, ICG Africa Report No. 66.
——, 2004. Biting the Somali Bullet. Nairobi/Brussels, ICG Africa Report No. 79.
——, 2004. Somalia: Continuation of War by Other Means? Nairobi/Brussels, ICG Africa Report No. 88.
International Republican Institute, 2006. Somaliland September 29, 2005 Parliamentary Election Assessment Report. Washington DC, IRI Report.
IRIN News, 2005. Somaliland Elections Peaceful Say Observers (3 October). Somalia News Report.
——, 2006. Controversy over extension of elders' term of office. Somalia News Report.
——, 2008. Somalia: TFG on Brink of Collapse. Somalia News Report.
Issa-Salwe, A., 1996. *The Collapse of the Somali State: The Impact of the Colonial Legacy*. London: HAAN Associates.
Jackson, R., 1987. Quasi-States, Dual Regimes, and Neoclassical Theory: International Jurisprudence and the Third World. *International Organization*, 41(4), pp. 519–49.
——, 1990. *Quasi-States: Sovereignty, International Relations and the Third World*. Cambridge: Cambridge University Press.
——, 1998. Surrogate Sovereignty? Great Power Responsibilities and 'Failed States'. Vancouver, University of British Columbia Insittute of International Relations Working Paper No. 25.
——, 2000. *Global Covenant: Human Conduct in a World of States*. Oxford: Oxford University Press.
Jama, F., 2006. The House of Representatives: Don't Just Talk the Talk; Walk the Walk to Save Somaliland. 26 August, *The Somaliland Times*, Hargeisa.
Jama, M., 2003. Somalia and Somaliland: Strategies for dialogue and consensus on governance and democratic transition. Oslo, UNDP Oslo Governance Centre Report.
Jessop, B., 1990. *State Theory: Putting the Capitalist State in its Place*. Oxford: Polity.
Johnson, R., 2003. *British Imperialism*. Basingstoke: Palgrave Macmillan.
Kahin, D., 2006. Degreeto Madaxweyne No. 117/052006: Soo jeedinta kordhinta muddada Golaha Guurtida (President's Request to the House of Elders, 2 May). Hargeisa, Somaliland Government Archives and Records.
——, 2006. Letter to Somaliland Guurti (24 April). Hargeisa, Somaliland Government Archives and Records.
Kahn, C., 2008. Conflict, Arms, and Militarization They Dynamics of Darfur's IDP Camps. Geneva, Small Arms Survey Report No. 15.
Kaplan, I., et al. (eds), 1969. Area Handbook for Somalia. Washington DC, Foreign Affairs Studies Series.
Kapteijins, L., 1994. Women and the Crisis of Communal Identity: The Cultural Constuction of Gender in Somali History. In: A. Samatar (ed.), *The Somali Challenge: From Catastrophe to Renewal*. London: Lynne Rienner, pp. 211–31.

King, C., 2001. The Benefits of Ethnic War: Understanding Eurasia's Unrecognized States. *World Politics*, 53(4), pp. 524–52.
——, 2001. Eurasia's Nonstate States. *East European Constitutional Review*, 10(4), pp. 524–52.
Kingston, P. and Spears, I. (eds), 2004. *States-Within-States: Incipient Political Entities in the Post-Cold War Era*. Basingstoke: Palgrave Macmillan.
Kölsto, P., 2006. The Sustainability and Future of Unrecognized Quasi-States. *Journal of Peace Research*, 43(6), pp. 723–40.
Laitin, D. and Samatar, S., 1987. *Somalia: Nation in Search of a State*. Boulder, CO: Westview Press.
Lamb, R., 2012. Political Governance and Strategy in Afghanistan. Washington DC, Center for Strategic and International Studies Report.
Leader, N., and Colenso, P., 2005. Aid Instruments in Fragile States. London, DfID Poverty Reduction in Difficult Environments Working Paper 5.
Levy, B. and Kpundeh, S. (eds), 2004. *Building State Capacity in Africa: New Approaches, Emerging Lessons*. Washington DC: World Bank Publications.
Lewis, I.M., 1957. The Somali Lineage System and the Total Genealogy: A General Introduction to Basic Principles of Somali Political Institutions. London/Hargeisa, Anthropological Research Report.
——, 1959. Clanship and Contract in Northern Somaliland. *Africa*, Volume 29, pp. 274–93.
——, 1961. *A Pastoral Democracy*. Oxford: Oxford University Press.
——, 1962. Historical Aspects of Genealogies in Northern Somali Social Structure. *Journal of African History*, 3(1), pp. 35–48.
——, 1963. Dualism in Somalian Notions of Power. *Journal of the Royal Anthropological Institute of Great Britain and Ireland*, 93(1), pp. 109–16.
——, 1965. *The Modern History of Somaliland: From Nation to State*. London: Weidenfeld and Nicholson.
——, 1991. The Recent Political History of Somalia. In: K. Barcik and S. Normark (eds), *Somalia: A Historical, Cultural and Political Analysis*. Uppsala: Life and Peace Institute, pp. 5–15.
——, 1993. *Understanding Somalia*. London: HAAN Associates.
——, 1994. *Blood and Bone: The Call of Kinship in Somali Society*. Lawrenceville, NJ: The Red Sea Press.
——, 2002. *A Modern History of the Somali*. Oxford: James Currey.
Lewis, I.M. and Farah, A., 1993. Somalia The Roots of Reconciliation: Peacemaking endeavours of contemporary lineage leaders and a survey of grassroots peace conferences in Somaliland. London, Action Aid Report.
Linder, W. and G. Lutz, 2004. Traditional Structures in Local Governance for Local Development. Berne, University of Berne, World Bank Institute Desk Study.
Lindley, A., 2005. Somalia Country Study. Oxford, Report on Informal Remittance Systems in African, Caribbean and Pacific Countries
Little, P., 2003. *Somalia: Economy Without a State*. Oxford: James Currey.

Lockhart, C., 2005. From Aid Effectiveness to Development Effectiveness: strategy and policy coherence in fragile states. London, ODI Senior Level Forum on Development Effectiveness in Fragile States Background Paper.

Logan, C., 2000. Overcoming the State-Society Disconnect in the Former Somalia: Putting Somali Political and Economic Resources at the Root of Reconstruction. Nairobi, USAID/REDSO Report.

Luce, W., 1960. Colonial Office Internal Memo Aden to London (23 January). London, Memo GH/8/21/2/53.

Luling, V., 1997. Come Back Somalia? Questioning a Collapsed State. *Third World Quarterly*, 18(2), pp. 287–302.

Lynch, D., 2004. *Engaging Eurasia's Separatist States*. Washington DC: US Institute of Peace Press.

Lyons, T. and Samatar, A., 1995. *Somalia: State Collapse, Multilateral Intervention, and Strategies for Political Reconstruction*. Washington DC: The Brookings Institution.

Maass, G. and Mepham, D., 2004. Promoting Effective States: A progressive policy response to failed and failing states.London, Institute for Public Policy ResearchReport.

MacGinty, R., 2008. Indigenous Peace-Making Versus the Liberal Peace. *Cooperation and Conflict*, 43(3), pp. 139–63.

——, 2010. Hybrid Peace: The Interaction Between Top-Down and Bottom-Up Peace. *Security Dialogue*, 41(4), pp. 391–412.

——, 2012. Routine Peace: Technocracy and peacebuilding. *Cooperation and Conflict*, 47(3), pp. 287–308.

MacGinty, R. and Richmond, O., 2013. 'The Local Turn in Peace Building: A Critical Agenda for Peace', *Third World Quarterly* 34(5), pp. 763–83.

McFaul, M., 2004–2005. Democracy Promotion as a World Value. *The Washington Quarterly*, 28(1), pp. 147–63.

Menkhaus, K., 1998. Somalia: Political Order in a Stateless Society. *Current History* 97(619), pp. 220–24.

——, 2005. Kenya-Somalia Border Conflict Analysis. Washington DC, USAID Conflict Prevention, Mitigation and Response Program for East and Southern Africa Report.

——, 2008. International Policies and Politics in the Humanitarian Crisis in Somalia. London, ODI Report for the Humanitarian Practice Network Issue 40.

Mennen, T., 2007. Legal Pluralism in Southern Sudan: Can the Rest of Africa Show the Way? *Africa Policy Journal*, Volume 3, pp. 49–73.

Migdal, J., 1994. Introduction. In: J. Migdal, A. Kohli and V. Shue (eds), *State Power and Social Forces: Domination and Transformation in the Third World*. Cambridge: Cambridge University Press, pp. 1–7.

Milliken, J. (ed.), 2003. *State Failure, Collapse and Reconstruction*. Oxford: Blackwell.

Moe, L.W., 2011. Hybrid and 'Everyday' Political Ordering: Constructing and Contesting Legitimacy. *Journal of Legal Pluralism and Unofficial Law*, 63, pp. 143–77.

——, 2013. Addressing Legitimacy Issues in Fragile Post-Conflict Situations to Advance Conflict Transformation and Peace-Building. Brisbane, University of Queensland and Berghof Foundation Somaliland Report.

Morton, A., 2005. The Age of Absolutism: Capitalism, the Modern State System and International Relations. *Review of International Studies*, 31(3), pp. 495–517.

——, 2005. The 'Failed State' of International Relations. *New Political Economy*, 10(3), pp. 371–79.

Morton, A. and Bilgin, P., 2002. Historicising Representations of 'Failed States': Beyond the Cold War Annexation of the Social Sciences? *Third World Quarterly*, 23(1), pp. 55–80.

Mukhtar, M., 1997. Somalia: Between Self-Determination and Chaos. In: H. Adam and R. Ford (eds), *Mending the Rips in the Sky: Options for Somali Communities in the 21st Century*. Lawrenceville, NJ: The Red Sea Press, pp. 49–64.

van Notten, M. 2006. *The Law of the Somalis: A Stable Foundation for Economic Development in the Horn of Africa*. S. MacCallum, ed. Trenton, NJ: The Red Sea Press.

Ntsebeza, L., 2004. Democratic Decentralisation and Traditional Authority: Dilemmas of land administration in rural South Africa. *The European Journal of Development Research*, 16(1), pp. 71–89.

Organisation for Economic Co-operation and Development, 2005. Principles for Good International Engagement in Fragile States. Paris, OECD Development Assistance Committee Fragile States Group Report.

Othieno, T., 2008. A New Donor Approach to Fragile Societies: The Case of Somaliland. London, Overseas Development Institute Opinion No. 103.

Ottaway, M., 2003. Promoting Democracy After Conflict: The Difficult Choices. *International Studies Perspectives*, 4(3), pp. 314–22.

——, 2003. Rebuilding State Institutions in Collapsed States. In: J. Milliken (ed.), *State Failure, Collase and Reconstruction*. Oxford: Blackwell, pp. 254–66.

Ottaway, M. and Mair, S., 2004. States at Risk and Failed States: Putting Security First. Washington DC, Policy Outlook for the Carnegie Endowment for International Peace and the German Institute for International and Security Affairs Democracy and Rule of Law Project.

Overseas Development Institute. 2005. Failed and Fragile States: How can the MDGs be achieved in difficult environments? London, Report of the ODI Spring 2005 Meeting.

Pankhurst, E., 1951. *Ex-Italian Somaliland*. London: Watts and Co.

Papagianni, K., 2008. Participation and State Legitimacy. In: C. Call and V. Wyeth (eds), *Building States to Build Peace*. London: Lynne Rienner, pp. 49–71.

Paris, R., 2004. *Building Peace After Civil Conflict*. Cambridge: Cambridge University Press.

Paris, R. and Sisk, T. (eds), 2008. *The Dilemmas of Statebuilding: Confronting the contradictions in postwar peace operations*. London: Routledge.
Pegg, S., 1998. *International Society and the De Facto State*. Aldershot: Ashgate.
——, 2004. From De Facto States to States-Within-States: Progress, Problems and Prospects. In: P. Kingston and I. Spears (eds), *States-Within-States: Incipient Political Entities in the Post-Cold War Era*. Basingstoke: Palgrave Macmillan, pp. 35–46.
Prime Minister's Strategy Unit, 2005. Countries at Risk of Instability: Future Risks of Instability. London, PMSU Report.
——, 2005. Countries at Risk of Instability: Practical Risk Assessment, Early Warning and Knowledge Management. London, PMSU Report.
——, 2005. Countries at Risk of Instability: Risk Factors and Dynamics of Instability. London, PMSU Report.
——, 2005. International Crisis Response and Peace Support Capabilities. London, PMSU Report.
——, 2005. Risk Assessment and Strategic Analysis Process Manual. London, PMSU Report.
Prunier, G., 1991. A Candid View of the Somali Naitonal Movement. *Horn of Africa*, 14(1–2), pp. 107–120.
——, 1994. Somaliland: birth of a new country? In: C. Gurden (ed.), *The Horn of Africa*. London: UCL Press, pp. 61–75.
——, 1997. Surviving Without the UN: Somaliland, a Forgotten Country. *Le Monde Diplomatique*. Paris.
——, 1998. Somaliland Goes it Alone. *Current History*, 97(619), pp. 225–8.
——, 2000. Somalia Re-Invents Itself. *Le Monde Diplomatique*. Paris.
Reece, G., 1952. Despatch to the Right Honourable Oliver Lyttleton, Secretary of State for the Colonies (9 March). London, Foreign Office Despatch No. 161/52.
Reno, W., 1999. *Warlord Politics and African States*. Boulder: Lynne Rienner.
——, 2001. External Relations of Weak States and Stateless Regions in Africa. In: M. Khadiagala and T. Lyons (eds), *African Foreign Policies: Power and Process*. London: Lynne Rienner, pp. 185–205.
——, 2003. Somalia and Survival in the Shadow of the Global Economy. Oxford, Queen Elizabeth House Working Paper No. 100.
Richards, R., 2012. The Road Less Traveled: Self-led Statebuilding and Non-Intervention in Somaliland. In: B. Bliesemann de Guevara (ed.), *Statebuilding and State Formation: The Political Sociology of Intervention*. London: Routledge, pp. 149–164.
Richards, R. and Smith, R.G., 2013. *Imagining the State: Legitimising Kurdistan and Somaliland*. Tartu, EWIS Workshops.
Roberts, D., 2007. Hybrid Polities and Indigenous Pluralities: Advanced Lessons in Statebuilding from Cambodia. *Journal of Intervention and Statebuilding* 1(3), pp. 379–402.
Robinson, W., 2004. *A Theory of Global Capitalism: Production, Class and State in a Transnational World*. Baltimore: Johns Hopkins University Press.

Rotberg, R. (ed.), 2003. *State Failure and State Weakness in a Time of Terror*. Washington DC: Brookings Institution Press.

Rotberg, R., 2002. The New Nature of Nation-State Failure. *The Washington Quarterly*, 25(3), pp. 85–96.

——, 2003. Failed States, Collapsed States, Weak States: Causes and Indicators. In: R. Rotberg (ed.), *State Failure and State Weakness in a Time of Terror*. Washington DC: Brookings Institute Press, pp. 1–28.

——, 2004. Strengthening Governance: Ranking Countries Would Help. *The Washington Quarterly*, 28(1), pp. 71–81.

——, 2004. The Failure and Collapse of Nation-States: Breakdown, Prevention and Repair. In: R. Rotberg (ed.), *Why States Fail: Causes and Consequences*. Princeton, NJ: Princeton University Press, pp. 1–50.

——, 2004. *When States Fail: Causes and Consequences*. Princeton, NJ: Princeton University Press.

Salamone, F., 1980. Indirect Rule and the Reinterpretation of Tradition: Abdullahi of Yauri. *African Studies Review*, 23(1), pp. 1–14.

Samatar, A., 1988. *Socialist Somalia: Rhetoric and Reality*. London: Zed Books.

——, 1989. *The State and Rural Transformation in Northern Somalia, 1884–1986*. Madison: University of Wisconsin Press.

——, 1994. *The Somali Challenge: From Catastrophe to Renewal?* London: Lynne Rienner.

Samatar, A. (ed.), 1994. *The Somali Challenge: From Catastrophe to Renewal?* London: Lynne Rienner.

Samatar, A. and Samatar, A., 2005. International Crisis Group Report on Somaliland: An Alternative Response. *Bildhaan*, 5(1), pp. 107–24.

Samatar, I., 1997. Light at the End of the Tunnel: Some Reflections on the Struggle of the Somali National Movement. In: H. Adam and R. Ford (eds), *Mending the Rips in the Sky: Options for Somali Communities in the 21st Century*. Lawrenceville, NJ: The Red Sea Press, pp. 21–38.

Selwyn Lloyd, J., 1960. British Consulate General Mogadishu Despatch to London (21 January). London, Foreign Office Telegram No. 34.

Shils, E., 1995. Nation, Nationality, Nationalism and Civil Society. *Nations and Nationalism*, 1(1), pp. 93–1118.

——, 2006. *Tradition*. Chicago, IL: University of Chicago Press.

Shivakumar, S., 2003. The Place of Indigenous Institutions in Constitutional Order. *Constitutional Political Economy*, 14(1), pp. 3–21.

Shuke, A., 2004. Traditional Leaders in Political Decision Making and Conflict Resolution. In: H. Adam, R. Ford and E. Adan Ismail (eds), *War Destroys, Peace Nurtures: Somali Reconciliation and Development*. Lawrenceville, NJ: The Red Sea Press, 147–68.

Sisk, T., 2013. *Statebuilding*. Cambridge: Polity.

Smith, R., 2007. *The Utility of Force: The Art of War in the Modern World*. London: Penguin.

Smith, R.G, 2013. Kurdistan: The Road to Independence. Unpublished Manuscript.

Somaliland Academy for Peace and Development (APD), 1999. A Self-Portrait of Somaliland: Rebuilding from the Ruins. Hargeisa, APD and Interpeace/War-torn Societies Project Report.

——, 2002. The Judicial System in Somaliland. Hargeisa, ADP Workshop Report.

——, 2004. The Somaliland Parliament: A Case Study. Hargeisa/Nairobi, Report for UNDP.

——, 2005. *Rebuilding Somaliland: Issues and Possibilities.* Lawrenceville, NJ: The Red Sea Press.

——, 2007. Arbitration Committee Addresses Deadlock. Hargeisa, Press Release on Deadlock between Executive and Lower House.

Somaliland Academy for Peace and Development (ADP) and Interpeace/WSP-International, 2003. Facilitating Somaliland's Democratic Transition. Nairobi/Hargeisa, Dialogue for Peace Somali Programme Report.

——, 2006. From Plunder to Prosperity: Resolving Resource-Based Conflict in Somaliland. Nairobi/Hargeisa, Dialogue for Peace Somali Programme Report.

——, 2006. Local Solutions: Creating an Enabling Environment for Decentralisation in Somaliland. Nairobi/Hargeisa, Dialogue for Peace Somali Programme Report.

——, 2006. A Vote for Peace: How Somaliland Successfully Hosted its First Parliamentary Elections in 35 Years. Nairobi/Hargeisa, Dialogue for Peace Somali Programme Report.

——, 2012. A Vote for Peace II: A Report on the 2010 Somaliland Presidential Election Process. Hargeisa/Nairobi, Dialogue for Peace Somli Programme Report.

Somaliland Government, 2001. Somaliland Constitution. Hargeisa.

——, 2001. Somaliland: Demand for International Recognition. Hargiesa, Ministry of Information Policy Document for the Government of Somaliland.

——, 2006. Somaliland: An African Success Story. Hargeisa, Report to G8 Arena.

Somaliland House of Elders, 2006. Ujeeddo: Go'aanka Korodhsiimada Mudada ilka Golaha Guurtida JSL (House of Elder's Extension of House of Elders, 6 May). Hargeisa, Somaliland Government Archives and Records.

——, 2006. Somaliland: A Model, Indigenous Owned Peace and Democratic Governance Building in the Horn. Hargeisa, Somaliland Upper House of Parliament Background Report.

——, date unknown. Somaliland Guurti: About Us. Hargeisa, Report compiled by Somaliland *Guurti*.

Somaliland House of Representatives, 2003. Go'zznka Ansixinta Qodobka 19aad Ee Mashruuc-Sharciga Doorashada Dadban Ee Golaha Guurtida and Hakinta Intiisa Kale (Bill for Indirect Election of the House of Elders). Hargeisa, Somaliland Government, House of Representatives Archives.

Somaliland Ministry of Foreign Affairs, 2002. The Case for Somaliland's International Recognition as an Independent State. Hargeisa, Ministry of Foreign Affairs Briefing Paper.

Somaliland NAGAAD and CONSONGO, 2005. Parliamentary Elections: Domestic Election Observers' Report. Hargeisa, NAGAAD and CONSONGO Report.

Somaliland National Electoral Commission, 2005. Report of the Parliamentary Election. Hargeisa, NEC Report.
——, 2005. Voters Manual: Parliamentary Elections 29 September 2005. Hargeisa, Voter Education Manual.
Somaliland Supreme Court, 2006. Soo jeedin Tallo-bixin Sharci (Response to President's Request for Legal Advice, 24 April). Hargeisa, Somaliland Government Archives and Records.
Somaliland Times. 2008. Somaliland Elections to be Held in December 2008 and March 2009. *Somaliland Times*, 24 May, Issue 331.
Spears, I., 2002. Africa: The Limits of Power-Sharing. *Journal of Democracy*, 13(3), pp. 123–36.
——, 2004. Debating Secession and the Recognition of New States in Africa. *African Security Review*, 13(2), pp. 35–48.
——, 2004. Reflections on Somaliland and Africa's Territorial Order. In: H. Adam, R. Ford and E. Adan Ismail (eds), *War Destroys, Peace Nurtures: Somali Reconciliation and Development*. Lawrenceville, NJ: The Red Sea Press, pp. 179–92.
——, 2004. States-Within-States: An Introduction to their Empirical Attributes. In: P. Kingston and I. Spears (eds), *States-Within-States: Incipient Political Entities in the Post-Cold War Era*. Basingstoke: Palgrave Macmillan, pp. 15–34.
State Failure Task Force, 1995. State Failure Task Force Findings I. College Park, MD, Centre for International Development and Conflict Management Report.
——, 1998. State Failure Task Force Reports: Phase II Findings. College Park, MD, Centre for International Development and Conflict Management Report.
——, 2000. State Failure Task Force Reports: Phase III Findings. College Park, MD, Centre for International Development and Conflict Management Report.
——, 2003. State Failure Task Force Findings IV. College Park, MD, Centre for International Development and Conflict Management Report.
——, 2005. State Failure Task Force Findings V. College Park, MD, Centre for International Development and Conflict Management Report.
Sweden, J., 2004. Somaliland's Quest for Recognition: A Challenge for the International Community. In: H. Adam, R. Ford and E.A. Ismail (eds), *War Destroys, Peace Nurtures: Somali Reconciliation and Development*. Lawrenceville, NJ: The Red Sea Press, pp. 169–78.
Terlinden, U., 2008. Emerging Governance in Somaliland: A Perspective from Below. In: E-M. Bruchhaus and M.M. Sommer (eds), *Hot Spot Horn of Africa Revisited*. Hamburg: LIT, pp. 51–67.
Terlinden, U. and Hassan, M., 2010. Somaliland: 'Home grown' peacemaking and political reconstruction. *Accord* 21: 76–9.
Thürer, D., 1999. The 'failed state' and international law. *International Review of the Red Cross*, Issue 836, pp. 731–61.
Tilly, C. (ed.), 1975. *The Formation of National States in Western Europe*. Princeton: Princeton University Press.

———, 1985. War Making and State Making as Organized Crime. In: P. Evans, D. Rueschemeyr and T. Skocpol (eds), *Bringing the State Back In* . Cambridge: Cambridge University Press, pp. 169–91.
Touval, S., 1963. *Somali Nationalism*. Cambridge, MA: Harvard University Press.
UK Government, 1957. Peace Talks at Burao: No Agreement Reached but Discussions Continue (19 October). London, Protectorate Report 125.
———, 2010. A Strong Britain in an Age of Uncertainty: The National Security Strategy. London, HM Government Strategy Document.
———, 2011. Building Stability Overseas Strategy. London, DfID, Ministry of Defence and FCO Strategy Report.
UK Secretary of State for the Colonies, 1960. Report of the Somaliland Protectorate Constitutional Conference Held in London (May). London, Report presented to Parliament.
United Nations Economic Commission for Africa, 2007. Relevance of African Traditional Institutions of Governance. New York, UNECA Report.
———, 2004. ADF IV Traditional Governance Focus Group Issues Paper. Addis Ababa, African Development Forum Paper.
United Nations, 1993. Resolution 814 (26 March 1993). New York, Security Council Resolution.
———, March 2002. Report of the International Conference on Financing for Development (Monterrey Convention). Monterrey, Mexico, Conference on Financing for Development Report.
United States Government, 2002. The National Security Strategy of the United States. Washington DC, The White House Strategy Document.
USAID, 2003. Proposed Typology in Order to Classify Countries Based on Performance and State Capacity. Washington DC, US Agency for International Development Report.
———, 2004. US Foreign Aid: Meeting the Challenges of the Twenty-first Century. Washington DC, US Agency for International Development Report.
———, 2013. What We Do: Democracy, Human Rights and Governance. Available at: http://www.usaid.gov.
Vallings, C. and Moreno-Torres, M., 2005. Drivers of Fragility: What Makes States Fragile? London, DfID Poverty Reduction in Difficult Environments Working Paper No. 7.
de Waal, A., 2002. Class and Power in a Stateless Somalia. London, Justice Africa Occasional Paper Series Discussion Paper.
Walls, Michael. 2006. Constitutional Crisis and the Challenge of Theocracy: Somaliland's Urgent Challenges. London, Report for Somaliland Focus.
———, 2009. Somaliland: Democracy Threatened – Constitutional Impasse as Presidential Elections are Postponed. London, Chatham House Briefing Note.
———, 2009. The Emergence of a Somali State: Building peace from civil war in Somaliland. *African Affairs*, 108(432), pp. 371–89.
Weber, M., 1964. *The Theory of Social and Economic Organisation (1947)*. edited by Talcott Parsons. New York: Free Press.

——, 1967. Politics as Vocation (1948). In: H.G. and C.W. Mills (eds), *From Max Weber: Essays in Sociology*. London: Routledge, pp. 77–128.

Weiner, M., 1996. Bad Neighbors, Bad Neighborhoods: An Inquiry into the Causes of Refugee Flows. *International Security*, 21(1), pp. 5–42.

West, H. and S. Kloech-Jensen, 1999. Betwixt and Between: 'Traditional Authority' and Democratic Decentralization in Post-War Mozambique. *African Affairs*, 98(393), pp. 455–84.

Williamson, J., 1994. In Search of a Manual for Technopols. In: J. Williamson (ed.), *The Political Economy of Policy Reform*. Washington DC: Institute for International Economics, pp. 9–28.

Woodward, S., 2011. State-Building and Peace-Building: What Theory and Whose Role? In: R. Kozul-Wright and P. Fortunato (eds), *Securing Peace: State-Building and Economic Development in Post-Conflict Countries*. London: Bloomsbury, pp. 87–112.

World Bank, 1989. Sub-Saharan Africa: From Crisis to Sustainable Growth. Washington DC, World Bank Report.

——, 1992. Governance and Development. Washington DC, World Bank Report.

——, 1994. *Governance: The World Bank's Experience*. Washington DC, The World Bank.

——, 2005. Additional Activities Note on Somalia. Washington DC, The World Bank Activities Note.

Yannis, A., 2003. State Collapse and its Implications for Peace-Building and Reconstruction. In: J. Milliken (ed.), *State Failure, Collapse and Reconstruction*. Oxford: Blackwell, pp. 63–80.

Young, J., 2005. Sudan: A Flawed Peace Process Leading to a Flawed Peace. *Review of African Political Economy*, 32(103), pp. 99–113.

Zartman, I. (ed.), 1995. *Collapsed States: The Disintegration and Restoration of Legitimate Authority*. Boulder, CO: Lynne Rienner.

Index

'acceptable' state 8, 10–11, 13–15, 17, 19, 22, 26, 29, 34, 56, 60, 115–16, 118, 120, 150, 177–8, 186, 190; *see also* liberal state
Afghanistan 33, 34, 120, 188
Africa 2, 3, 11, 12, 19, 54, 57*fn*, 64, 75, 76, 83, 89, 129, 180, 190
An Agenda for Peace 30–31
authority 4–5, 21, 31, 42, 45, 46, 48, 73–4, 78, 101, 125, 134, 136, 143, 144, 149, 182; *see also* traditional authority
autonomy 28, 38, 47–9, 80–81, 124, 186, 190

Barre, Siad 63, 87–92, 96–9, 100, 132, 150
    and clan 87–9, 90–91
    impact on clan governance 88–9
    Isaaq and the north 89–91, 96–7, 99, 99*fn*, 128, 130, 132
blood money (*diya*) 65, 69, 70, 71, 72, 78, 127
blueprint 11–12, 14, 15, 16, 24–5, 27, 32, 34, 35, 38, 47, 58, 60–61, 175–6, 180, 181, 182–3, 188–9, 190–91, 193
Bosnia 24, 34
Boutros-Ghali, Boutros 30–31, 35, 37; *see also An Agenda for Peace*
British Somaliland Protectorate 76–9, 82, 83*fn*, 84, 86–7, 90–91, 92, 97, 102, 143; *see also* colonial rule
    benign neglect 77–8, 79, 80–81, 150
    clan 77–9

civil war, Somalia 96–100, 104, 125, 126–131, 132–3
civilian (*beel*) administration, Somaliland 105–9, 136–7, 138, 139

clan 16, 17, 61, 63–75, 78–81, 92, 95–6, 136, 144, 179; *see also* clan system; elders; *Guurti* (House of Elders)
    co-existence 65, 70–72, 132, 134, 136, 142, 149
    colonial rule 75–81
    conflict resolution and reconciliation 65, 68, 71–3, 74, 102–105, 110, 124, 132–3, 134, 135–6, 187
    governance 2, 13, 14, 61, 63–6, 67–70, 71, 92, 95–6, 124, 126, 127, 142, 175, 181, 184
    identity 65–70, 85–6, 91–2, 102
    law and justice 65, 69–70, 69–70*fn*, 74
    politics and government 15, 64, 66, 67–8, 71, 85–6, 87–91, 92, 95, 102–103, 108, 113–14, 119, 126–7, 136, 142–5, 150–51, 155, 174–5, 179, 184, 187, 190
    provision 79, 79*fn*, 91–2, 95–6, 100, 126, 130, 131
    romanticising of 17, 150, 190
    stability and security 68, 71, 74, 132, 149, 164, 187
    and statebuilding 16, 61, 74, 102–103, 124–5, 134, 135, 150–51, 153, 187
clan system 63–5, 65–6, 67–8, 71, 72–3, 74–5, 78–9, 92, 95–6, 97, 98, 102, 104, 106–107, 119, 123, 126, 127, 128, 132–3, 141, 142–3, 145, 174, 179, 181, 184, 187; *see also* clan
    disruption to 64–5, 67, 74–5, 78–81, 85–6, 87–9, 91–2, 95, 126, 143
    organisation and structure 64–6, 68–9, 73–4, 142
clannism 85–6, 88, 89, 92, 113, 127
colonial rule 63, 64, 67, 75–82, 83, 92
    British 75–81, 81–2*fn*, 134, 143, 150, 179

Italian 75, 77, 78, 79, 80, 81, 82, 83, 89, 179
community councils (*shir*) 68, 69, 72, 101, 104, 105, 119, 133, 134, 135, 138, 149, 175
compliance and conformity 13, 15, 36, 38, 177
compromise, *see* negotiation
conflict prevention 31–3, 68
conflict resolution 31, 42, 65, 66, 71–3, 100–101, 102–105, 110, 119, 146
consensus 42, 46, 66, 68, 72–3, 74, 98, 106, 124, 140*t*, 153, 169, 171, 172, 175, 187
constitution, Somaliland 106, 110–15, 119–20, 138–9, 140–41, 141–2, 145, 147, 154, 155–60, 167, 168, 169, 170
 ambiguity 112–13, 119–20, 141, 154, 155–8, 169, 170*fn*, 172
 referendum 111, 117, 138, 140
corruption 22, 32, 33, 54, 85–6, 87, 88, 108, 115, 162
council of elders (*guurti*) 61, 68–70, 72, 74, 98*fn*, 101, 105–106, 119, 125, 128, 129, 130, 132–3, 134, 135, 138, 139*t*, 149, 168, 175; *see also* elders; *Guurti* (House of Elders)
coup 63, 82, 85, 87–8, 97, 108
customary, use of term 12*fn*
customary law (*xeer*) 68, 69, 70–71, 72, 74, 78*fn*, 102, 105, 109, 119, 125, 126, 127, 150

de facto states, *see* unrecognised states
decolonisation 5, 19, 20, 40, 78, 80–81, 81*fn*, 82, 82*fn*, 83, 87
democracy 11, 13, 32–5, 37, 43–4, 48, 52, 101, 110, 115, 116, 117–18, 119, 125, 132, 179
democratic elections 3, 32, 35, 59, 110–12, 113–15, 116, 118*fn*, 140*t*, 141, 146–8, 154, 156, 158, 159, 160, 161, 162, 163, 168, 170–71; *see also* House of Representatives; presidential elections
Dervish 76–7
development 2–4, 8, 9–11, 12, 20, 27–8, 29–34, 36, 38, 39, 42, 44, 47, 54, 77–8, 96, 97, 124, 145, 146, 148 161, 162–3, 169–70, 171, 177, 180, 181–2, 186, 188
development-security 31–4
deviance 11, 12–16, 23–6, 38, 40, 47–8, 120–21, 123, 141, 150–51, 180, 181, 182, 184, 187–8, 190, 193
diaspora 13*fn*, 65, 66, 67, 96, 104, 108, 116, 138, 139–40*t*, 150, 154, 165, 167, 173, 175, 181, 184, 185
domestic support 57, 59, 177–8, 180; *see also* legitimacy; statebuilding, domestically-led

East Timor 34, 58
Egal, Mohammed Ibrahim 105, 107, 108–10, 110–11, 112–13, 115, 117, 137, 138, 140*t*, 141, 142, 146, 159, 160–61, 168
elders 61, 67–9, 72–3, 73–4, 78, 79*fn*, 89, 99–101, 102–103, 105–107, 108, 111, 119, 125, 126–31, 132–3, 134, 135, 136–7, 139–40*t*, 142, 143–4, 145, 147, 149, 153, 159–60, 164, 168, 170, 175, 184, 191; *see also* council of elders; *Guurti* (House of Elders)
 definition 73–4
election v. selection 141, 142, 155–60, 162–71, 173; *see also Guurti* (House of Elders)
Ethiopia 64, 75, 76, 81*fn*, 89–91, 98–9, 128–30, 131, 134, 178, 182–3
exclusion 11, 12, 15, 25–6, 37, 41, 43, 59, 124, 183, 188, 189, 190
expectations gap 17, 40–41, 44, 49, 51–3, 57–8, 61, 181–2, 192
extension, power of 111*fn*, 112*fn*, 115, 145, 147–9, 154, 156–9, 161, 162, 171; *see also Guurti* (House of Elders); self–extension crisis
extraversion 10–11, 118, 177, 178

failed state 1, 2, 4–5, 7–8, 9–10, 13, 16, 17, 19–20, 20–25, 29, 32–4, 36–8, 48, 56*fn*, 61, 63, 93, 95, 100, 120, 189
 fixing 8, 9, 20, 23–5, 29, 32–4, 37, 39, 47–8, 181–2

familiar/unfamiliar, *see* known/unknown
federalism 127, 132
flexibility 14, 47–8, 60–61, 150–51, 153, 154, 155–6, 161, 169, 176, 183–4, 186, 189, 190–91; *see also* statebuilding
foundations for state 3, 15, 36, 44, 50, 53–4
 Somaliland 15, 70, 82, 87, 93, 96, 98, 101, 102–103, 105–108, 115, 118–19, 124, 126, 133, 136–7, 143, 149, 153, 160, 164, 170, 173, 175, 176, 192
fragile state, *see* failed state

good governance 4–6, 8, 10, 16, 20, 22–4, 30–36, 37–8, 39, 41, 48–9, 56
governance 2, 6, 9–11, 13–14, 16–17, 19–20, 22–5, 26, 29–30, 31, 33, 35–6, 38, 40, 45, 48, 49, 52, 55–7, 60, 61, 63–75, 79, 81–2, 88–9, 92, 95–6, 101, 103, 105, 106, 112, 116, 119, 120, 124, 125, 126–7, 129, 131, 133, 136, 139*t*, 142–5, 146, 149–51, 153, 160, 163, 169, 172–4, 177–8, 181–2, 184, 186, 188–9, 192; *see also* clan, traditional authority
 reform 9, 11, 16, 24, 28, 30–31, 35, 39–40, 182, 186, 189, 191
Guurti (House of Elders) 13–14, 101–104, 111–12, 115, 118–19, 123–51, 153–75, 185, 187
 advisory/mediation role 112, 115, 129, 133, 135, 137, 141–2, 145–8, 162, 164–5, 170–71, 172, 174
 as bridge 17, 61, 131, 144–6, 148, 149–50, 165, 170, 174
 and democracy 118*fn*, 138, 144–5, 147–8, 149, 150–51, 153, 164, 165, 166–8, 170–71, 172, 187
 changing nature of 135, 138, 146–8, 149–50, 153, 154–5, 157, 159–60, 162–4, 168–73, 174
 co-option of 148, 157, 159–60, 161–2, 167, 168, 169, 172
 destabilising 12, 123–4, 166–7
 familiar 144–5, 149, 171
 future of 138, 154–5, 158, 160, 162–73, 174, 187
 institutionalisation of 103, 106, 107, 111–12, 118, 123–7, 129, 130–31, 132, 135, 137, 139, 140–48, 150–51, 154, 156, 163, 174–5, 184
 internal-external placement 118, 135, 136, 138, 144–6, 148, 165
 as 'King Makers' 103, 107, 135, 137
 legislative role 112, 125, 140, 141–2, 148, 165, 167, 168, 170
 membership 111, 111*fn*, 140–41, 155–60, 162, 163, 164, 166, 167
 peace, security and stability 104, 105, 110, 112, 118, 132–3, 134, 135–6, 138, 140, 145–6, 147–8, 150, 153, 158, 165–6, 169
 and politics 138, 141, 145–6, 147–8, 149–50, 153, 154, 156–7, 160, 161, 163, 167, 170, 174
 reconciliation 112, 129, 131, 132–3, 134–7, 138, 145–6, 148, 150, 163
 representing the clan 111–12, 141, 142–146, 165–6, 171, 172
 romanticising of 16, 150, 190
 safety net 143, 145–6, 147–8, 156, 184
 self-extension 156–8, 161–2, 164, 167, 173, 174
 sovereign power 103, 107, 135, 136–7, 143–5, 146, 156, 164–5, 184
 as spine 107, 112, 119, 123, 136–7, 164–5, 169, 170
 symbolic role 73, 112, 125, 139, 142, 145–6, 149, 163, 170–71, 172, 173, 174, 175

House of Representatives 103, 111, 112, 113, 115, 140, 141, 142, 145, 146–7, 157–9, 160–62, 163, 164–6, 166–8, 170–71, 172
 2005 election 114–15, 146–7, 158, 160, 163
human security 6, 9, 21, 30, 35
hybrid 12–14, 16–17, 102–103, 106, 110–15, 116, 118, 120–21, 125, 138, 150–51, 154–5, 160, 163–4, 166, 172, 173–5, 178, 180–81, 190; *see also* Somaliland

idea of state 44, 49–52, 57, 60, 153–4, 176, 192; *see also* nation; political culture
ideal state 2, 8, 9–11, 11–15, 17, 22–5, 28–9, 34, 37–8, 39, 44, 48, 50, 55, 59, 61, 120, 151, 173, 175, 177, 186, 189, 191, 193; *see also* 'acceptable' state; liberal state; 'successful' state
identity 28, 45, 49–50, 57, 64, 65–7, 70, 74, 82, 85, 96, 102, 121, 123–4, 176, 178–9, 187; *see also* clan; nation
indigenous governance 2, 7, 9–11, 14–15, 17, 38, 39–40, 41, 43, 47–8, 55–7, 59–60, 63, 74, 79, 95, 101, 103, 120, 124, 144, 146, 154, 166, 177, 180–82, 183–4, 187–8, 189–90, 191–2
institutional state 4, 5, 10, 34–6, 37, 41–4, 47–9, 57, 59, 96, 101, 104–106, 109, 118, 121, 123, 141–2, 178, 192; *see also* statebuilding
institutions 14–15, 20, 22, 24, 25, 31–4, 34–6, 37–8, 39–40, 41–3, 44–9, 49–51, 52–3, 57, 58–61, 66, 67–8, 73–4, 81, 83, 88, 96, 101, 104–106, 108–109, 111, 113, 117–18, 119, 121, 123–5, 126, 129–30, 133, 135–8, 141–8, 150–51, 162–3, 165–8, 173–6, 178, 179, 181–2, 184, 187, 190, 192; *see also* state; statebuilding
  norms 27–8
  teaching and learning 26–8, 150–51
internal-external expectations 16, 38, 40, 43, 48–9, 51–2, 55–7, 60, 106, 124, 125, 144–5, 148, 150–51, 169–70, 178–9, 180, 181, 183, 191, 192–3; *see also* new-old
  balance 38, 43, 48–9, 51, 52, 57, 60–61, 92, 96, 106, 115–18, 151, 160, 169, 171, 173–6, 178, 187, 191, 192–3
international institutions 8, 11, 13, 26–9, 30, 177
intervention 6, 7, 8, 10, 12, 13, 17, 24, 33–4, 37, 39, 41, 56, 180–83,
186, 191; *see also* liberal interventionism
ideational 8, 27, 150–51, 186
intra-government relationships 153–176
Iraq 25, 33, 34, 41
Isaaq 86, 90, 91, *91fn*, 97, 98–9, *99fn*, 100–102, 109, 127–8, 129, 130–31, 132, 134, 136, 140, 150
Islamic law (*shari'a*) 69, 72, 78, 95
isolation, *see* non-intervention

Kahin, Dahir Rayale 110, 111, 114, 147–8, 157–60, 161–2, 172
  2003 election 114, 146–7, 161
known/unknown 6, 8, 11, 12, 16, 23–6, 27, 29, 38, 47–8, 49, 98, 117, 123, 124, 131, 144–5, 150–51, 153, 164, 169, 180, 184, 188, 189–91, 193
Kosovo 34, 58
Kulmiye 113, 114–15, 147, 159, 160–61, 166, 171
Kurdistan 53*fn*, 58, 58*fn*

Law 19 155–160, 161
legitimacy 3–5, 6, 7–8, 9, 13, 14–15, 17, 20, 22, 24, 26, 31, 35, 36, 38, 39–61, 95–6, 103, 118–21, 123, 124, 126, 133, 142–3, 144, 145, 147, 149, 153, 160, 168, 176, 177–9, 180–81, 182, 184, 189, 190, 192; *see also* internal-external expectations; Somaliland; state
  and non-democratic rule 51, 121, 144, 181
legitimacy gap 41, 49–59, 144–5, 153, 176, 181; *see also* internal-external expectations
liberal framework 10, 12–14, 21–6, 29, 33–6, 38, 39–40, 42, 47–8, 57, 60, 120–21, 124, 150–51, 180, 189–90
liberal interventionism 8, 25, 27, 35–6, 43, 52, 56, 181, 186, 191
liberal state 2–3, 6–11, 14–15, 19–20, 22–6, 29–30, 34–8, 44, 48–9, 52, 54–6, 59, 61, 115–18, 120, 124, 150–51, 177–8, 180, 181, 186, 189, 190–91, 192
liberal statebuilding, *see* statebuilding

liberation movements 89, 92, 97, 98*fn*, 128, 129; *see also* Somali National Movement
liberation struggle, Somaliland 97–101, 103, 125–6, 127–31; *see also* Somali National Movement
local capabilities, *see* indigenous governance
local ownership 17, 40–41, 43–4, 45–8, 57, 96, 126, 133, 150, 183–4, 187, 189, 191–2

mediation 66, 74, 104, 110, 125, 129, 131, 133, 141, 145–8, 149, 163, 170, 172, 174
militias 65, 90–91, 97, 103, 105–6, 139*t*
    demobilisation 105–106, 107, 135, 187
model 9, 10–11, 12–13, 15–16, 22, 24–5, 28–9, 29–30, 34–5, 36–8, 47, 59–60, 120–21, 178, 180–81, 186, 190–91, 192–3
modern state, *see* 'acceptable' state; liberal state; 'successful' state
modernisation 10, 29–30, 54–5, 65–6, 164, 166–7, 171, 173, 175, 181, 184
Montevideo Convention on the Rights and Duties of States 4
multi-party democracy 3, 110, 116, 139, 140, 150, 153

narrative 32–3, 50–51, 149–50, 174–5, 176, 178–9, 187
nation 44–9, 50–51, 57, 60, 65, 81–2, 86, 117, 124–6, 155; *see also* identity
nation-building 44–7, 60–61, 96, 102*fn*, 117, 118, 123–6, 172, 175–6, 178–9
National Charter 105–106, 109, 110, 111, 112*fn*, 138
negotiating the state 14, 16–17, 42, 44, 60–61, 119, 145, 149, 174–6, 178, 191
negotiation 14, 16–17, 31, 37, 44, 46, 61, 66, 68, 70*fn*, 71, 72–3, 74, 79*fn*, 83, 87, 95, 104, 107, 110, 113, 115, 119, 128, 130, 132–3, 134, 136, 138, 145, 146–7, 149–50, 162, 169–71, 172, 174–6, 178

nepotism 85–8
new-old 11–14, 17, 59, 75, 96, 106, 112, 116, 118, 119, 125, 145, 148, 149–51, 153, 160, 162–71, 172–3, 174–6, 178, 181, 184, 187
nomadic 64, 65–6, 67–8, 71, 79, 99, 114*fn*, 141, 142–3
non-intervention 12, 13*fn*, 102*fn*, 104–105, 115–16, 150, 176, 180, 183, 184–6, 187
non-Western, *see* deviance; political organisation
norms 5–8, 9–10, 12–15, 19–24, 26–9, 35–6, 37–8, 39, 46, 52, 54–6, 61, 95, 115–18, 120–21, 123, 150–51, 177, 180, 186, 188–90, 192; *see also* liberal framework; state reproduction 26–8, 38, 47
North-South divide, *see* Somali unification

Ogaden War 89–91, 97, 99, 128
    impact on north 90–91, 97, 99
'one size fits all' 8, 11, 14, 24–5, 27, 38, 58, 120

patron states 56, 58, 177–8
patronage 77, 81, 89–91, 161–2
Peace Charter 105–106, 140*t*, 147
peacebuilding 31–5, 37, 42, 48, 55, 59, 74, 132–3, 134, 135, 141, 153, 182
political community 42, 45–7, 49–51, 52, 57, 125; *see also* nation
political culture 7, 48, 50–51, 55, 124, 176
political goods 6–8, 10, 23, 25, 31, 33–4, 41, 47, 95, 109, 115, 127
political organisation 4, 11, 23–5, 34–6, 47–8, 64, 74, 120, 180
    non-Western 23–5, 35, 48, 50–51, 120, 180–81, 182, 187–8, 190; *see also* deviance
political parties 85–6, 113–14, 146, 147–8, 161, 163; *see also* Kulmiye; UCID; UDUB
post-conflict 1, 31–2, 37, 41–2, 44, 45, 47, 49, 100, 120, 125, 133, 150, 153, 184, 188, 191
power relationships 120, 138, 160, 163, 182–3, 191, 193

presidential elections 111, 113, 114–15, 146–8, 154, 158, 159, 161, 162, 170
presidential power 103, 105, 107, 111–13, 138, 141–2, 154, 157–60, 161–2, 168, 169, 172

recognition 10–15, 16, 51, 52–3, 55–7, 58, 60–61, 85*fn*, 101–102, 106, 111, 115–18, 119, 123, 127, 163, 164, 166, 175, 176, 177–9, 180–81, 185–6, 192–3; *see also* unrecognised states
recognition strategy 11, 13, 55–7, 101–102, 118, 121, 177–8, 193
reconciliation 13, 31, 37, 42, 66, 73, 116, 119, 124, 129, 132–3, 134, 136, 138, 146, 148, 163, 170, 174, 175
reconciliation, post-conflict 2, 37, 42, 73, 100–101, 104, 105, 110, 119, 124–5, 129, 131, 132–3, 134, 135, 137, 138, 143, 145, 150, 170, 187
representation 83–4, 97, 106, 112–13, 136, 140, 141, 153, 158, 171
reproduction 26–9, 38, 47

safety net 143, 145–6, 147–8, 156, 184
Sanaag and Sool 107, 133, 147, 170
security 2, 3–4, 6–8, 9–10, 16, 20, 25, 26, 29, 30–34, 36–8, 39, 42, 64, 66, 71, 95, 102–104, 105–10, 112–13, 115, 126, 131, 135, 139*t*, 141, 143, 147, 149, 159, 168–9, 187, 189, 191
self-extension crisis 141, 147–8, 154–63, 169, 170–71, 172, 173, 193; *see also* election v. selection; *Guurti* (House of Elders)
Sheikh Conference 104, 135, 139*t*
social contract 7, 47, 50, 70, 102, 192
socialisation 27–9, 35–6, 115–16
societal responsibility 23–4, 133
socio-political change 33, 34, 38, 39, 41, 44, 45, 49, 58, 60–61, 123, 124, 125, 145, 153, 177, 179, 192
Somali, the 13–14, 16, 17, 63–75, 79
Somali nationalism 80–84, 86, 87, 88–9*fn*
Somali National Movement (SNM) 96, 97–101, 102–103, 104–106, 116, 119, 124–5, 126–33, 134–7, 139–40*t*, 145, 150; *see also* transitional administration
clan 97–8, 99, 100–101, 125, 126–32, 143
democracy 98, 103, 106, 116, 131, 136, 138, 173
Ethiopia 98–9, 128–9
guurti/Guurti 98, 101, 103, 126–31, 132–3, 134, 135, 150, 156
origins and intent 97–8, 100, 101, 103, 106, 116, 143
political and military wings 97–8, 103, 116, 131–2
post-war tensions 100, 102–104, 105–106, 109–110, 132–3, 138–9
support for 97, 98–9, 100, 127–8, 130–31
Somali unification 81–87, 92
Acts of Union 82, 83–5*fn*, 102
colonial legacies 81–3
North-South gap 83–6, 87, 89, 90–91, 92, 102
problems with 82–6, 87, 92, 100
Somalia 1–2, 8*fn*, 12–13, 15, 16–17, 25, 30–31, 61, 63–4, 65–6, 68, 73, 75–6, 79–82, 83–7, 88–91, 92–3, 95–100, 102, 104–105, 113–14, 115, 116, 118–20, 123, 125, 126–31, 132, 135, 143, 149–50, 175, 180, 182–3, 184, 185*fn*, 186
al Shabaab 2, 25*fn*, 65
Union of Islamic Courts 25*fn*, 65, 158
Somalia government 1–2, 25, 30–31, 82–87, 87–92, 95, 97–8, 104, 113–14, 119, 120, 125, 127, 132, 143
Somaliland 1–2, 11–13, 15–17, 25–6, 61, 63–5, 67, 69, 71, 75, 92, 95–121, 123–151, 153–176, 177–187, 190, 192–3; *see also Guurti* (House of Elders); Somaliland statebuilding
clan 16, 96, 101, 102, 104, 109, 111–13, 119, 123–6, 131–3, 134–8, 142–5, 153–4
conflict 103–104, 109–10, 135, 138–9
conflict resolution and reconciliation 100–101, 104, 125, 132–3, 145, 150, 153

declaration of independence 13, 92, 96, 97, 102, 135
democracy 13, 61, 101, 110–11, 114–15, 116, 117–18, 119, 125, 144–6, 149, 150–51, 153–4, 160, 162, 164, 165, 166–9, 171, 172, 179, 180
deviance 12, 14, 16, 25–6, 61, 120–21, 123, 124, 150–51, 184, 186
familiar/unfamiliar 16–17, 26, 121, 142–7, 150–51, 153, 180
flexibility 145, 150–51, 153, 154, 156
future of 154, 162–71, 173–5, 179, 181, 187
government 61, 69, 71, 104, 106–107, 109–15, 118, 123, 135, 140–47, 181
hybrid 12–14, 17, 102, 106, 110–15, 116, 118, 120, 125, 126, 138, 142–4, 150–51, 153, 154–5, 160, 163, 164–71, 172–3, 174–6, 178–9, 180–81, 184, 190
identity 123–4, 175–6, 178–9, 187
institutions 96, 101, 106, 108–11, 118, 121, 125, 140–47, 168, 169
internal-external 12, 16–17, 41, 61, 92, 106, 115–18, 125, 150, 160, 169, 173–6, 178–9, 181, 183–4, 187
learning from 15–17, 181, 186–92
legitimacy 118–19, 121, 123, 124, 126, 133, 143, 144–5, 147, 149, 153, 160, 178, 180, 184
and models 12, 15–16, 180–81, 186, 193
modern statehood 12–14, 16, 109, 115, 119, 145–7, 150–51, 154, 164, 166–7, 173, 175, 177, 179, 180, 184
problems and obstacles 110–11, 115, 119–20, 133, 149, 154–6, 162–71, 172–6, 179
recognition 13, 15, 101, 106, 111, 115, 116–18, 119, 123, 163, 164, 166, 176, 177, 178–9, 180–81, 183, 186
recognition strategy 106, 115–16, 117–18, 123, 177, 179
traditional authority and governance 12, 14–16, 61, 67, 69, 71, 72, 74, 102, 118, 120–21, 123–51, 153, 154, 160, 164, 166–7, 180–81, 184
Somaliland National Conferences 101, 105, 119, 131–40, 139–40t
Berbera 107, 134, 135, 139t
Borama 104–105, 107, 108, 109, 136–7, 140t
Burco 101, 102, 103, 105, 135–7, 139t
Hargeisa 110, 138–9, 140t, 146
Somaliland statebuilding 1–2, 12, 14–15, 16–17, 61, 63, 96, 101–109, 115, 116–18, 118–22, 123–6, 133, 134, 137, 142, 145, 146, 148, 149, 150–51, 153–5, 160, 162–4, 165, 169–70, 172–3, 174–6, 177–8, 179, 180–81, 183, 187–93; see also Guurti (House of Elders); Somaliland
nation-building 82, 116, 118, 123–6, 172, 175–6, 178–9, 187
South Ossetia 55fn, 58
sovereignty 3, 6, 8, 12–14, 19, 21, 47, 51, 55–6, 57, 58, 117, 124, 135, 136, 177–9, 181, 182, 184, 186, 189
externally exercised 47, 57, 124, 182–3
state; see also liberal framework; liberal state
concept and evolution of 15–16, 19–20, 25, 42, 45, 51, 181
criteria and assessment 4–7, 19–24, 29, 181, 186
expectations of 1, 3–7, 9–10, 15, 16, 19–20, 22–23, 27–30, 33, 34–6, 38, 40–41, 43–4, 45, 47–52, 54–61, 92, 124, 150–51, 155, 179, 180, 183, 186–92
state failure, see failed state
state formation 6, 11–14, 19, 40, 44, 53–5, 105, 116, 125, 145, 173, 176, 185fn, 187, 191, 192
state-society 8, 24, 33, 35, 41, 43–9, 51–2, 59–60, 61, 120, 124, 126, 130, 136, 143, 144–5, 153, 164, 165, 166, 174–6, 178–9, 180, 183–4, 187, 190–91, 192
statebuilding 2–3, 10–11, 13–16, 20, 25, 27–9, 33–40, 39–61, 34–40, 42–45, 47–49, 51–52, 59, 120–21, 123–4,

124, 181–2, 186, 188, 175–6, 180, 188, 192–3; *see also* state; statebuilding, domestically-led
alternatives to liberal state 15, 25–6, 35, 38, 47–8, 51, 58, 120–21, 180–81, 83
exclusion 25–6, 41, 120–21, 183
flexibility 14, 47–8, 60–61
as ideological exercise 34–5, 39, 48
institution building 33–6, 39, 42–4, 48–9, 57, 59–60
limitations and problems of 34–5, 37, 39, 41–43, 45, 47, 49, 52, 57, 59–60, 176, 181–3, 186, 188–92
long-term v. short-term 41, 47, 54, 60–61, 80, 189
as peacebuilding 31, 33–4, 42, 55, 59, 181, 191
as a process 11, 14, 16, 17, 29, 37, 39, 40, 44, 54, 57, 60–61, 119, 126, 151, 153–5, 169, 173, 175–6, 178, 187, 191–2, 193
reproduction 26–27, 29, 38, 47
technocratic approach 32–5, 39–41, 43, 49, 57, 59–60, 181–2, 191–2, 192–3
statebuilding, domestically-led 1, 2, 16, 17, 28, 52–3, 55, 57, 58, 60, 104–106, 120, 125, 149, 150–51, 163, 175–6, 177–8, 183, 184, 186, 188, 193
Structural Adjustment Programmes (SAPs) 10, 28
'successful' state 7–8, 9, 11, 12–14, 20, 22–6, 29, 36–8, 39–40, 45, 48, 56, 60, 116, 166, 177, 180, 181, 186, 189, 190
Sudan 182–3
Supreme Court 111, 112, 114*fn*, 157–9, 160–61, 164
'survival strategy' 55, 55*fn*, 177; *see also* unrecognised states

Tamil Eelam 55*fn*, 58
teaching and learning 26–9, 59, 61, 118, 164, 187–8

technocratic elites 29–30, 116, 162, 164, 175, 187
template, *see* blueprint
Tilly, Charles 53–4
tradition 66–7, 72, 73–4, 112, 140–41, 142, 144, 145–6, 149, 151, 162, 169, 170, 173–5, 182, 184, 190
use of term 12*fn*, 73
traditional authority 4, 10–11, 12–15, 16–17, 40, 59, 61, 65–67, 68, 69, 70, 71, 73, 78–9, 81, 88–9, 95, 98, 102, 112, 118–21, 124–6, 127, 129–30, 132–9, 141–8, 149–50, 153–5, 160, 162–6, 169–71, 172–3, 174–6, 178, 180–82, 184–8, 190, 192; *see also Guurti* (House of Elders); Somaliland
transitional administration, Somaliland 100–101, 102, 103–104, 105, 108, 135, 136–7; *see also* Somali National Movement; Tuur
trust/distrust 11–12, 29, 40, 42, 44, 47–8, 51, 60, 72–3, 74, 90, 98, 108, 123, 124, 125, 128, 129, 131, 134, 137, 143–4, 148, 149, 153, 159–60, 167, 172, 182, 187, 190, 191; *see also* known/unknown
Tuur, Abdulrahman Ahmed Ali 100–101, 103–104, 108, 136

UCID 113, 160–61, 166, 171
UDUB 113, 114, 115, 160–61, 164, 165, 167
United Nations 6, 8*fn*, 19, 30, 31, 33, 80, 81, 90, 102*fn*, 104, 109, 149, 185, 186
Security Council Resolution 814 31
United Nations Operation in Somali II (UNOSOM II) 30–31, 104
United Somali Congress (USC) 97, 128
unrecognised states 10–12, 17, 52–8, 61, 92, 101, 121, 177, 179, 181, 192–3

Weberian state 3–5, 21, 34, 36, 42, 50*fn*, 51, 54, 56*fn*, 181–2, 184
Westphalia 3–4, 5, 19–20, 50*fn*
World Bank, The 12, 30, 123, 167